To Mary Ellen

in memory of her Feast
Mary the Queen

[signature]

May 31, 1961
New York

FOUNTAIN OF JUSTICE

FOUNTAIN OF JUSTICE

A Study in the Natural Law

by John C. H. Wu, LL.B., J.D., LL.D.

Professor of Law
Seton Hall University School of Law

Formerly Chief Justice of the
Provisional Court of Shanghai

SHEED AND WARD · NEW YORK · 1955

To Sheng Mu, Teh Lan, and Erh Chieh
in love and gratitude

CONTENTS

PROLOGUE

SOME BASIC NOTIONS

PART ONE
THE NATURAL LAW AND OUR COMMON LAW

Section I.

The Common Law in Its Old Home

Section II.

The Common Law in Its New Home

PART TWO
IN THE SCHOOL OF CHRIST

EPILOGUE
THE ART OF LAW

PROLOGUE

SOME BASIC NOTIONS

SOME BASIC NOTIONS

As the present book is addressed not only to lawyers who are interested in the fundamental problems of legal philosophy, but also to educated people with no special knowledge of the law, I find it necessary to begin with a general introduction in order to clarify some of the basic ideas and terms which constitute the woof and warp of the whole book. What, for instance, is meant by law, and how many kinds of law are there? What is natural law, what is human law, what is the essence of law, what is the end of law? What are the relations between the eternal law, the natural law, and positive law? What is Divine positive law, what is human positive law? What are the sources of human law? What is the common good? What is speculative reason, what is practical reason? What is teleological jurisprudence, and what is conceptualistic jurisprudence?

It is clear that to answer these questions adequately would take a whole volume. The best I can do here is to offer a synopsis of my philosophy of law, in which the above questions will be dealt with briefly, each in its proper place. I have said "my" philosophy of law, not because I am particularly possessive, but because I am too diffident to claim that my philosophy can represent any school. It is true that I draw largely upon the Holy Scriptures and the works of St. Thomas, but there are Christians and Christians, and there are Thomists and Thomists, and I certainly dare not assert that my line of legal thinking represents *the* Christian or *the* Thomistic philosophy of law. I shall be sufficiently happy if the reader does not find in my ideas anything unchristian. When other writers have proclaimed themselves proudly to be Kantians, Hegelians, Marxists, Benthamites, Platonists, Confucianists, Darwinians, Spinozists, and so forth, why should I be ashamed of being a Christian philosopher of law? I shall be more than grateful if Christianity is not ashamed of me. But I beg my non-Christian readers to bear with me when they come across any passages in this book which flow from faith rather than from natural reason. As I have believed, so have I spoken. But it is hoped that there is enough in this book to appeal to the natural reason of every reader. There is still another matter for which I beseech the reader's indulgence. Since this Prologue serves as a background for the main body of the book, a certain number of overlappings will be unavoidable.

The Need of a Philosophy of Law

When we speak of law, we ordinarily mean *human* law, the law that regulates the transactions and relations between men in their social life, the law that defines their rights and duties, civil liability and criminal responsibility, and prescribes the remedies for wrongs and the proper procedure for complaining and setting up defenses. Why, then, do we not confine our study strictly to *human* law, and why should we bring in such things as theology, philosophy, ethics, sociology, economic theories? The answer is twofold. In the first place, the profession of law is not a mere craft for making a living, as the layman is inclined to think—perhaps not without a certain justification, when he observes the narrow intellectual interests of the lawyers he may happen to know. As Justice Holmes testified, "One heard Burke saying that law sharpens the mind by narrowing it. One heard in Thackeray of a lawyer bending all the powers of a great mind to a mean profession. One saw that artists and poets shrank from it as from an alien world. One doubted oneself how it could be worthy of the interest of an intelligent mind."[1] "And yet," he said to himself, "law is human—it is a part of man, and of one world with the rest."[2] Like all men, lawyers too desire happiness. "And happiness," said Holmes, "I am sure from having known many successful men, cannot be won simply by being counsel for great corporations and having an income of fifty thousand dollars. An intellect great enough to win the prize needs other food besides success. The remoter and more general aspects of the law are those which give it universal interest. It is through them that you not only become a great master in your calling, but connect your subject with the universe and catch an echo of the infinite, a glimpse of its unfathomable process, a hint of the universal law."[3] "It seems to me," he further declared, "that for men as they are, the law may keep its every-day character and yet be an object of understanding wonder and a field for the lightning of genius."[4]

Secondly, we may be allowed to go a step further than Justice Holmes, and to observe that the law, even in its every-day character, necessarily contains "an echo of the infinite" and "a hint of the universal law." Moreover, so far as the ideals of life are concerned, the distinction between an ordinary man and a man of genius does not appear to me as marked as the words of Holmes would lead us to believe. As a matter of fact, Holmes himself has said, "If you convince a man that another way of looking at things is more profound, another form of pleasure more subtle than that to which he has been accustomed—if you can make him really see it—the very nature of man is such that he will desire the profounder thought and the subtiler joy."[5] Thus, he shows a great faith in the perfectibility of human nature as such. To him, "the business of a law school is not sufficiently described when you merely say that it is to teach law or to make lawyers. It is to teach law in the grand manner, and to make great lawyers."[6] As students of law cannot all be men of genius, it is plain that Holmes wanted law to be taught in the grand manner to men of ordinary intelligence.

But my own point is that there is no other way of teaching law except in the grand manner, for the simple reason that one cannot really know the law without taking account of its sources. If only we delve into the cases deep enough, we should find it literally true that "the sparks of all sciences are raked up in the ashes of the law."[7] You may think that this is an outmoded way of looking at the law. But a great modern master of the common law has testified to the same truth. In a lecture to law students, Justice Cardozo said:

> You think perhaps of philosophy as dwelling in the clouds. I hope you may see that she is able to descend to the earth. You think that in stopping to pay court to her, when you should be hastening forward on your journey, you are loitering in by-paths and wasting precious hours. I hope you may share my faith that you are on the highway to the goal. Here you will find the key for the unlocking of bolts and combinations that shall never be pried open by clumsier or grosser tools. You think that there is nothing practical in a theory that is concerned with ultimate conceptions. That is true perhaps while you are doing the journeyman's work of your profession. You may find in the end, when you pass to higher problems, that instead of its being true that the study of the ultimate is profitless, there is little that is profitable in the study of anything else.[8]

Cardozo was not trying to win the students to philosophy. He was trying to win them to law. He was giving an inside view of the law. "Implicit in every decision where the question is, so to speak, at large, is a philosophy of the origin and aim of law, a philosophy which, however veiled, is in truth the final arbiter. It accepts one set of arguments, modifies another, rejects a third, standing ever in reserve as a court of ultimate appeal. Often the philosophy is ill co-ordinated and fragmentary. Its empire is not always suspected even by its subjects. Neither lawyer nor judge, pressing forward along one line or retreating along another, is conscious at all times that it is philosophy which is impelling him to the front or driving him to the rear. None the less, the goad is there. If we cannot escape the Furies, we shall do well to understand them."[9]

I may add that in a majority of cases, the question is "at large." I may further add that even when a lawyer is doing the journeyman's work of his profession, the Furies are at work in him, although he does not understand them. It is usually the unconscious philosophy of a man which is the most doctrinaire and stubborn.

Let me then present my philosophy of law in all candidness, without claiming for it any finality but only as one point of view among others.

Human Law as a Compound of Natural Law and Positive Law

In order to understand what human law is, we must have some notion of the eternal law, and particularly of the natural law, which is not only the origin from which all human law is derived, but constitutes an essential part of it. As St. Thomas has said, "Every law enacted by man enjoys the character of law to the extent that it is derived from the natural law."[10] The human sovereign is, indeed, subject to God and to the law, because it is from them that he derives his authority.

Speaking of the king, Bracton wrote:[11]

It is true that in the receiving of justice the king stands in an equal position with the least in his kingdom. On the other hand, it is also true that in power he is superior to all. Even so, the heart of the king ought to be in the hand of God, so that his power may not be unbridled. Let him therefore apply the bridle of temperance and the reins of moderation, lest unbridled power should lead to lawlessness. For, as the servant and vicar of God, the king can do nothing on earth save that which he may lawfully do. Nor is it any answer to say that "what the king wills has the force of law" (Dig., i. 4. 1), because it is followed up at the end of that provision by these words: "as by the Lex Regia which was passed concerning his power"; that is, not everything that the will of the king rashly conceives, but what by the council of the magnates, with the authority of the king, and after due deliberation, has been rightly determined, has the force of law. His power is a power of law, not of lawlessness, and since he is the author of law, he must not give occasion to lawlessness, but only give birth to laws; and he whose office is to prohibit others to do wrong should never commit the very thing in his own person. In short, the king should use his power to do right as the vicar and servant of God on earth, for that alone is the power of God, while the power to do wrong is from the devil and not from God; and of him whose works he does the king will be the servant. Therefore, as long as he administers justice, he is the vicar of the eternal king, but he would be a servant of the devil if he turns aside to do injustice. The term "king" connotes good government, not reckless domination; because a king is a king when he governs well, but a tyrant when he oppresses the people with violence. (Cf. Isidore, Etym. ix. 3.) Let him therefore temper his power by law, which is the bridle of all power, so that he may live according to law, for human laws are sanctified when they bind their maker, and moreover "it is worthy of the majesty of the reigning king to avow to be bound by the law." (Cod. i. 14. 4.) Indeed, "nothing is so fitting to a ruler as to live according to law," and "to submit his authority to law is a greater thing than empire." (Cod. i. 14. 1.) For "it is good to attribute to the law what the law has attributed to him, for it is the law which makes him king."

This is true of all human power, be it legislative, judicial or executive. The force of a law, a judicial decision, or an administrative act depends on the extent of its justice, and justice means nothing else than conformity with the law of nature. Human law, being derived from the law of nature, is subject to it, and if in any point it is directly contrary to the law of nature, "it would no longer be law but a corruption of law."[12]

To illustrate the intrinsic force of the law of nature, take the case of *Robinson v. Continental Insurance Co. of Mannheim* (1915), 1 K.B. 155. There an alien enemy is made a defendant in an action before an English court. It is held that the action properly lies against him. The next question is: Can he appear and defend himself either personally or by counsel? The answer of Judge Bailhache is significant. "I think," he says, "he certainly can. To allow an action against an alien enemy to proceed and to refuse to allow him to appear and defend himself would be opposed to the fundamental principles of justice. No state of war would, in my view, demand or justify the condemnation of a man unheard." In other words, to hold otherwise would be so arbitrary and unreasonable as to constitute a perversion of law. As Nicodemus said to the Pharisees, "Does our law judge a man unless it first give him a hearing and know what he does?" (John 7:51). But the question is whether *any* law can do this kind of thing without losing its essential character as law. The fact that such a thing has been done by certain states at certain periods of their history does not turn lawlessness into law. The words of St. Augustine come to mind: "Without justice, what are kingdoms but gangs of robbers?" (*City of God*, Bk. IV, 4).

All systems of human law contain, in varying proportions, natural-law principles and positive rules. The former are immutable. They are not made, as are positive rules, by human authority, although they may be declared by it; therefore they are not subject to change. In the words of Pope Leo XIII: "Of the laws enacted by men, some are concerned with what is good or bad by its very nature; and they command men to follow after what is right and to shun what is wrong, adding at the time a suitable sanction. But such laws by no means derive their origin from civil authority; because just as civil society did not create human nature, so neither can it be said to be the author of the good which befits human nature, or of the evil which is contrary to it. Laws come before men live together in society, and have their origin in the natural, and consequently in the eternal, law. The precepts, therefore, of the natural law, contained bodily in the laws of men, have not merely the force of human law, but they possess that higher and more august sanction which belongs to the law of nature and the eternal law." Of the positive rules of law, the same Pontiff has this to say: "Now there are other enactments of the civil authority, which do not follow directly, but somewhat remotely, from the natural law, and decide many points which the law of nature treats in a general and indefinite way. For instance, though nature commands all to contribute to the public peace and prosperity, still whatever belongs to the manner and circumstances and conditions under which such service is to be rendered must be determined by the wisdom of men and not by Nature herself."[13]

Thus, positive law is really but an implementation of the natural law and has to vary with the changing circumstances and conditions of social life. It takes both elements to constitute a living system of human law. St. Thomas has given an apt instance of it: "It is the law of nature that he who does evil should be punished; but that he should be punished in any specific way is a kind of determination (particularization) of the law of nature."[14] We may add that these particular determinations should be revised from time to time so as to keep abreast of the advancing civilization of man. To take another example, it is one of the principles of natural law that justice should be done to every man. No reasonable man can deny this principle. But as to what is just under particular circumstances, reasonable men can and often do disagree. St. Thomas has brought out this point very clearly in dealing with the question whether the judicial precepts of the Old Law bind forever. The objector maintains that they bind forever. "The judicial precepts," so runs the objection, "pertain to the virtue of justice: for judgment is said to be the exercise of justice. But justice is *perpetual and immortal,* says the Book of Wisdom (1:15). Therefore the binding force of the judicial precepts is perpetual."[15] St. Thomas's reply to this objection is characteristically judicious: "Justice indeed must be observed at all times. But the determination of what is just by human or divine enactment must vary with the different circumstances of mankind."[16] What St. Thomas means by "divine enactment" is the divine positive law, which is not part of the natural law. The Old Law embraces three kinds of precepts, the ceremonial, the judicial and the moral. Only the moral precepts belong to the natural law.

The principles of the natural law are permanent and comprehensive; but just because they are comprehensive, they have an elasticity when they come to be applied. The positive rules are variable and subject to change by human authority; but as long as they remain in force, they are rigid in application. Because the principles of natural law are broad and elastic in their application, many a superficial jurist is led to deny their intrinsic immutability. Likewise, because the positive rules are clear-cut and rigid in their application, the unwary are led to deny their intrinsic changeability. One must beware of these pitfalls. As Lord Penzance said, "Law is, or ought to be, the handmaid of justice, and inflexibility, which is the most becoming robe of the latter, often serves to render the former grotesque."[17]

The Definition of Law

It is not easy to arrive at a complete definition of law. To be in any way adequate, a definition of law must take account of its essence, its end, and its process (genesis and growth). Philosophers and jurists of different ages and schools have attempted to answer the question: What is law? Mostly they have paid special attention to one aspect or one kind of law, to the neglect of other aspects or kinds. Some conceive of the law ontologically, others teleologically, and still others functionally. Some think principally of the eternal law, others of the natural law, and still others of the positive law.

In *Minos*, attributed to Plato, we find the statement: "Law seeks to be the finding out of reality."[18] Chrysippus is quoted by Diogenes Laertius as saying: "The common law, going through all things, is the same with Zeus who administers the whole universe."[19] These evidently have reference to the eternal law. The same is true of Hooker's words: "Of law there can be no less acknowledged, than that her seat is the bosom of God, her voice the harmony of the world; all things in heaven and earth do her homage, the very least as feeling her care; and the greatest as not exempted from her power."[20]

Cicero was thinking of the natural law when he said: "Law is the highest reason, implanted in nature, which commands what ought to be done and prohibits the contrary."[21] Celsus was thinking of the process and the end of law when he said that "law (*ius*) is the art of what is good and equitable."[22] The positivists have laid exclusive emphasis upon the will and power of the political sovereign as the ultimate source of all law, forgetting that it is the law that makes the political sovereign. The pragmatists have emphasized the enforcement as the life of law. Cardozo, for instance, writes: "A principle or rule of conduct so established as to justify a prediction with reasonable certainty that it will be enforced by the courts if its authority is challenged, is, then, for the purpose of our study, a principle or rule of law."[23] He looks at the law chiefly as a process and his approach is predominantly psychological. The saving grace of this definition lies in the fact that it leaves the door open to the principles of natural law, which, if the courts think rightly, will be a strong ground for their decision and therefore constitute a solid basis for our prediction. But this definition is one-sided, because it neglects the essence of the law.

Comparatively the most adequate definition of the law is that of St. Thomas: "It is nothing other than a certain rule of reason for the purpose of the common good, laid down by him who is entrusted with the welfare of the community, and promulgated."[24] This definition takes care of the essence as well as the end and the process of the law. The essence of the law is conformity to reason, the end is the common good, and the process consists in gradual realization of its essence through a progressive attainment of the end, by means of legislation, promulgation, judgment and enforcement. The definition comprehends all kinds of law: the eternal law, the natural law, the human law, and the revealed Divine law of the Old and the New Dispensation.

The Eternal Law

Wherever there is order, there is law. The whole cosmos is an ordinance of Divine Reason. God, who is its Creator, is also its Lawgiver, its Judge and its King. He governs the whole creation according to the plan of His Divine Providence for the good of all. This plan is called the eternal law. The eternal law must not be identified with the Word, because it is not a Person like the Word, but an Idea. But, as St. Thomas has pointed out, the eternal law is specially related to the Word. The Word is not made, but begotten by the Father expressing Himself wholly in the uncreated. All things were made through the Word expressing them as they are in the Father's knowledge. "And among other things which are expressed through this Word, the eternal law itself is also expressed through the same."[25]

No one can know the eternal law as it is in itself, except the Blessed, who see God in His essence. The eternal law is the fountainhead of both the physical order and the moral order. We see it darkly through the mirror of its effects. Poets and philosophers of all ages have experienced momentary transports, when they are struck by the ineffable wonders of the universe and the mysterious harmony between the physical order and the moral order. The realization that the same Love and Wisdom that kindle and enlighten our hearts give life and order to the whole mysterious universe, sends us into raptures.[26] In our workaday moments, our vision is fragmentized. We know that the law of the Decalogue, the law of gravitation, the law of conservation of energy, the Mendelian law, the law of diminishing returns, and criminal and civil law, all belong to different orders of laws. But when we reflect that God is the sole Lawgiver, whose intention we read with more or less accuracy, we begin to see the fundamental unity of all kinds of laws. Then we shall be in a position to sing with David:

> The heavens show forth the glory of God: and the firmament declareth the work of his hands.
> Day to day uttereth speech: and night to night showeth knowledge. (Ps. 18:1-2.)

And in the same breath we shall celebrate the wonders of the moral law:

> The law of the Lord is unspotted, converting souls: the testimony of the Lord is faithful, giving wisdom to the little ones.
> The justices of the Lord are right, rejoicing hearts: the commandment of the Lord is lightsome, enlightening the eyes. (Ps. 18:7-8.)

All these are but the effects of the eternal law, which, as it is in itself, is hidden among the clouds. As the Psalmist has it:

> The Lord is King: let the earth exult, let the many islands be glad.
> Clouds and darkness surround him: justice and right are the support of his throne. (Ps. 96:1-2.)

While the eternal law in its essence is beyond our powers of comprehension, it is enough for us to know that "all laws to the degree that they share in right reason, to that degree are they derived from the eternal law."[27] It is because physical law and moral law share a common origin in the eternal law that both are rooted in the reality of things and belong to the same universe. However little we may know about the eternal law, this transcendental reference is an indispensable starting point of a sound philosophy of law.

One of the commonest errors of modern thinkers is to hold that physical law is objective, while moral law is subjective; for the former has to do with what is true, while the latter has to do with what is good. But it cannot be too much emphasized that if the good is not founded in Reality or Being, it would not be good at all, just as truth would not be truth if it did not correspond with Reality. On this point, I want to introduce a passage from Frank Sheed dealing with the distinction between physical law and moral law and at the same time showing that both are rooted in ontological Reality:

> A very brief consideration of the laws by which our universe is run shows us two rather different sets of laws, what we may call physical law and moral law. The practical distinction for us is that physical law is God's ordinance as to how all things *must* act, moral law is His ordinance as to how spiritual beings *ought to* act. There is an element of choice in the operation of the moral law which does not exist in the operation of the physical law. But the element of choice, although it is there, may not be precisely what we think. That fire burns is a physical law, at times extraordinarily useful for man, at times catastrophic. But, useful or catastrophic, fire still burns. At first sight the moral law seems different. It tells us that we ought to do this and ought not to do that, and in those very terms implies that we are free to choose whether we will do this or that, whereas there is no freedom of choice about being burned if we put our hand in the fire. But in actual fact the moral law merely casts into the form of a command something that is already as much a law of nature as that fire burns. God's command to us not to bear false witness implies that we are free to bear false witness if we choose; but

to bear false witness—even if we do not know of God's command and no question of sin arises—will damage us spiritually
just as certainly as to put our hands into the fire will damage
us bodily. We can if we choose bear false witness: we can if
we choose put our hand into the fire: in either event we shall
be damaged. In other words physical laws and moral laws *are*
laws because we are what we are. If we were asbestos instead
of flesh, fire would not burn us; if we were stags, adultery
would not damage us either. Physical law or moral law, to
know what it is, is to know the reality of things: to act in accordance with it, is to act by the reality of things. And that is
sanity.[28]

While I am on this subject, I cannot resist the urge to quote a
magnificent passage from Pius XII, because every word in it rings
true.

It is impossible to observe with attention the universe, corporeal and spiritual, physical and moral, without being struck
with admiration at the sight of the order and harmony that
reign throughout all the various grades in the scale of being.
In man, up to that line of boundary where his unconscious activity ends and the conscious and free action begins, that order
and that harmony are strictly realized according to the laws
placed by the Creator in the existing being. Beyond that line
the ordaining will of God is still in force; however, its actualization and its development are left to the free determination
of man, which can be either conformed or opposed to the
Divine Will.

In this field of conscious human action, of good and evil, of
command, permission and prohibition, the ordaining will of
the Creator is manifested through the moral commandment of
God written in nature and in revelation, as also through the
command and the law of legitimate human authority, alike in
the family, in the State, and in the Church. If human activity
regulates and directs itself according to these norms, it remains naturally in harmony with the universal order willed by
the Creator.

In this is found the answer to the question of true law and
false law. The mere fact that the legislative power declares a
rule to be obligatory in the State does not, in and of itself,

make it a true law. The "criterion of simple fact" is valid solely for Him who is the Author and the Supreme Norm of all law, God. To apply it indiscriminately and definitively to the human legislator, as if his law were the supreme norm of right, is the error of juridical positivism in the proper and technical sense of the word. This is the error which is at the root of state absolutism, and which is tantamount to the deification of the state itself.[29]

There is a true realism, and there is a false realism. There is a true existentialism and a false existentialism. True realism and existentialism start from the fundamental insight that of the Supreme Being alone can we say that His Existence is His Essence, and, as a corollary from this initial perception, that in all other beings existence falls short of essence and carries within itself an aspiration to the essence. Without this aspiration, existence is a mere empty husk with no living kernel inside; and this is precisely what false realism and existentialism would lead us to. This aspiration of the existential to embody more and more fully the essential is rooted in, and evoked by, the very nature of the Supreme Being, who is Reality Itself.

To put it more plainly, with God reality is a fact; but with us reality must be achieved. Our reality consists in realization, in a continuous process of progressive realization. True realism differs from false realism in that it perceives the aspiration to the essence as a necessary constituent of existence. It differs, on the other hand, from mere idealism in that it sees the aspiration in the context of ontological Reality. A true realism would echo the words of the Psalmist: "Deep calleth on deep, at the noise of Thy flood-gates" (Ps. 51:8).

The Natural Law

St. Thomas defines the natural law as "a participation in the eternal law by the rational creature."[30] It is important to know the distinction between the eternal law and the natural law, if we are to avoid the pitfall of unwarranted dogmatism. The eternal law is the Plan of Divine Providence, and therefore it is absolutely perfect. The natural law, on the other hand, is only an imprint of the eternal law on the natural reason of man, which is finite and cannot be absolutely perfect. No one has brought out this distinction in clearer terms than St. Thomas himself: "Human reason is not able to participate completely in the dictates of divine reason but only in its own mode, and imperfectly. Now, in respect to speculative reason, there is in us, through a natural participation in divine wisdom, a knowledge of certain general principles, but not a particular knowledge of each and every truth as it is possessed by divine wisdom. Likewise, in respect to practical reason, man naturally shares in the eternal law as to certain general principles, but not, however, as to the particular determinations of each one of them, although they are contained in the eternal law."[31]

St. Thomas further distinguishes practical reason from speculative reason. Speculative reason deals mainly with cause and effect, while practical reason deals mainly with end and means. The former has for its object *the true*, while the latter has for its end the *good*. The former deals with facts and factual relations, while the latter deals with values and their relative importance, and involves the choice of ends and the determination of the means thereto. In consequence of this difference in subject matter, practical reason, to which law belongs, is differently situated from speculative reason with regard to certitude.

"Since speculative reason deals chiefly with necessary relations which cannot possibly be other than they are, truth is found without any defect in particular conclusions just as it is found in general principles. But practical reason deals with contingencies, among which are human actions, and therefore, although there is some necessity in the general principles, the further you descend to particular conclusions, the more you find the lack thereof."[32]

This insight is of paramount importance to all students of law. Most of the errors of modern jurists can be traced to a lack of clear understanding of the nature and limitations of practical reason. Those who are dogmatically inclined have sought necessity or perfect rectitude not only in the general principles but also in matters of detail. On the other hand, the sceptics have denied necessity not only in matters of detail but also in general principles. Mr.

Justice Holmes, for instance, was right when he applied his "cynical acid"[33] to the over-assertions of the dogmatists. When the economic doctrine of laissez-faire was fortified by the legal doctrine of the liberty of contract, when free and ruthless competition found a sacred sanction in the Darwinian theory of struggle for existence and survival of the fittest, when labor was considered a mere commodity and the labor contract was treated on a par with any other contract of purchase and sale, when reasonable social legislation was denounced by the courts as paternalism, when, in short, the legal system was being dehumanized in the name of the natural law, even the "cynical acid" served as a timely antidote.

But Justice Holmes went to the other extreme when he made a sweeping denial of the natural law. In his own words, "It is not enough for the knight of romance that you agree that his lady is a very nice girl,—if you do not admit that she is the best that God ever made or will make, you must fight. There is in all men a demand for the superlative, so much so that the poor devil who has no other way of reaching it attains it by getting drunk. It seems to me that this demand is at the bottom of the philosopher's effort to prove that truth is absolute and of the jurist's search for the criteria of universal validity which he collects under the head of natural law."[34] In this he denied too much. For men cannot live on cynical acid alone, however useful it may be in dissolving "legal conceptualism."

A word should be said about the meaning of "conceptualistic jurisprudence" or "legal conceptualism," which the reader will often come across throughout this book. The term is a translation of *"Begriffsjurisprudenz"* which Ihering coined to describe all tendencies in legal thinking opposed to his own *"Wirklichkeitsjurisprudenz,"* which means a jurisprudence of realities.[35] Of course, the science of law, like all sciences, cannot dispense with concepts, but the legal conceptualists use them as ends in themselves, and not as a means to an end, which is always the administration of justice. They put the law in a technical shape, which makes it seem to belong to speculative reason like a causal law, and tends to hide its teleological motive. In many cases, this proves to be a labor-saving device for the judge, who, instead of resorting every time to value-judgment and intuition like another Solomon, would need only to start from a legal concept as a major premise, use the facts of the case as the minor premise, and deduce a conclusion almost automatically. Some jurists have compared this process to the slot-machine. You put a coin in at the right slot, and behold! out comes the thing desired. (Sometimes it doesn't, as my secretary tells me, but that is an accident.)

I remember when I was sitting in a police court in Shanghai, every morning there were brought to me hundreds of cases of minor infractions of traffic regulations, each to be fined not more than a dollar. If I had had to resort each time to equity or a balancing of interests, the mental strain would have killed me long ago. In such cases, the judicial slot-machine worked perfectly. There was the municipal ordinance, there were the facts, and the result came out just as certainly as the physical law that fire burns. For the most part, the legal order looks like the natural order, although it is artificially set up by positive law. But unfortunately not all cases are as simple as that, and the trouble comes when a judge begins to regard the artificially set up "natural order" as though it were really a part of the eternal order of things. When the judge allows his thought processes to be reduced to the application of the crystallized formula and entirely forgets the mother-liquor of justice and equity, he is likely to turn the law into a Procrustean bed. So he must be reminded of what Sir Thomas Browne has said, "When natural logic prevails not, artificial logic too often faileth," and of what Justice Evatt has declared, "Ratiocination is good, but common sense is necessary."[36] Now, what they have called "natural logic" and "common sense" is kindred to what St. Thomas has called "the natural law" and "practical reason," whose basic principle is to pursue the good and avoid the evil.

Take, for instance, the concept of possession. The classical jurists analysed "possession" into two elements, the *corpus,* or the body, and the *animus,* or the soul. The *corpus* denotes a person's physical control over a thing; while the *animus* denotes his intention to occupy it to the exclusion of others. Now, the whole idea of possession originated in primitive society when many things were still ownerless and therefore could be acquired by prior occupation. It is clear that in such a situation some definite and unmistakable criteria must be set up to distinguish a "true" possession from a "false" possession, in order to prevent private feuds and a relapse into a condition of anarchy. The classical concept of possession was arrived at in the light of that situation. It had a pragmatic origin, and must not be regarded as an *a priori* axiom. But in the nineteenth century, most judges had come to treat it as an abstract axiom isolated entirely from its origin and its end of maintaining peace and justice, and to apply it without regard to the practical consequences.

Let one illustration suffice. In the case of *Young v. Hitchens*, 6 Queen's Bench, 606 (1844), the undisputed facts were as follows: The plaintiff had drawn his net partially round the fish in question, leaving open a space of about seven fathoms, which he was about to close with a stop net; that two boats, belonging to the plaintiff, were stationed at the opening, splashing the water about for the purpose of terrifying the fish, so that they would not pass through the opening; and that, at this time, the defendant rowed his boat up to the opening, and the disturbance, and the taking of the fish complained of, took place. The learned Sergeant left to the jury the question of fact whether the fish were at that time in the plaintiff's possession, and also other questions of fact on the other issues. Verdict for plaintiff on all the issues, with damages separately assessed, namely, 568 £. for the value of the fish, and 1 £. for the damage done to the net. But in the Queen's Bench, the judgment was reversed. Lord Denman, C.J., said, "It does appear almost certain that the plaintiff would have had possession of the fish but for the act of the defendant; but it is quite certain that he had not possession. Whatever interpretation may be put upon such terms as 'custody' and 'possession,' the question will be whether any custody or possession has been obtained here. I think it is impossible to say that it had, until the party had actual power over the fish. It may be that the defendant acted unjustifiably in preventing the plaintiff from obtaining such power: but that would only show a wrongful act, for which he might be liable in a proper form of action." Patteson, J., said, "I do not see how we could support the affirmative of these issues upon the present evidence, unless we were prepared to hold that all but reducing into possession is the same as reducing into possession."

These opinions savor of excessive technicality. They lay too much emphasis on the physical element of possession. If it was practically certain that the partially enclosed fish would have been completely enclosed but for the act of the defendant, the court should have concluded that there was possession, if they knew that law was not mathematics but an instrument of justice. But they were enslaved by the tyranny of concepts. This is what Ihering meant by "a jurisprudence of conceptions," which Dean Pound would call "mechanical jurisprudence."[37]

St. Thomas's philosophy of the natural law saves us, on the one hand, from such a "jurisprudence of conceptions" and, on the other hand, from a purely utilitarian and pragmatic jurisprudence. He steers carefully between a naive and unconscious dogmatism which attributes cosmic validity to all ideas one may happen to hold, and a sheer psychological relativism which recognizes no objective standards of right and justice. He is neither a porcupine, with too many spines, nor a jellyfish with no spine. His philosophy of law is opposed to mechanical jurisprudence, because it is teleological, maintaining that law is ordained to the common good, as its *telos*. This is why Ihering, who was the author of *Der Zweck im Recht*, or *Law as a Means to an End*,[38] should have praised St. Thomas so highly. Ihering had not read St. Thomas when he wrote his book. It was only after the first edition was published that he came to study the work of St. Thomas. In the second edition of *Der Zweck im Recht*, which was published in 1886, he wrote some significant words about the Saint: "Now that I have come to know this vigorous thinker, I cannot help asking myself how it was possible that truths such as he has taught should have been so completely forgotten among our Protestant scholars. What errors could have been avoided if people had kept these doctrines! . . . For my part, if I had known them earlier, I probably would not have written my whole book; for the fundamental ideas which I have treated here are found expressed in full clarity and in a convincing manner by this powerful thinker."[39] Considering the tremendous influence of Ihering on contemporary jurists, one can easily see how *modern* the ideas of St. Thomas must be. In fact, they are neither ancient nor new, but belong to the *philosophia perennis*. But while Ihering was wise enough to see the teleological aspect of St. Thomas's legal philosophy, he did not seem to realize its ontological basis. He did not absorb St. Thomas's philosophy of the natural law, which is the foundation of all positive law.

To St. Thomas, the basic precepts of the natural law are immediate dictates of man's natural reason. They are self-evident principles. The first precept is that *good is to be done and evil is to be avoided*. All other precepts are based upon this. Whatever practical reason naturally apprehends as good or evil to man as man belongs to the precepts of the natural law as something to be done or avoided. He places human goods on three levels.[40] First, life as such is a good, and therefore "whatever conduces to the preservation of human life, and to the elimination of its obstacles, belongs to the natural law." Secondly, the procreation and education of offspring is a good. Therefore, whatever preserves the integrity of the family and promotes its welfare belongs to the natural law. Thirdly, man being a rational creature, he has a natural inclination to know the truth about God and to live peacefully and harmoniously in human society. Therefore, whatever secures religious and intellectual freedom, whatever establishes justice, peace and order in society belongs to the natural law.

It should be noted that St. Thomas does not regard the natural inclinations of man as in themselves constituting the principles of the natural law. He treats them only as the natural materials to be regulated by reason. In his own words: "All the inclinations of human nature of any parts whatsoever, for instance the concupiscible and irascible parts, belong to the natural law insofar as they are ruled by reason."[41] In other words, the natural law is a dictate of natural reason concerning natural goods. It is for reason to evaluate, affirm, approve, correct, and co-ordinate the natural goods or values in a proper relationship.

For instance, life is a good, but under certain circumstances it is the clearest duty to sacrifice it for a higher good. As the Chinese sage Mencius says, "I desire life. I also desire justice. But if I cannot have both, I shall have to let life go and take justice."[42] In a well-known shipwreck case, *United States v. Holmes*[43] Justice Baldwin said, "The sailor (to use the language of a distinguished writer) owes more benevolence to another than to himself. He is bound to set a greater value on the life of others than on his own. And while we admit that sailor and sailor may lawfully struggle with each other for the plank which can save but one, we think that, if the passenger is on the plank, even 'the law of necessity' justifies not the sailor who takes it from him." This opinion illustrates the point that one has no right unreasonably to sacrifice another's life in order to save one's own life, and that in the light of reason there are higher values than human life, to say nothing of material interests. It is significant that the Justice announced that "The law of nature forms part of the municipal law." There is a hierarchy of values in the order of nature. As Francis Bacon says in *Chudleigh's Case*[44] "Life and liberty are more precious than lands or goods." It may be added that justice and duty are even more precious than life and liberty.

St. Thomas considers all the moral precepts of Holy Scripture as precepts of the natural law. It is impossible in this article to treat the moral precepts in detail. Happily, Christ Himself has given us a fundamental view of the law. Once a doctor of the Law, putting Christ to the test, asked Him, "Master, which is the great commandment in the Law?" His answer was: "*Thou shalt love the Lord thy God with thy whole heart, and with thy whole soul, and with thy whole mind.* This is the greatest and the first commandment. And the second is like to this: *Thou shalt love thy neighbor as thyself.* On these two commandments dependeth the whole law and the prophets" (Matt. 22:35–40).

On another occasion, defining further the love of our neighbor, Christ uttered the Golden Rule: "All things therefore whatsoever you would that men should do to you, do you also to them. For this is the law and the prophets" (Matt. 7:12). In these words, Christ is commenting only on the moral precepts of the Old Law, and does not pass beyond the realm of natural reason and natural law. Confucius has likewise formulated a golden rule of life: "What you do not desire for yourself must not be inflicted upon another." These two golden rules, one positive and one negative, flowing directly from the first principle of the practical reason: *good is to be done and evil is to be avoided*, constitute the highest norms for the social life of man. All other precepts of the natural law are concretizations of these, e.g., *Honor thy father and thy mother, Thou shalt not kill, Thou shalt not commit adultery, Thou shalt not bear false witness against thy neighbor, Thou shalt not covet thy neighbor's house* (Exodus 20:12–17). There are further concretizations, such as: *If a fire breaking out light upon thorns, and catch stacks of corn, or corn standing in the fields, he that kindled the fire shall make good the loss* (Exodus 22:6). No one can reasonably deny the justice of this. Even some of the judicial precepts, addressed specifically to the judges, seem to flow from natural reason, such as: *The innocent and just person thou shalt not put to death . . . Neither shalt thou take bribes, which even blind the wise and pervert the words of the just; Thou shalt not follow the multitude to do evil; neither shalt thou yield in judgment to the opinion of the most part, to stray from the truth* (Exodus 23:7, 8, and 2). The last precept is of special significance for us moderns: we should remember that it is the truth, and not the majority view or public opinion, that a judge ought to follow.

The basic precepts of the natural law, so far as human law can embody them, are well declared in Justinian's *Institutes:* "The precepts of the law are these: to live honorably, to injure no one, and to give every man his due."[45] It is plain that to give every man his due and to injure no one is a juridical application of the Golden Rule in its positive and negative phases. "To live honorably" means, according to Savigny, "to preserve moral worth in one's own person."[46] In the human law, this precept, as Roscoe Pound has pointed out, "is represented . . . by the doctrines as to good faith in transactions, the rules as to the illegality of corrupt bargains, the various doctrines which recognize *boni mores* and attach consequences to violations thereof."[47]

Human Law

The eternal law, the natural law and human law form a continuous series. The whole series may be compared to a tree, with the eternal law for its root, the natural law for its trunk, and the different systems of human law for its branches. Wherever the soil is not too thin and the climate favorable, the tree sends forth its splendid flowers of justice and equity and yields the fruits of peace and order, virtue and happiness. Indeed, peace is the fruit of justice. Formally, the eternal law and the natural law belong to higher orders than human law; but materially, human law is richer and furnishes a more interesting field for study, because it embodies, *within the limits of its capacity*, part of the natural law together with certain positive or conventional rules and measures which vary with time and circumstances.

According to St. Thomas, as we have seen, the law of nature is the foundation of all human law. No positive enactment which runs counter to the law of nature can be regarded as law. For instance, "Human law can never concede that a man may lawfully be put to death without just cause."[48] The primacy of natural law over positive law is the fundamental starting point of the Thomistic philosophy of law. On the other hand, St. Thomas is equally emphatic on the point that the law of nature is inadequate to the task of regulating the affairs of men in society. To the objection that, "If human laws were derived from natural law, it would follow that they too would be the same for all people, but this obviously is not the case," St. Thomas replies: "The general principles of the natural law cannot be applied in the same way to all because of the great diversity in human affairs. Hence arises the diversity of positive laws among the various peoples."[49]

The truth is that human laws are derived from the natural law in two ways: first, by way of conclusion from premises; secondly, by way of determination of certain generalities. In his own words, "Some things are derived from the general principles of natural law by way of conclusions: thus the precept that *'one must not kill'* can be derived as a certain conclusion from the principle that *'evil should be done to no man.'*[50] Other things, however, are derived by way of determination: thus it is the law of nature that he who does evil should be punished; but that he should be punished in any specific way is a kind of determination of the natural law."[51]

For example, all systems of human law prohibit murder and

treason. This very uniformity bespeaks the sameness of their origin. But the punishments provided by the laws of different States differ greatly from one another. For punishment is only a means to an end. In the choice of the means, human judgment is bound to differ from country to country, from period to period, and from individual to individual.

There is no better illustration of the variability of human judgment than the recent case of *Rosenberg v. United States* (1953), 73 S. Ct. 1151, where the question is which of two different provisions concerning penalty should have been applied. Two statutes are involved, the Espionage Act of 1927 and the Atomic Energy Act of 1946. The first contains the provisions that if the acts are committed *in time of war*, the culprit *shall be punished by death or by imprisonment for not more than thirty years*. The second provides that the penalty of death or imprisonment for life may be imposed only upon recommendation of the jury. The trial court had applied the first act and sentenced the defendants to death without recommendation of the jury. The crime was commenced in 1944, more than two years before the Atomic Energy Act was passed, and the conviction was had under the Espionage Act. There can be no question about the legality of the conviction. The question is whether, in view of the fact that *when the sentence was passed* there was already in existence a later Act requiring recommendation of the jury, the court could still apply the earlier Act in this respect.

The opinions of the Justices of the Supreme Court are divided into three lines. The majority take the line that "Each Act is complete in itself and each has its own reason for existence and field of operation." They therefore hold that since the conviction was under the Espionage Act, it was not improper to apply the penalty as provided in the same Act. Justice Douglas, on the other hand, declared: "Some say, however, that since *a part* of the Rosenbergs' crime was committed under the old law, the penalties of the old law apply. But it is a law too elemental for citation of authority that where two penal statutes may apply—one carrying death, the other imprisonment—the court has no choice but to impose the less harsh sentence."

Justices Black and Frankfurter take still another line. They are noncommittal as to whether the majority or Justice Douglas is right. They only criticize the proceeding of the Supreme Court as being too much in a rush. In the words of Justice Black: "I think this question should be decided only after time has been afforded counsel for the Government, and for the defendants, to make more informed arguments than we have yet heard, and after this Court has had an opportunity to give more deliberation than it has given up to this date. This I think would be more nearly in harmony with the best judicial traditions." Justice Frankfurter said: "The Government could of course have charged a conspiracy beginning in 1944 and ending on July 31, 1946, the day before the Atomic Energy Act, 42 U.S.C.A. Sec. 1801 et seq., came into effect. It did not do so. That fact is of decisive importance." It is of decisive importance, that is, to make the question a substantial one. He does not decide the question, for as he says, "nothing I am saying may be taken to intimate that I would now sustain the last claim made in behalf of the Rosenbergs." "But I am clear," he continues, "that the claim had substance and that the opportunity for adequate exercise of judicial judgment was wanting." His point is: "More time was needed than was had for adequate consideration. . . . Without adequate study there cannot be adequate reflection; without adequate reflection there cannot be adequate discussion; without adequate discussion there cannot be the searching and fruitful interchange of informed minds which is indispensable to wise decision and which alone can produce compelling opinions." "This case," he concludes, "is an incident in the long and unending effort to develop and enforce justice according to law. The progress in that struggle surely depends on searching analysis of the past, though the past cannot be recalled, as illumination for the future. Only by sturdy self-examination and self-criticism can the necessary habits for detached and wise judgment be established and fortified so as to become effective when the judicial process is again subjected to stress and strain. American criminal procedure has its defects, though its essentials have behind them the vindication of long history. But all systems of law, however wise, are administered through men and therefore may occasionally disclose the frailties of men. Perfection may not be demanded of law, but the capacity to counteract inevitable, though rare, frailties is the mark of a civilized legal mechanism."

This case well illustrates the thesis of St. Thomas that human law deals with contingent matters, and though there is necessity in the general principles, the more we descend to the details the less necessity and certainty we encounter. The two different rules of penalty are both particular determinations of the natural law; or rather, of one of its conclusions, that treason should be punished. As determinations they are neither absolutely right nor, on the other hand, altogether arbitrary. Both are more or less proportionate to the end, which is to inhibit the crime of treason through fear of punishment.

In law the proportion between means and end cannot be expected to possess mathematical exactitude. For it is a sign of lack of scientific culture to expect exactitude where no exactitude can be had in the nature of things. For instance, in a case of self-defense, *Sikes v. Commonwealth*, Court of Appeals of Kentucky, 1947, 304 Ky. 429, 200 S.W. 2d 956, Commissioner Stanley has said, "Man-made law is not blind to human nature; at least self-preservation. So one is not held accountable for taking the life of another in resistance to an attack which from its nature creates a reasonable apprehension of imminent danger of losing one's own life or of suffering great bodily harm. Naturally, lesser correlative degrees of attack and defense receive the same sanction of the law. Generally speaking, the reciprocal standard or measure of force and violence is the same. It is essential that the defensive act not be excessive or disproportionate to the force involved in the attack. But the person under attack is not required to measure the force necessary to protect himself 'with as much exactness as an apothecary would drugs on his scales.' The measure is what in the exercise of a reasonable judgment under the circumstances is required to avert the danger. That is all the law demands." As Justice Holmes puts it, "Detached reflection cannot be demanded in the presence of an uplifted knife." (*Brown v. United States*, 1921. 256 U.S. 335.)

To return to the *Rosenberg case*, substantively the decision of the Court is probably right. The fact that the Espionage Act of

1917 mentions explicitly "in time of war" and that some of the acts of the defendants were begun and completed in time of war, gives a strong point to the majority opinion. The fact that the defendants continued their activities after the war was concluded cannot cancel the war-time character of their former acts. Justice Douglas's point would be valid if the two acts covered exactly the same factual situation, which they do not seem to do. But on such a complicated and novel question, no one can speak with absolute confidence. The natural law does not help us here. From the standpoint of the judicial process, the views of Justices Black and Frankfurter seem to represent not a mere "determination" but a "conclusion," however remote, of the natural law, and as such deserve serious consideration. The very fact that natural reason is inadequate to the decision of concrete cases emphasizes the need of what Lord Coke calls "artificial reason," whose exercise requires a great deal of study and deliberation.

Nature and Art in Jurisprudence

The making of a great jurist requires in a high degree the moral virtue of justice and the intellectual virtue of prudence. In the words of Bracton, "Jurisprudence perceives what is due to each man, and justice renders it to him. For justice is a virtue, while the prudence of law is a science."[52] Jurisprudence is, therefore, the science of justice. As Dr. Miriam T. Rooney has said, "The science of judging what is just, in so far as human reason is competent to determine it, is called jurisprudence."[53]

That the cultivation of this science of justice has need not only of natural reason but of "artificial reason" has been eloquently advocated by Lord Coke. On the one hand, he was one of the staunchest supporters of the law of nature. The influence of his doctrine upon American jurisprudence has been tremendous. I need only cite a few instances. In *Bank v. Cooper*, 2 Yerg. 599, 603 (1831), Justice Green said, "There are eternal principles of justice which no government has a right to disregard. It does not follow, therefore, because there may be no restriction in the Constitution

prohibiting a particular act of the legislature, that such act is therefore constitutional. Some acts, although not expressly forbidden,
may be against the plain obvious dictates of reason. 'The common law,' says Lord Coke, 'adjudgeth a statute so far void.'" In
1866, Chief Justice Chase declared, in *License Tax Cases*, 5 Wallace
462, 469, that "there are, undoubtedly, fundamental principles of
morality and justice which no legislature is at liberty to disregard."
In 1910, in *Monongahela B. Co. v. U.S.*, 2166 U.S. 177, 195, Justice
Harlan said in all frankness that "the courts have rarely, if ever, felt
themselves so restrained by technical rules that they could not find
some remedy, consistent with the law, for acts, whether done by
government or by individual persons, that violated natural justice
or were hostile to the fundamental principles devised for the protection of the essential rights of property." Only recently Coke
was cited together with Bracton by the Supreme Court of New
Jersey.[54]

But what is of special significance for jurisprudence is the fact
that Lord Coke, who was such a great advocate of the natural law
and natural reason, should also have been the one who saw so clearly
the indispensable role of "the artificial reason" in the making and
learning of human law.

Now Coke has been made a victim of ridicule by certain modern
writers for saying that the common law is "the perfection of reason." This seems to me to be an instance of thoughtless scoffing.
What he actually said was:

> For reason is the life of law, nay the common law itselfe is
> nothing else but reason; which is to be understood of an arti-
> ficiall perfection of reason, gotten by long study, observation,
> and experience, and not of every man's naturall reason; for
> *Nemo nascitur artifex.*[55]

If I am not mistaken, he did not mean that the common law was perfect by nature, but rather that it was constantly being perfected by
art, by the cumulative experience of many generations. What he
was emphasizing was the necessity of patient study and long rumi-
nation before the student could assimilate the spirit of the common
law. We must not rely solely upon our own abstract ratiocination,

we must feed our minds with the knowledge and experience of juridical realities. This recalls to my mind a wise saw of Confucius: "Thinking without study is perilous: study without thinking is vain."[56] But the passage I like best in Coke is where he compares the learning of law to drawing water from a well.

> Our student shall observe, that the knowledge of the law is like a deepe well, out of which each man draweth according to the strength of his understanding. He that reacheth deepest, he seeth the amiable and admirable secrets of the law, wherein I assure you the sages of the law in former times (whereof sir William Herle was a principall one) have had the deepest reach. And as the bucket in the depth is easily drawn to the uppermost part of the water, (for *nullum elementum in suo proprio loco est grave*)[57] but take it from the water, it cannot be drawne up but with great difficultie; so albeit beginnings of this study seem difficult, yet when the professor of the law can dive into the depth, it is delightfull easie and without any heavy burthen so long as he keepe himselfe in his own proper element.[58]

We owe to Coke the beautiful phrase: "The gladsome light of jurisprudence."[59] Were it not for the eternal and natural law, there would be no "gladsome light." Were it not for the human refinement of natural reason there would be no "jurisprudence."

The Sources of Human Law

The natural law is not only the foundation of human law, but constitutes one of its essential "sources." In many countries of codified law, this source is explicitly recognized. For instance, in the Austrian Code of 1811, it is provided that when a case is not covered by the statutes and cannot be decided even by analogy, "then it is to be decided in accordance with the principles of natural law in the light of a careful gathering of facts and their mature consideration" (Section 7). Article 21 of the Louisiana Civil Code reads: "In all civil matters, where there is no express law, the judge is bound to proceed and decide according to equity. To decide equitably, an appeal is to be made to natural law and reason, or received usages, where positive law is silent." Similarly, the Swiss Civil Code contains the provision: "Where the law expressly leaves a point to the discretion of the judge, or directs him to take circumstances into consideration, or to appreciate whether a ground alleged is material, he must base his decision on principles of justice and equity" (Art. 4).

Superficially it may seem as though, in all these instances, it is the positive law that gives authority to the natural law. But in reality the positive law here is only declaratory of the natural law. In the very nature of things, it is impossible for a human authority to foresee all the infinitely variable and ever-changing conditions and circumstances of human affairs so as to regulate them with comprehensive particularity. As St. Thomas says, "No man's wisdom is so great that he can anticipate every single case, and so he is not able to set forth in words adequately those things which bear upon the purpose he has in mind. Even if a legislator could consider every case, yet to avoid confusion, he ought not to set forth all of them: but he should enact laws to cover the most common occurrences."[60]

The natural law, from which human law is derived, continues to hold, as it were, a residuary power in the decision of particular cases. This is also true of the common-law countries, where the body of the law is built upon customs and precedents. As C. K. Allen has written, "If it is true that precedents are employed only to discover principles, so it is true that principles are employed to discover justice. . . . Nobody claims that the law always achieves ideal moral justice, but whatever the inevitable technicalities of legal science may be, they exist for the prosecution of one aim only, the aim of the judge's office: to do justice between litigants, not to make interesting contributions to legal theory. This dominant purpose all precedents, all arguments, and all principles must subserve; and when precedents do not help, enlightenment must be found elsewhere. Hence arise those cases 'of first impression' which are by no means uncommon in the courts, even at this day when so many permutations and combinations of circumstances have been considered and recorded. To what, then, do the judges turn? To those principles of reason, morality, and social utility which are the fountainhead of English law and of all law. The judge is not embarrassed by the absence of 'authority' in clear cases of this kind, for no authority is needed for the affirmation of the very essence of the law."[61]

This is but a confirmation of the classic statement made by Judge Willes: "Principles of private justice, moral fitness and public convenience . . . when applied to a new subject, make common law without a precedent" (*Miller v. Taylor,* 1769. 4 Burr. 2303, 2312). Even in the interpretation and construction of statutes and contracts, reason exercises a controlling role. As Judge Earl says in *Riggs v. Palmer* (1889. 115 N.Y. 506): ". . . all laws and contracts may be controlled in their operation and effect by general, fundamental maxims of the common law. No one shall be permitted to profit by his own fraud, or to take advantage of his own wrong, or to found any claim upon his own inequity, or to acquire property by his own crime. These maxims are dictated by public policy, have their foundation in universal law administered in all civilized countries, and have never been superseded by statutes."

If, then, the natural law is an essential part of human law, it is clear that the end of human law—the common good to which human law is ordained—cannot consist solely in the principle of utility to the body politic; it must above all include the higher values proper to man as man. It must be emphasized that the notion of common good is much broader than that of the public welfare of the State. It includes this, but it also includes virtue. As St. Thomas says, "the purpose of human law is to lead men to virtue, though not abruptly but step by step."[62] Again, he says, "The principal purpose of human law is to bring about the friendship of man to man."[63] Even this is not the ultimate end of human law. "The goal of human life and of society is God."[64] As law is made for man, not man for law, so no human law can be called just and reasonable which tends to frustrate the ultimate end of man.

But human law has its limits; it can only contribute toward the common good within the limits of its capacity. Although all human law is derived from the first precept of the natural law: *Goodness is to be done and evil is to be avoided,* it does not belong to human law to prescribe all the acts of every virtue or to repress all vices. Human law has often been a subject of ridicule to laymen; when they see that the law does not prohibit all the vices nor prescribe all the virtues, they infer, quite unwarrantably, that law is immoral, or at least amoral. They do not realize that there are limits to effective legal action. Human law does not approve the vices which it refrains from prohibiting; nor does it frown upon the virtues which it does not think it wise to prescribe for the present. In fact, certain moral obligations, which ordinarily are not recognized by the law as legal obligations, may acquire legal significance under exceptional circumstances. This shows that the law is not indifferent to virtue, but has to consider its own limits and the conditions of the time and place. As St. Thomas reminds us, "Human law regards the mass of men the greater part of whom are imperfect in virtue. And therefore human law does not forbid all evil acts from which men of virtue abstain, but only the more serious vices from which the greater part of men are able to abstain. . . . Otherwise imperfect men, being unable to obey such precepts, would fall into worse evils."[65]

Human law often has to weigh all the values involved, and to choose the lesser evil. Not infrequently good morals and public policy come into conflict, as in the case of *Mogul v. McGregor*, 23 Q.B.D. (1889), where the public policy in favor of freedom of trade seems to tip the scales of justice against the requirement of good morals. Lord Bowen says, "No man, whether trader or not, can . . . justify damaging another in his commercial business by fraud or misrepresentation. Intimidation, obstruction and molestation are forbidden. . . . But the defendants have been guilty of none of these acts. They have done no more against the plaintiff than pursue to the bitter end a war of competition waged in the interests of their own trade. . . . To say that a man is to trade freely, but that he is to stop short at any act which is calculated to harm other tradesmen, and which is designed to attract business to his own shop, would be a strange and impossible counsel of perfection." But it is to be noted that where grave moral duties are involved, such as the duty not to commit fraud or misrepresentation or to use intimidation, no amount of public policy can turn the balance against them.

Good morals constitute an essential ingredient of the common good. In fact, public order and good morals are the twin-motors of the legal mechanism. In the Chinese Civil Code,[66] they appear almost always in pairs. A few samples will do. "A custom is applicable in civil matters only when it is not contrary to public order or good morals" (Art. 2). "Liberty may not be restricted in a manner contrary to public order or good morals" (Art. 17). "A juristic act which is contrary to public order or good morals is void" (Art. 71). Both of these norms are indicative of the common good, and therefore belong to the natural law. But their concretization and implementation are matters left to the "artificial reason," which cannot claim to absolute rectitude.

Rationalism, Voluntarism and Realism

There have been innumerable discussions as to whether the essence of law consists in reason or in will. Now, it is plain that both reason and will enter into the making of law. Take, for instance, the principle laid down in the 14th Amendment of the United States Constitution, that no State shall "deprive any person of life, liberty or property, without due process of law." It is clearly the *will* of the people of the United States that all the States of the Union should observe this principle in their executive, legislative and judicial activities. But it is equally clear that the principle itself is a principle of *reason*. To be more precise, it is a principle derived by way of conclusion from the precept of the natural law that injustice, being an evil, is to be avoided. In every law both reason and will are present, but the question is which is the essence of the law. Evidently will alone does not constitute the law. The very idea of law is opposed to willfulness. As St. Thomas says, "All law proceeds from the reason and the will of the lawgiver. Divine and natural law proceed from the reasonable will of God, but human law proceeds from the will of man regulated by reason."[67] It is noteworthy that St. Thomas does not speak of the natural law in terms of "the will of God, regulated by reason," because the will of God cannot be otherwise than reasonable. As Dr. Peter J. Stanlis says, "Since God is a spirit infinitely perfect, there cannot really be any separation of the Divine Mind and the Divine Will. . . . Therefore, whether a law is just because God has willed it, or whether God has willed it because it is just, is a problem which does not exist for God."[67a] In other words, the question whether the obligation of the eternal and natural laws is founded on the will or the reason of God is pointless, because in God Love and Wisdom are one. The same cannot be said of the will of the human lawgiver. In order to constitute law, the human will must be *regulated by reason*. St. Thomas is most emphatic on this point. Someone argued in favor of the will-theory: "The law impels those who are subject to it to act aright. But to impel to act is properly a function of the will; therefore law does not pertain to reason but rather to the will, in accordance with which even the jurist says: *Whatever pleases the sovereign has the force of law*."[68] St. Thomas's reply is incisive: "Reason derives the power of impelling to act from the will. It is from the fact that one wills the end that reason dictates those things which are ordered to the end. But the willing of those things which are ordered to the end, to have the character of law, *must be regulated to some extent by reason*. And in this sense is to be understood the expression that the will of the sovereign has the force of law: otherwise the will of the sovereign would be an injustice rather than a law."[69] Human law, then, may be compared to a train in motion, with will as the motive power, reason as the engine on the track, leading to the common good as its destination. Will may perhaps be said to constitute the existential element of the law, while reason is its essence. The progress of law is measured by the degree in which it embodies its essence.

The modern German jurist Gustav Radbruch says that law is a "judgment of value." Its primary form is: "This is necessary for the sake of justice and the general good. It is an idea as sinister as it is unreal to see the power of law exclusively in its threatening voice of command, or even only in the sanction, in the compulsion by which it enforces its command."[70]

Likewise Chief Justice Vanderbilt of New Jersey says, "For the most part our law has been hammered out on the anvil of private litigation by lawyers and judges. When cases go up on appeal, the judges regularly state the reasons for their decisions in published opinions. These opinions reveal the place of reason and experience in the development of the law, and we habitually think of reason and experience as the controlling factors in the law rather than the physical force of the state which actually stands behind it."[71] These thoughts come near to the insight of St. Thomas.

To deserve the name of law, all human law must be consonant to reason in a threefold sense. First, it must not be contrary to any dictates of the natural reason; secondly, it must be ordained to the common good, which is the *raison d'être* of law; thirdly, the means it employs must be in reasonable proportion to the end. The justice of a law depends upon how well it fulfills these conditions. This, of course, does not mean that any system of human law could be a perfect embodiment of reason. In fact, as St. Thomas has said, "It seems natural to human reason to advance gradually from the imperfect to the perfect."[72] The universal precepts of the natural law are, of course, unchangeable; but human law, which is derived from the natural law by way of particular determinations and by way of concrete conclusions, must adapt itself to the ever-varying conditions of human culture and civilization. Furthermore, inasmuch as natural law is bound up with human reason, as human reason grows, so does natural law. This is why St. Thomas says that natural law can change by way of addition. As Jacques Maritain has put it, "Natural law is an unwritten law. Man's knowledge of it has increased little by little as man's moral conscience has developed. . . . The knowledge which our moral conscience has of its law is doubtless still imperfect, and very likely it will continue to develop and to become more refined as long as humanity exists. Only when the Gospel has penetrated to the very depth of human substance will natural law appear in its flower and its perfection."[73]

St. Thomas's philosophy of law is rational but not rationalistic. He knows the importance of reason, but he also has a historical sense. He believes in the gradual development of rationality in the course of time. He avoids the errors of both rationalism and irrationalism. The sound kernel in modern rationalism is its emphasis on reason, but the source of its errors lies in its ignorance of the distinction between speculative reason and practical reason. Many jurists deal with the law as though it belonged to speculative reason, just as the natural sciences do. Inevitably they fall into the illusion of certainty. Others, revolting against the search for an illusive certainty, tend to think lightly of reason, and resort too readily to animal faith, will, intuition, feeling, emotion, sentiment, experience and inarticulate value-judgment. Finding that speculative reason does not work in the practical affairs of men, in ethics and in law, and not knowing the true nature of practical reason, they throw reason overboard and resort to history and psychology, which can only explain but not justify. Any attempt at justification is suspected as a piece of rationalization. Many modern thinkers are like the flounders leaping from the frying-pan to the fire. I think that Kant's misconception of "practical reason" and his relegation of it to the position of sentiment and faith is chiefly responsible for most of the errors of modern philosophy.

For jurisprudence and other moral sciences, nothing is more important than to distinguish the Thomistic conception of practical reason from the Kantian conception of it. With St. Thomas, practical reason is contrasted with speculative reason; with Kant, it is set up as the opposite of "pure reason," making it appear as though practical reason were something impure, called "reason" only by courtesy. To St. Thomas, both practical reason and speculative reason are essentially the same faculty. There is only one reason. Speculative reason is reason confronted with one type of problem, having mainly to do with cause and effect. Practical reason is the same reason confronted with another type of problem, having to do mainly with ends and means. The difference between the two lies in the subject-matter dealt with; it does not lie in the reason itself.

St. Thomas's position in this matter is defined very clearly as follows:

> The same sort of certitude is not to be expected in all fields of scientific inquiry. *The well-disciplined mind will not demand greater certitude than the subject will offer, nor be content with less.* To accept mathematical truth on rhetorical

persuasions is almost a crime; so also to exact mathematical demonstrations from an orator.[74]

The degrees of certitude hinge on the nature of things. Physical sciences offer a greater degree of it, moral sciences a lesser; but the rationality is the same in both.

Kant's position is stated in his *Critique of Pure Reason* as follows:

> From the critical point of view, the doctrine of morality and the doctrine of science may each be true in its own sphere; which could never have been shown had not criticism previously established our unavoidable ignorance of the real world, and limited all that we can know scientifically to mere phenomena. I have therefore found it necessary to deny knowledge of God, freedom and immortality, in order to find a place for faith.[75]

It is clear, then, that the whole critical system of Kant rests upon an "in-order-to," a pious motive. It is praiseworthy as a philosopher's *fiat*, but as an intellectual vision it falsifies reality by superimposing upon it a violent bifurcation. For, after all, is reason so faith-proof, or faith so reason-proof, as Kant made it out to be? The modern mind, subtilized by deeper psychological and metaphysical insights, can hardly be satisfied with a segregation of faith and reason so clear-cut and so extremely uncritical. Whitehead has somewhere said that the medieval age was an age of faith based upon reason, while the modern age is an age of reason based upon faith.[76] The fact is, there is faith in reason and reason in faith. Here, as everywhere, there is a twilight zone in which the one shades imperceptibly into the other.

In the last analysis, there is no essential difference in rationality or knowability between physical, moral, and aesthetical sciences. As E. I. Watkin has queried, "How does the intuition that reason is trustworthy differ from the intuition that a sunset is beautiful or cruelty wrong?"[77]

But because Kant reduced practical reason to faith and moral sentiment, his followers were split into two main groups. One group discarded "practical reason" altogether from their systems, and applied the methods of "pure reason" even to moral sciences;

while the other group became irrationalists, romantics, voluntarists, pragmatists, and philosophers of "as if." Even those who declared independence from the domination of Kant, like Hegel, Nietzsche, and the early Bergson of the creative evolution, were influenced by Kant, inasmuch as theirs were attempts to demolish the dualism of Kant by arbitrarily objectivizing the subjective. Hegelianism, especially, is extreme irrationalism dressed in the garb of reason; materialism dressed in the garb of the spirit. It remained for Marx to take off the garb.

In brief, by a *fiat* of will, Kant confined reason and knowledge to the phenomenal world, in order to make room for moral sentiment, will, intuition, feeling and faith, which he groups together under the name of practical reason and judgment.

Thus, the practical reason, as Kant understood it, was no reason at all! It is a different faculty from the pure reason. The Kantian bifurcations between the phenomenal world and the noumenal world, between physical science and ethical doctrine, between logical certainty and moral certitude, between reason and faith, are all too clear-cut to be true to reality. They have a certain basis in the ontological, and as mental schemata they may be helpful to clear thinking. But once your mind is fixed on the schemata, it tends to mistake them for distinctions that inhere in reality itself, and instead of clear thinking the result would be "confusion twice confounded."

As Professor Louis de Raeymaeker observes:

> Kantianism is a form of philosophical positivism, at least as regards theoretical or speculative reason. It preaches a subjectivistic formalism, which forbids this theoretical reason to make any incursion into transphenomenal reality; but Kant did not rest satisfied with this agnosticism. He believed that he had discovered in practical reason the means to get at the domain of noumena, which had been irredeemably closed to speculative philosophy.
>
> Kant's procedure was imitated by many philosophers, for there are very few who resign themselves to ignoring completely what goes beyond phenomena. The defenders of Kantian agnosticism have quite frequently entered into the paths

of irrationalism,—those of feeling, of action, or of some fundamental intuition—in order to discover a satisfactory explanation of reality.[78]

Even from a purely phenomenological point of view, Kant's dualism is an oversimplification of things. It was John Dewey who said: "We live in a world which is an impressive and irresistible mixture of sufficiencies, tight completeness, order, recurrences, which make possible prediction and control, and singularities, ambiguities, uncertain possibilities, processes going to consequences as yet indeterminate. They are mixed not mechanically, but vitally like the wheat and tares of the parable."[78a] This comes close to the Thomistic view of *empirical* reality, which "is neither a kind of solid homogeneous mass which has the same sense throughout, nor a swarm of profoundly unrelated particles, but nuanced and differenced from within."[78b] Thus the Thomistic position in the philosophy of experience is *pluralistic* rather than dualistic.

Such, too, is juridical reality. Jurisprudence must face the whole juridical reality and tackle it with a true scientific temper. It must not arbitrarily isolate that part of juridical reality which can be reduced to neat and clear-cut categories and build itself an ivory tower. A jurist with a true scientific temper will not deal with the law as if it belonged to speculative reason. He will deal with his data as they are, not as he wishes them to be. He will not call justice an irrational ideal, simply because it does not fit in with "pure reason" in the Kantian sense.

Among the Neo-Kantians there are two main schools, represented by Stammler[79] and Kelsen.[80] The former treated the problem of justice with the method of pure reason. The latter, who seems to have a more objective understanding of Kant's system, especially of the implications of Kant's conception of practical reason—which is really no reason, but sentiment—dropped the problem of justice as an irrational idea,[81] and dismissed it from jurisprudence, which must be rational. I have a high respect for both. They have made lasting contributions to jurisprudence, each in his own field. I think Stammler's theory of the Right Law keeps legal speculation from degenerating into sheer positivism; and Kelsen's theory of different stages of the legal order and a hierarchy of juridical norms is a valuable contribution to analytical jurisprudence. But because both Stammler and Kelsen accepted uncritically Kant's naive bifurcation of pure reason and practical reason, the results have been affected by the erroneous starting point. Stammler's system is a revised rationalism, under the flag of critical idealism, while Kelsen's "pure theory of law" is sheer positivism, excluding from the domain of jurisprudence the "irrational" idea of justice as mere emotion. One wonders whether it is justice or rather its exclusion from the concept of law that is irrational.

It was Goethe who said, "He who shies away from the idea finally does not even have the concept."[82] Stammler would understand this much better than Kelsen. To my mind, "the idea" has to do with the *essential*, while "the concept" has to do with the *existential*. Legal positivists, who shy away from the *essential*, will end by missing even the *existential*.

Thomism furnishes the answer to both rationalism and irrationalism, or voluntarism. To the former it says that law does not belong to speculative reason, which deals with causes and effects, but to practical reason, which deals with means and ends. The one has to do with natural phenomena, which are called "necessary things" because they cannot be otherwise than they are. The other has to do with human actions, which are called "contingent matters" because human beings are endowed with free will as well as with reason, and they differ from each other both in the valuation of the ends and in the choice of the means thereto. In the case of speculative reason, there is necessity both in the generalities and in the particularities. But in the case of practical reason, there is necessity only in the general principles, and the more we descend to the matters of detail the less necessity we find. If men were angels, or if Adam had not fallen, this might have been different. As it is, probability must be the guide of life in matters of detail.

To the irrationalists, on the other hand, Thomism would say that practical reason is still reason, and not an inarticulate judgment or blind volition, and that although "general propositions do not decide concrete cases,"[83] they are nevertheless the indispensable foundation on which the judicial edifice must be built. Although, as St. Thomas says, there is no absolute rectitude in matters of detail, there is still a relative rectitude. In these matters he does not speak in terms of all reason or no reason, but in terms of the "more or less reasonable." "In the dealings of man, you cannot attain demonstrable and infallible proof, but it is sufficient that you attain a certain conjectural probability, such as an orator would use in his art of persuasion."[84] St. Thomas is realistic through and through, empirically as well as ontologically. As Heinrich Rommen has pointed out, the difference between empiricism and philosophical realism lies in the fact that while the former remains content with what is in the foreground, the latter, with its delight in knowledge, pierces beyond the cheerfully affirmed actuality to that which is in the background.[85]

Individualism, Collectivism and Personalism

Non-Catholic writers often think of the Catholic theory of society as being collectivistic. Nothing can be farther from the truth. The foundation of the Catholic social philosophy is the dignity of the human person.[86] In this it is directly opposed to Fascism and Communism, which are truly collectivistic. For them the group is all-important, while the individual members have no importance of their own except as cells of the body politic. The group is the end, while the individual is only a means. All rights are created by the State. There is no law above the State, and there are no natural rights inherent in the human person as such. The State can give, and the State can take away. Thus, Caesar usurps the position of God. The interests of the political society become the sole criterion of right and wrong. The Soviet Penal Code, for instance, states the end of law in these terms: "The aim of the penal legislation of the R.S.F.S.R. is to protect the socialist state of the workers and peasants and the established order therein against socially dangerous acts (crimes) by applying to persons committing such acts the measures of social defence provided for in the present code."[87] Thus, it identifies the common good completely with the collective good of the state, or rather of a particular class. Those who are not peasants or workers have no legal standing before the state, and may be ruthlessly "liquidated" as being "socially dangerous." The state is, in fact, identified with a single class. As Vyshinsky says, "Law is the totality (a) of the rules of conduct, expressing the will of the dominant class and established in legal order, and (b) of customs and rules of community life sanctioned by state authority —their application being guaranteed by the compulsory force of the state in order to guard, secure, and develop social relationships and social orders advantageous and agreeable to the dominant class."[88] "Soviet law," he further says, "is the aggregate of the rules of conduct established by the authority of the toilers and expressive of their will. The effective operation of these rules is guaranteed by the entire coercive force of the socialist state in order to defend, to secure, and to develop relationships and arrangements advantageous and agreeable to the toilers, and completely and finally to annihilate capitalism and its remnants in the economic system, the way of life, and human consciousness—in order to build a communist society."[89] This is positivism pushed to its logical end. The will of the dominant class becomes the essence of law, and reason becomes the handmaid of will.

As Lon Fuller has pointed out, "On almost every point of substance . . . , Aristotle and the philosophy of Marxian Communism are at opposite poles. . . . Almost every one of his major premises is opposed in some degree by the tenets of Soviet legal and moral philosophy. That man is a responsible agent settling his own relations to his fellows; that penalties should be founded on, and be proportionate to, some kind of fault or short-coming; that ethical and legal questions are subject to rational examination in isolation from the economic organization of a particular society—all of these propositions would meet contradiction in varying degrees from Soviet philosophers."[90]

When it is remembered to how great an extent the ideas of Aristotle were assimilated by St. Thomas Aquinas, whom we may regard as the representative Catholic philosopher of law, it is easy to realize how far the Catholic position is from collectivism. In the words of a modern Thomist, "That a human community can constitute a substantial whole is clearly denied by St. Thomas. The ultimate substance is the person. No higher containing compound exists, nor anything like an 'Over-Soul.' Despite his strong sense of the naturalness of some groupings, St. Thomas never thinks they evolve into things-in-themselves, organisms with lives of their own apart from the individuals comprising them, corporate personalities that swallow up lesser persons."[91]

Man is the end, while society is only a means, although a necessary means. According to Pius XII, this is true even of the Mystical Body of Christ. He has brought out the distinction between the Mystical Body and any human society, on the one hand, and any physical body, on the other, so clearly that no serious student of the Catholic philosophy of society can afford to neglect his words. "Whereas in a physical body the principle of unity joins the parts together in such a way that each of them completely lacks a subsistence of its own, on the contrary in the Mystical Body the cohesive force, intimate though it is, unites the members with one another in such a way that each of them wholly retains his own personality. A further difference is seen if we consider the mutual relation between the whole and each individual member; for in any living physical body the sole final purpose for which each and every individual member exists is for the benefit of the whole organism, whereas any social structure of human beings has for its ultimate purpose, in the order of utilitarian finality, the good of each and every member, inasmuch as they are persons."[92] The social philosophy of the Church, therefore, is *personalistic* rather than collectivistic.

On the other hand, personalism should be sharply distinguished from individualism. The former treats human beings as integral moral persons; the latter treats them mainly as economic units. Personalism would, for instance, lay the greatest stress on the dignity of labor, while individualism would regard labor as a mere commodity which is regulated like other goods by the economic law of supply and demand. Where individualism thinks almost exclusively of natural rights, personalism would consider natural duties as well. Matter is the principle of individuation; so individualism is bound to lead to materialism. Spirit is the principle of personality; so personalism has as its goal the perfection of the human being, which can never be attained without the cultivation of love and justice.

In the American Bishops' Statement of 1953 on *Man's Dignity* is to be found a clear exposition of the golden mean between individualism and collectivism. "The Christian view," it reads, "avoids the opposing extremes of individualism and collectivism, both of which are grounded on false concepts of liberty—either the unfettered liberty of individualism, which gives the 'individual' the right to ignore society; or the unfettered liberty of dictatorship, which gives the government the right to ignore the person by absorbing him into a race or class, thus destroying his freedom of choice. The false liberty of individualism wrecks society by defining freedom as individual license; the false liberty of dictatorship wrecks humanity by defining freedom as the right of the dictator to nullify the person—a right which he claims to derive from social necessity."[93]

Now we are in a position to understand the Christian notion of the common good. It primarily means the intrinsic goods given by God to men as men. These goods are common to all. The notion of the common good also includes the collective good of the State and other social organizations, but this collective good is only a means to the implementation of the primary ends of the law. It should further be remembered that the ultimate common good is God. Both the individual person and society are under God and His law.

Approached from every point of view, love is the fulfillment of the law.

NOTES

1. O. W. Holmes, *Collected Legal Papers* (Harcourt, 1920), pp. 164–5.
2. *Ibid.*, p. 195.
3. *Ibid.*, p. 202
4. *Ibid.*, pp. 276–7.
5. *Ibid.*, p. 37.
6. *Ibid.*, p. 37.
7. Sir Henry Finch, *Nomotechnia* (1613), quoted by Richard O'Sullivan in *The King's Good Servant* (Newman, 1948), p. 19.

8. Cardozo, *The Growth of the Law* (Yale University Press, 1924), p. 23.
9. *Ibid.*, pp. 25–6. Judge Robert N. Wilkin has likewise testified: "The principles, standards and precepts of Natural Law are continually employed by courts as the constitutions, statutes and precedents are interpreted and applied to the ever-varying circumstances of life. They are employed also in the interpretations of wills, contracts, conduct and relationships of life. They are part of man's nature and cannot be separated from life" (*Proceedings of the Natural Law Institute,* 2 [1948], p. 147).
10. *Summa Theologica,* I–II, 95. 2. *in corpore.* Unless otherwise noted, the passages from the *Summa* which I have quoted in this book are new translations done with the generous co-operation of Rev. Anthony Lo Gatto of Brooklyn, N.Y.
11. Translated from Bracton, *De legibus consuetudinibus Angliae,* ed. by Woodbine (1915), folios 107a and 107b. All passages from Bracton quoted in this book have been done by me with the generous help of Rev. Edward Synan of Seton Hall University.
12. St. Thomas, *S. T.,* I–II, 95. 2. *in corp.*
13. From Encyclical Letter *Libertas Praestantissimum,* June 20, 1888. See *The Great Encyclical Letters of Pope Leo XIII* (Benziger, 1903), pp. 141–2.
14. *S. T.,* I–II, 95. 2. *in corp.* It should be noted that a "determination" of the natural law is the product of empirical reason and can claim no finality.
15. *S. T.,* I–II, 109. 3. 1.
16. *Ibid., ad* 1.
17. *Combe v. Edwards* (1878), 3 Probate Division 142.
18. *Minos,* 315 A.
19. Diogenes Laertius, *Lives of the Philosophers,* VII, 88.
20. Hooker, *Ecclesiastical Polity,* I, Sec. 16. I am using a modernized text.
21. Cicero, *De legibus,* I, 6.
22. Justinian, *Digest,* 1, 1, 1.
23. Cardozo, *The Growth of the Law,* p. 52.
24. *S. T.,* I–II, 90. 4. *in corp.*
25. *S. T.,* I–II, 93. 1. *ad* 2.
26. This is the ultimate vision in Dante's *Divine Comedy.* In the Confucian classic *The Golden Mean,* we find this: "These moral laws form the same system with the laws by which the seasons succeed each other and the sun and moon appear with the alternations of day and night." (Ku Hung Ming's translation.) Even Kant had his moments of breaking through his self-created prison of dualism.
27. *S. T.,* I–II, 93. 3. *in corp.*

28. Sheed, *Theology and Sanity* (Sheed & Ward, 1946), pp. 137–8. In
    a recent essay, Prof. George W. Goble says, "Love, friendship,
    sympathy and beauty are no less real because they cannot be put
    into logical terms" (*American Bar Association Journal*, Vol. 41,
    p. 403). If he uses the word "real" not merely in the empirical sense
    but also in the ontological sense, I should agree with him perfectly.
29. This passage is from His Holiness's Allocution to the Tribunal of
    the Sacred Romana Rota, delivered on November 13, 1949, at the
    Inauguration of the Juridical Year. The full title is "Law and Con-
    science: the Objective Norms of Law," published in Pius XII,
    Discorsi agli Intellettuali: 1939–1954 (Rome, 1954). It is a most
    penetrating critique of modern juridical positivism; and at the same
    time it lays down the fundamental starting point for the philosophy
    of natural law.
30. *S. T.*, I–II, 91. 2. *in corp.*
31. *Ibid.*, 91. 3. *ad* 1. This distinction between the eternal law and the
    natural law is forgotten by the speculative philosophers of the natu-
    ral law, with the result that human reason takes the place of Divine
    Reason, and presumes to legislate for the universe. Hegelianism,
    which is speculative philosophy at its worst, even applies the laws
    of becoming to God. See Sheed, *Communism and Man* (Sheed &
    Ward), Chap. I on "What Hegel Thought."
32. *Ibid.*, 94. 4. *in corp.*
33. *Collected Legal Papers*, p. 174.
34. *Ibid.*, p. 310.
35. Rudolf von Ihering (1818–1894) is regarded by many as the greatest
    jurist of the nineteenth century. Holmes called him "a man of
    genius" (*The Common Law*, p. 208). He was a German scholar
    with an American sense of humor. His style of writing is lively. Be-
    sides his monumental works such as *Der Geist des römischen Rechts*
    ("The Spirit of Roman Law," of which no English translation has
    been made) and *Der Zweck im Recht* (the first volume of which
    has been translated under the title of *Law as a Means to an End*
    and published in the "Modern Legal Philosophy Series"), he wrote
    a book called *Scherz und Ernst in der Jurisprudenz* ("Humor and
    Sober Truth in Jurisprudence"), which contains a witty essay,
    "*Im juristischen Begriffshimmel*" ("In the Heaven of Legal Con-
    cepts"). An English version of this is available in Cohen and Co-
    hen, *Readings in Jurisprudence and Legal Philosophy* (New York,
    Prentice-Hall, 1951), pp. 678 ff. In this humorous essay, he makes
    fun of all those legal pedants who indulged in hairsplitting reason-
    ings without any idea of the *purpose* of legal institutions.
36. See Browne, *Christian Morals* (Bonn's ed.), p. 111; and Justice Evatt
    in *R. v. Connare*, 61 C.L.R. 620.

37. See Roscoe Pound, "Mechanical Jurisprudence," *Columbia Law Review*, Vol. 8 (1908), pp. 1 ff. One of the salient trends in contemporary jurisprudence is the increasing awareness in judges of the "underlying philosophy" or "rationale" or "purpose" of a rule of law. American jurisprudence is more and more saturated with the spirit of equity and natural justice, which looks to substance rather than form. Even in dealing with the statute of limitations, moral considerations are not completely excluded. For instance, Judge Francis says, "The statute of limitations is not a club in the hands of a wrongdoer, whether a wilful or an unintentional one; it is a prod in the back of the victim, the prod being powered by the conspicuous nature of the adverse use" (108 A. 2d 458, at 464).
38. See *supra*, note 37.
39. This is to be found in a note on p. 161 of the second volume of *Der Zweck im Recht* (1886).
40. *S. T.*, I–II, 94. 2. *in corp.*
41. *Ibid.*, 94. 2. *ad* 2.
42. *The Works of Mencius*, Bk. I, Part II, Chap. 10, Pr. 1.
43. Circuit Court, E.D. Pennsylvania, 1842. 1 Wall. Jr. 1, 26 Fed. Cas. 360.
44. *Works* (Spedding's ed., 1879), Vol. VII, p. 634.
45. *Institutes*, 1. 1. 3. These words were taken from Ulpian.
46. Savigny's words are to be found in his *System des heutigen römischen Rechts*, Vol. I, pp. 407 *et. seq.* The deep Christian foundation of Savigny's philosophy can be gauged from what he said: "The universal aim of all law may be derived from the moral orientation of human nature, as it is represented in the Christian philosophy of life" (*Ibid.*, pp. 53–4).
47. Pound, "The End of Law as Developed in Juristic Thought," *Harvard Law Review* (1914), p. 609.
48. *S. T.*, I–II, 100. 8. *ad* 3.
49. *Ibid.*, 95. 2. *ad* 3.
50. From this it is clear that "conclusions" are concretizations of "good" and "evil." Thus, they have to do with *values* and proximate *ends*. "Determinations," on the other hand, have to do with the *means* of implementing ends. Conclusions bear a lineal relation to the primary precepts of the natural law, while determinations bear a collateral relation. In the words of Archbishop A. G. Cicognani, "All human laws and precepts are fundamentally the necessary conclusions, or more minute determinations of the general principles of the natural law. Human laws are therefore proximately or remotely reducible to the natural law" *Canon Law* (Newman, 1949), pp. 25–6.
51. *S. T.*, I–II, 95. 2. *in corp.*

52. *De legibus*, fol. 36.
53. Rooney, *Lawlessness, Law, and Sanction* (Catholic University, 1937), p. 70.
54. *State v. Otis Elevator Co.* (1953), 95 A. 2d 715, 721-2, where Chief Justice Vanderbilt quoted Bracton and Coke. See also Dean Erwin N. Griswold, *The 5th Amendment Today* (Harvard University Press, 1955), p. 33, where, commenting on the classic pronouncement of Bracton on the King being under God and the Law, he observes: "These words, I am proud to say, are inscribed in their original Latin—*Non sub Homine sed sub Deo et Lege*—over the portal of the Harvard Law School."
55. Coke on Littleton, 97b. The Latin maxim may be rendered as: "No one is a born artist."
56. *The Analects of Confucius.*
57. "No element is heavy in its own place." To render the sense better, "Nothing is heavy in its own element."
58. Coke on Littleton, 71a.
59. Coke on Littleton, Epilogue.
60. *S. T.*, I–II, 96. 6. *ad* 3.
61. C. K. Allen, *Law in the Making*, 5th ed. (Oxford: at the Clarendon Press 1951), pp. 276–7.
62. *S. T.*, I–II, 96. 2. *ad* 2.
63. *Ibid.*, 99. 2.
64. *Ibid.*, 100. 6.
65. *Ibid.*, 96. 2. *ad* a.
66. English translation by Chin-Ling Hsia.
67. *S. T.*, I–II, 97. 3. *in corp.*
67ª. *Newman Review*, Vol. 4, p. 36.
68. *Ibid.*, 90. 1. 3.
69. *Ibid.*, 90. 1. *ad* 3.
70. *Law Quarterly Review*, Vol. 3, p. 534.
71. Vanderbilt, *Law and Government in the Development of the American Way of Life* (University of Wisconsin, 1951), p. 10.
72. *S. T.*, I–II, 97. 1. *in corp.*
73. Maritain, "The Philosophical Foundations of Natural Law," in *Natural Law and World Law: Essays to Commemorate the Sixtieth Birthday of Kotaro Tanaka* (Yuhikaku, 1954), p. 137.
74. Commentary, Ethics, I, Lect. 3. I am using the translation of Thomas Gilby, in his *St. Thomas Aquinas: Philosophical Texts* (Oxford, 1951), p. 9.
75. See Fulton Sheen, *The Philosophy of Religion* (Appleton, 1948), p. 38.
76. I came across this idea many years ago in his *Science and the Modern World*, but I have not been able to locate the page.

77. *The Catholic Center* (Sheed & Ward), p. 105.
78. *The Philosophy of Being* (Herder, 1954), pp. 5–6.
78ᵃ.*Experience and Nature*, p. 47.
78ᵇ. Gilby, *Between Community and Society*, p. 14.
79. Rudolf Stammler (1856–1938) was generally considered the greatest legal philosopher of the present century. Of him Pound wrote: "Stammler has undoubtedly been the strongest influence in philosophical jurisprudence in the present century" (*Harvard Law Review*, Vol. 51, p. 448). The importance of his position lies in the fact that he was writing at a time when positivism was at its height and natural law was at its lowest ebb, and that he advocated, by adapting the method of Kant, the universal validity of the fundamental principles of justice, which he classified into two categories: (1) the principles of respect, (2) the principles of participation. His system was transcendental idealism, not transcendental realism. His idea of "universal validity" was confined to the human mind. He did not claim any ontological basis for the idea of justice. In the early twenties, I was studying under him as a private pupil. I already felt that his system was a half-way house between reality and the mind. I had difficulties with what seemed to me an excessive formalism in his system. I wrote an article in which I maintained that the concept of law presupposed the law as a thing in itself, and therefore one could not know the law completely through conceptual knowledge alone. Perception was just as important as conception, and over and above conception and perception, we needed to resort to "intellectual intuition." In one word, it took the *whole* mind to know the law. To my immense surprise, my great teacher said, "This is so far the most formidable criticism that my philosophy has met with!"

But Stammler's contribution to jurisprudence cannot be gainsaid. He was combatting the prevailing positivism in a language that it could understand.

His best-known book was *Die Lehre vom dem richtigen Rechts* (1902), ("The Theory of Right Law"), which was translated into English and published in 1925 in the "Modern Legal Philosophy Series" under the title *The Theory of Justice*.

Similar in tendency but a little more metaphysically inclined is the Italian jurist Giorgio del Vecchio. Although generally labeled a Neo-Kantian, he is in fact a humanist pure and simple. His *Philosophy of Law* has recently been translated into English and published by the Catholic University of America Press (1953). In his foreword to the book, Dr. Brendan Francis Brown has very ably brought out the inadequacies of del Vecchio's system, which "does not reach the scholasticism of François Geny." One cannot help wishing that the works of Geny and the other great French jurist, Georges Ripert, be translated into English.

80. Hans Kelsen desires "to free the concept of law from the idea of justice" (*General Theory of Law and State*, [Harvard, 1945], p. 5). As an orthodox Kantian dualist, Kelsen sees only two alternatives: either identify law with justice or isolate law completely from justice; and he chooses the latter course. To my mind, the statement of these alternatives is purely arbitrary. Law is neither identical with justice nor separable from it. When the very *Fragestelling* (or the way of presenting the question) is wrong, all discussions pro and con are like talking to the wind.

81. See Kelsen's essay "The Metamorphoses of the Idea of Justice" in Paul Sayre, *Interpretations of Modern Legal Philosophers* (Oxford, 1947), pp. 390 ff.

82. Quoted in Gustav Radbruch, "Legal Philosophy," in *The Legal Philosophies of Lask, Radbruch, and Dabin* (Harvard, 1950), p. 72.

83. Justice Holmes dissenting in *Lochner v. New York* (1905), 198 U.S. 45 at 74.

84. *S. T.*, I–II, 105. 2. *ad* 8.

85. Heinrich Rommen, *The Natural Law* (Herder, 1947), p. 166.

86. In the words of Pius XII: "Whatever happens, whatever change or transformation may take place, the purpose of all social life remains the same, ever sacred, ever obligatory: the development of the personal values of man, who is made in the image of God." (Broadcast on Christmas, 1942. English translation by Canon G. D. Smith.) One of the consequences of this doctrine is the dignity of labor: "The dignity of the human person normally demands the right to the use of earthly goods as the natural foundation for a livelihood; and to that right corresponds the fundamental obligation to grant private property, as far as possible, to all" (*Ibid.*).

87. Article 1.

88. Vyshinsky, *The Law of the Soviet State* (Macmillan, 1948), p. 50.

89. *Ibid.*

90. *Problems of Jurisprudence* (ed. Temporary, Foundation Press), p. 65.

91. Gilby, *Between Community and Society* (Longmans, 1953), p. 114.

92. Encyclical Letter *Mystici Corporis Christi* (1943), Chap. III. (English translation by Canon G. D. Smith.)

93. St. Peter had summed up the social philosophy in a few simple words: "Free men, but the liberty you enjoy is not to be made a pretext for wrong-doing; it is to be used in God's service. Give all men their due; to the brethren, your love; to God, your reverence; to the king, due honor" (I Peter 2:16–17).

PART ONE

THE NATURAL LAW AND OUR COMMON LAW

THE NATURAL LAW AND OUR
COMMON LAW

Introductory Note

THIS essay is based upon an address delivered at the Symposium on the Natural Law held by the Guild of Catholic Lawyers of New York, December 5, 1953. A whole day was devoted to this symposium. There were four speakers: Professor John E. McAniff dealt with "The Natural Law—Its Nature, Scope, and Sanction"; Judge Charles S. Desmond with "Natural Law and the American Constitution"; Professor Oscar Halecki with "The Natural Law and International Affairs Today"; and I with "The Natural Law and Our Common Law."

This subject was assigned to me in the letter of invitation which Judge Thomas E. Rohan, then President of the Guild, sent me in the name of the Guild. I naturally felt honored by this invitation, but I was not a little surprised that those who were brought up in the common law should have called upon me, a foreigner, to speak about it. It is true that I have always had a secret love for the common law, but how the Catholic lawyers of New York could have known my secret love mystified me then, as it still does. However, the invitation came as a challenge to me, and I accepted it manfully. If I was carting coal to Newcastle, it was the Newcastlers who had ordered it.

The address was later expanded and published in *Fordham Law Review*, March, 1954. I have here further revised and expanded it, so as to fit it to the rest of the book.

Some preliminary explanations are called for. The meaning of "natural law" I have dealt with in the Prologue. As to the term "common law," I am using it in its broadest sense as an equivalent of the whole system of Anglo-American jurisprudence. Thus, it covers all departments and branches of the law, whether public law or private law, whether the decisions of the "law" courts, "equity" courts, or any other tribunals. I am looking at the common law not microscopically but macroscopically. I am interested here in its basic principles and features and in its characteristic methods and attitudes.

The outstanding characteristic of the common law is that it is a system of law built up by the judges from case to case, especially in the field of civil law. It thus presents a marked contrast to the legal systems of the Continental countries, which have each a civil code for the judges to apply in their decisions. The first question the common law judge asks himself when confronted with a case is, Are there any previous decisions to serve as the precedent or at least an analogue for the instant case? There are, of course, statutes in the common-law countries; but even the statutes are looked at in the context of judicial interpretation and tradition.

The judicial opinions of the common-law countries are much more interesting than those of the Continental countries. The latter proceed deductively from the general to the particular. In form, at least, they are syllogistic. A French decision usually runs this way: "Considering that the law is thus and so, considering that this case is thus and so . . . therefore we have decided thus and so." Of course, some practical reasons are often smuggled through the interstices of the syllogism. But the form is deductive, and this is repulsive to those who are habituated to the more frankly empirical, experimental and inductive ways of the common law. The common-law judges do not start with a major premise. They must first try to arrive at one, and in this process of searching for a major premise to govern the case before them, they employ all kinds of methods and surmises, such as analogy, "would be" (which usually takes the form: *Any other rule would entail certain undesirable or unreasonable consequences*); "as if" (which is applied when two admittedly different situations are practically the same so far as law is concerned); and the method of differentiation (which is resorted to when a precedent sought by a party to be applied to the case is for reasons of justice "distinguished out of existence" by the judge). The experimental, dynamic and concrete nature of the common law makes it a much more thought-provoking and profitable study than the judicial decisions of the Continental courts.

Another feature of the common law is to be found in the dissenting opinions, unknown in the Continental systems. In China, for example, which adopted a modern civil code, no dissent is permitted, still less published. The logic is that once the people should know that even the judges could disagree on a point of law, respect for the law would be shaken. Not so in the common-law countries. You often find a court narrowly divided on a particular question. Many of the U.S. Supreme Court decisions, on the most vital constitutional issues, are 5 to 4 decisions. Dissents are frequent also in the state courts. Yet the people, on the whole, have as great a respect for the law as you can find anywhere in the world. The people do not expect a judge to be infallible; they expect him only to be honest and fair, candid and reasonable. The frank expressions of differences of opinion on the part of the judges, therefore, inspire the confidence of the whole nation in their conscientiousness and strengthen the reign of law rather than weaken it. This tradition makes the law appear just what it is: a typically human institution, not superhuman or less than human.

The practical temper of Anglo-American jurisprudence is further to be seen in its emphasis on the law of procedure. A right, to be effective, must be protected, and its protection mainly takes the form of giving redress for its infringement. When your rights are not violated by another, you generally stay away from the courts. It is only when some right of yours is violated that you would resort to the court for a remedial measure, without which your right would go without protection. Like a matter-of-fact housewife, the common law believes that the proof of the pudding is in the eating. It is important to have a right, but it is equally important to have a decent and efficient system of procedure by which redress can be had for its infringement. This not only implements the right but in a real sense sanctions it. The writ of Habeas Corpus, for instance, is a necessary complement to the right of personal liberty. Substantive law without the law of procedure would be like a body without feet.

There are innumerable judicial utterances of the importance of procedure. A recent reminder of it is found in the decision of a court in California:

> Judicial absolutism is not a part of the American way of life. The odious doctrine that the end justifies the means does not prevail in our system for the administration of justice. The power vested in a judge is to hear and determine, not to determine without hearing. When the Constitution requires a hearing, it requires a fair one, one before a tribunal which meets established standards of procedure. It is not for nothing that most of the provisions of the Bill of Rights have to do with matters of procedure. Procedure is the fair, orderly, and deliberate method by which matters are litigated. To judge in a contested proceeding implies the hearing of evidence from both sides in open court, a comparison of the merits of the evidence of each side, a conclusion from the evidence of where the truth lies, application of the appropriate laws to the facts found, and the rendition of a judgment accordingly (Justice Vallée in *In re Buchman*, 267 P. 2d 73).

So far we have viewed only the modality of the common law. From the standpoint of its underlying philosophy, we may say that its idea of justice is mainly derived from the Christian ideology, which insists upon the dignity and equality of men, as expressed in Bracton's words that "the king is . . . under God and the law," and in the words of Justice Miller that "no man in this country is so high that he is above the law." On the whole, we may also say that the judges have kept constantly in mind the ideal of fairness and good faith, that they have tried to base their decisions on reasonableness rather than on arbitrariness, that, thanks to their practical common sense, they have persistently groped after the happy mean, even when consciously they might have thought merely of finding a compromise between conflicting interests, and that there is often an inarticulate spiritual idealism even when they speak only in terms of property rights. This is due to the Christian tradition, which has constituted the vital air which the judges, willy-nilly, have imbibed from their childhood. Even the prevalence of positivist and materialistic philosophies of life has not been able to crush out the spark of Christian love in the center of their hearts. Taken all in all, the common law has not departed very far from the Christian tradition of the natural law, which does not think of power and rights in isolation from their correlative responsibility and duties. It is only when the judges have espoused a fundamentally materialistic philosophy of law, but insisted upon calling it natural law, that the common law has become disfigured beyond recognition and the natural law itself been brought into disrepute.

At present, jurisprudence faces an uncertain future; it must take one direction or another; it is pregnant with great hopes, but the perils are just as great. To my mind, what we need most is a true spirit of catholicity and the moral courage to face the problems head-on, which alone can help us arrive at a new vital synthesis.

THE COMMON LAW IN ITS OLD HOME

CHAPTER I

THE COMMON LAW AS A
CRADLE CHRISTIAN

SOME prominent English and American jurists have spoken of the common law in terms of "our lady." In fact, Justice Cardozo and Sir Frederick Pollock have used the beautiful expression "our lady of the common law." I do not know whether either of them fully realized the implications of this title. To a Catholic, it is likely to suggest the image of Our Lady tenderly holding the Divine Infant in her arms. If the common law is Our Lady, then the natural law is the Divine Infant that she holds in her embrace. In appearance, it is Our Lady who holds the Divine Infant. In reality, it is the Divine Infant who holds Our Lady. We know that the Divine Infant is none other than the *Word,* Who "was in the beginning with God." But it is easier for us to seek Him in the arms of Our Lady. This gives you an idea of how I am going to approach the subject which has been assigned to me: "The Natural Law and Our Common Law."

To speak plainly, my method will be empirical and historical. At least, I shall start from the fullblooded experience of the common law. We may mount higher and higher, until we attain a transcendental vision of the natural law, or even of the eternal law. But our starting point must be a juridical experience.

In comparing the natural law to the Word Incarnate, I am aware that Our Lord enters into humanity not as an Idea but as a Living Person. Similarly, in comparing the common law to Our Lady, I by no means forget that Our Lady is purity itself, while the common law, in the happy phrase of Lord Mansfield, "works itself pure by rules drawn from the fountain of justice."[1] Even this is true only when the common law is at its best. When at its worst, it becomes, as Tennyson says, a "lawless science," a "codeless myriad of precedent," a "wilderness of single instances."

Whenever I come across a bad decision, I am reminded of an interesting dialogue in *Faust* between the student and Mephistopheles:

> Student. I can never bring myself to like Jurisprudence.
> Mephisto. I do not blame you there, for I know only too well what kind of science it has come to be. All rights and laws are transmitted like an eternal disease from generation to generation, and carried along from place to place. Reason becomes a sham, welfare a plague; and you are heir to all this, and hence miserable is your lot. There is no longer any inquiry after the law which is born with us.[2]

But when the common law is at its best, the country under its beneficent rule becomes truly a land

> Where Freedom slowly broadens down
> From precedent to precedent.[3]

Whatever you may say of its defects, which are incidental to all human institutions, there can be no denying that the common law has one advantage over the legal system of any country: it was Christian from the very beginning of its history.

In connection with the laws of Ethelbert, which saw the light around 600 A.D., Maitland writes, "Germanic law has no written memorials of the days of its heathenry. Every trace, but the very faintest, of the old religion has been carefully expurgated from all that is written, for all that is written passes under ecclesiastical hands. Thus we may guess that a new force is already beginning to transfigure the whole sum and substance of barbaric law, before that law speaks the first words that we can hear."[4]

Some decades before the laws of Ethelbert, Emperor Justinian had promulgated his magnificent *Corpus Juris Civilis* explicitly "*In the name of Our Lord Jesus Christ.*" Roman law had reached its perfection when English law was just beginning to prattle like a baby. No one could have foreseen that the latter was destined, in the centuries to come, to grow into a more glorious system of law than its predecessor. Justice Holmes was not boasting when he said that "Our law has reached broader and more profound generalizations than the Roman law, and at the same time far surpasses it in the detail with which it has been worked out."[5]

No doubt there are many causes for this superiority; but in my humble opinion, the most important is that, while the Roman law was a deathbed convert to Christianity, the common law was a cradle Christian. In preparing this study, I have gone to the very origins, and have been thrilled to find that many sages of the common law are also Saints of the Church. King Ethelbert is a Saint, and it is well known that up to the days of Henry VIII, a light was always kept lighted before his tomb.[6] It was St. Theodore who planted the Christian law of marriage on the soil of England.[7] Edward the Confessor was noted not only for his laws but for his just administration, which caused him to reign in the hearts of the people. His selfless devotion to the welfare of the people made them love his law and government. He has been described as "a man by choice devoted to God, living the life of an angel in the administration of his kingdom, and therefore directed by Him."[8] "The laws and customs of good King Edward" became a household saying for all succeeding generations. His life illustrates the truth that "love therefore is the fulfilment of the law."[9] My impression is that the common law was not only founded on justice, but, what is more important, rooted in grace. It gradually assimilated the principles of natural law, not as an abstract theory, but as vital practical rules of human conduct.[9a] The leaven worked slowly, but steadily.

After the Norman Conquest, holy and learned clerics like Lanfranc, St. Thomas à Becket, John of Salisbury, and many others continued to infuse natural-law principles into the common law. It may be said that Canon Law was the nurse and tutor of the common law. The very name "common law" was derived from the "*ius commune*" of the canonists.[10] It was not till the twelfth century that the name began to be generally used by the lawyers, to denote not so much the general custom of the realm as the custom and judicial tradition of the king's court.[11] Thus, the predominantly judicial origin of the common law was clear from its beginning.

As you know, "legal memory"[12] of the common law goes back only as far as the coronation of Richard I, September 3, 1189. Let us take a look at that age. Pollock and Maitland tell us that

> English law was administered by the ablest, the best educated, men in the realm; nor only that, it was administered by the selfsame men who were "the judges ordinary" of the church's courts, men who were bound to be, at least in some measure, learned in the canon law. At one moment Henry had three bishops for his archjusticiars. The climax is reached in Richard's reign. We can then see the king's court as it sits day by day. Often enough it was composed of the archbishop of Canterbury, two other bishops, two or three archdeacons, two or three ordained clerks who were going to be bishops and but two or three laymen. The majority of its members might at any time be called upon to hear ecclesiastical causes and learn the lessons in law that were addressed to them in papal rescripts.[13]

To Pollock and Maitland, "Blackstone's picture of a nation divided into two parties. 'the bishops and clergy' on the one side contending for their foreign jurisprudence, 'the nobility and the laity' on the other side adhering 'with equal pertinacity to the old common law' is not true." On the contrary, "It is by 'popish clergymen' that our English common law is converted from a rude mass of customs into an articulate system, and when the 'popish clergymen,' yielding at length to the pope's commands, no longer sit as the principal justices of the king's court, the creative age of our medieval law is over."[14]

CHAPTER II

THE MAGNA CARTA

Iᴛ is not possible to understand the spirit of the common law without taking a look at the Magna Carta, which lies at its very foundation. But I can only deal briefly with it here. To put the whole thing in a nutshell, King John, who had been law-abiding in the early years of his reign, became more and more oppressive and capricious in his later years, to such an extent that the barons whose interests were directly affected could no longer bear with him. By combined forces they compelled John to pledge himself to certain terms which would secure their rights of liberty and property from arbitrary invasions by the king. This was the political origin of the Magna Carta. In form a donation, a grant of franchises freely made by the king, in reality it was a treaty extorted from him by the feudal lords, a treaty which threatened him with the loss of his land if he would not abide by its terms. By c. 61 of the Charter of 1215, for instance, power is given to twentiy-five barons to distrain the land of the king if he should infringe their rights.

Historically, this was in no sense a "popular" movement. But the significance of the Magna Carta is as profound as it is far-reaching. "For in brief," as Pollock and Maitland sum it up, "it means this, that the king is and shall be below the law."[15] But if the king is below the law, nobody else, not even the victorious barons, could be above it. This idea of the supremacy of God and the law over all human beings was a powerful leaven which was bound in the course of time to permeate the whole mass of the people, although it started from the upper layers. That the charter was procured at the point of the sword does not decrease its value. On the contrary, it made it a living thing rather than a mere generous gesture on the part of a benevolent monarch without any claim of right on the part of the subjects.

Of special importance for the cause of the natural law are the guarantees of the rights and liberties of the Church and the freemen. I shall content myself with reproducing two of such provisions:

> From Chapter I: "First, we have granted to God, and by this our present charter have confirmed for us and our heirs for ever, that the English Church shall be free and shall have her rights and liberties, whole and inviolable." From Chapter 29: "No freeman shall be taken or imprisoned or disseised of his free tenement, liberties or free customs, or outlawed or exiled or in any wise destroyed, nor will we go upon him, nor send upon him, unless by the lawful judgment of his peers, or by the law of the land. To none will we sell, deny, or delay right or justice."

With reference to the last quotation and other provisions of a similar nature, Pollock and Maitland have made a thoughtful observation: "Even in the most famous words of the charter we may detect a feudal claim which will only cease to be dangerous when in course of time men have distorted their meaning."[16] For one thing, the king's justices were no peers of earls and barons. If these words were taken literally, it would seriously block the way to the unification of the judicial system. But somehow in the actual course of legal and political evolution, the logic of life got the better of the logic of words. For another thing, the Charter only guarantees the rights of "freemen," which does not include most of the peasants called "*villani*." Ownership of land was the mark of a freeman, and the only form of ownership then known was the freehold. But later the lawyers invented the institution of "copyhold," and many tenants, originally not freemen, became copyholders, whose only visible title consisted in the court rolls made out by the steward of the manor on a tenant's being admitted to any parcel of land. Although the copyhold was held at the will of the lord, yet the lord could not take it back arbitrarily, for even his will was subject to the customs of the manor. In the course of time, copyholders became as secure and free as any freeholder, so that Coke could write: "But now copy holders stand upon a sure ground, now they weigh not Lord's displeasure, they shake not at every sudden blast of wind, they eat, drink, and sleep securely."[17] This means that the blessings of the Magna Carta had been extended to them as a matter of course, although they were not in the contemplation of the barons who fought for the Charter.

By the time of Lord Mansfield, the "freeman" of the Magna Carta had become an equivalent of "everyman," so that in the famous *Sommersett's Case* he could declare: "Villeinage, when it did exist in this country, differed in many particulars from West India slavery. The Lord never could have thrown his villein, whether *regardant* or *in gross*,[18] into chains, sent him to the West Indies, and sold him there to work in a mine or in a cane-field. At any rate, villeinage has ceased in England, and it cannot be revived. The air of England has long been too pure for a slave, and every man is free who breathes it. Every man who comes into England is entitled to the protection of English law, whatever oppression he may heretofore have suffered, and whatever may be the color of his skin: '*Quamvis ille niger quamvis tu candidus esses.*' [However black he is and however white you are.] Let the negro be discharged."[19]

Thus the protective arm of the Magna Carta stretched not only over every Englishman but over every human being who set foot on English soil. There was no change in the words, nor was there any real distortion of their meaning, in spite of the statement of Pollock and Maitland to the contrary. We should look upon the Magna Carta as a stone thrown into a lake, causing ever-widening concentric circles until the whole expanse of the water is embraced. In fact, this is the way all the fundamental principles of the common law have grown.

But I cannot dismiss the Magna Carta without mention of Cardinal Stephen Langton, Archbishop of Canterbury, who was actually the soul of the whole movement. To me it is not without significance that the father of the Magna Carta was also the author of the magnificent hymn to the Holy Ghost, *Veni Sancte Spiritus*.[20]

The same Spirit that inspired that hymn motivated and energized, on a lower plane, the movement which was crowned by the Magna Carta; and I think that the same Spirit has enlivened the common law by breathing into it the liberalizing influence of natural justice and equity.

If the clerics had merely converted a rude mass of customs into an articulate system, it would, indeed, have been an admirable intellectual achievement, but the system would not have acquired the vitality at which all students of the common law have marvelled. My own surmise is that the vitality of the common law is due to the leaven of the Spirit. The clerics did more than produce a vessel of barren clay; they started a living tradition.

CHAPTER III

THE AGE OF BRACTON

THE reign of Henry III (1216-72) is, to my mind, the most important period in the history of the common law. As Pollock and Maitland have observed, "At the end of that period most of the main outlines of our medieval law have been drawn for good and all; the subsequent centuries will be able to do little more than to fill in the details of a scheme which is set before them as unalterable."[21] It was the age in which the "Father of the Common Law,"[22] Bracton, accomplished his great work. Like all men of supreme achievement, he was born at the right time. The law had been slowly developing for many centuries; there was an abundance of material awaiting the creative thought of a man of genius to order and synthesize it in a living system. His treatise *De legibus et consuetudinibus Angliae* "is the crown and flower of English medieval jurisprudence."[23] He drew from many sources, but his native wit organized them into a harmonious whole. He learned his Roman Civil Law from Azo of Bologna;[24] he absorbed his Canon Law principles from Gratian's *Decretum* and the *Decretals* of Gregory IX. The Roman Law gave him the method of treating his native materials and filling the gaps. He wove a doctrine out of the *plea rolls*, and dealt with the judgments of Pateshull and Raleigh just as Azo had dealt with the opinions of the Roman jurisconsults and the later glosses. Like a true Englishman, equipped with the casuistic method, he introduced the use of cases in presenting the law. In his *Note Book*, he had collected no less than two thousand cases; and in his *Treatise* he made use of five hundred. Of course, he did not arrive at the doctrine of *stare decisis;* but there is no denying the fact that he was the first to hit upon the idea of developing the law by the method of analogy. Similar facts should lead to similar decisions.[25] He veritably discovered a new method of studying juridical realities and solving actual problems of law, a method which has its roots in the sure-footed Anglo-Saxon habit of dealing with things as they arise instead of resorting to abstract conceptions. This concrete way of looking at the law springs from the Anglo-Saxon mentality and finds in it a fertile soil. This is why his seminal thought has grown into a magnificent tree in the course of time; and this is why he may properly be called the father of the common law.

A word must be said also of the system of writs,[26] which Bracton helped to develop, though he did not invent them. This emphasis on procedure and remedies is, again, typical of the practical sense of the Anglo-Saxons. In this respect, they are really more akin to the Romans than to the modern Romanists.[27] They are too Roman to receive wholesale the *Corpus Juris* of an ancient age. As Maitland and Pollock have put it, "more Roman than the Romanists," they "made the grand experiment of a new formulary system. . . . Those few men who were gathered at Westminster round Pateshull and Raleigh and Bracton were penning writs that would run in the kingless commonwealths on the other shore of the Atlantic Ocean; they were making right and wrong for us and for our children."[28]

In yet another sense is Bracton the father of the common law. As we have already seen, the common law is a cradle Christian; but it was not until the thirteenth century that the Christian element of the common law came to some sort of maturity. Bracton, with his extraordinary power of assimilation, succeeded in formulating a truly Christian philosophy of law.

His greatness lies not so much in originality as in the fact that he sums up all that was best in the legal and political philosophy of his time. In expounding the coronation oath, for instance, he says that the king must pledge himself to three things—first, that he will do what lies in his power to secure for the Church of God and all Christian people true peace in his time; second, that he will forbid all rapine and wrong-doing among all classes of people; third, in all his judgments he will promote equity and mercy as he hopes for mercy from a clement and merciful God.[29] In fact, according to Bracton, the king is instituted and elected for the very purpose of doing justice to all. The king is God's vicar and minister on earth, and it is his duty to distinguish right from wrong, the equitable from the inequitable, that his subjects may live honestly, that no man shall injure another, and that each may receive his due and make his reasonable contribution in return.[30] If the king does justice, he is a minister of God; if he does injustice, he becomes an agent of the devil. He is above his people, but he is under God and under the law, for it is the law that makes him king. On this point, I would like to introduce a splendid passage.

> The king himself, however, ought not to be under man but under God, and under the Law, because the Law makes the king. Therefore, let the king render back to the Law what the Law gives to him, namely, dominion and power; *for there is no king where will, and not Law, wields dominion.* That as a vicar of God he ought to be under the Law is clearly shown by the example of Jesus Christ whose place he takes on earth. For although there lay open to God, for the salvation of the human race, many ways and means beyond our telling, His true mercy chose this way especially for destroying the work of the devil: He used, not the force of His power, but the counsel of His Justice. Thus He was willing to be under the Law, "that He might redeem those who were under the Law." For He was unwilling to use power, but judgment. Thus also the blessed parent of God, the Virgin Mary, mother of the Lord, who by a unique privilege was above the Law, for the sake of giving an example of humility did not recoil from following lawful ordinances. The king should act likewise, lest his power remain unbridled.[31]

"*There is no king where will, and not the Law, wields dominion.*" Here the idea of the supremacy of the law is formulated in the clearest terms. The essence of law is not will and force, but judgment and the counsel of justice. In another passage he declares: "*Iuris enim prudentia agnoscit, et justitia tribuit cuique suum est.*

Item justitia virtus est, iuris prudentia scientia est."[32] This may be rendered as: "The prudence of law perceives what is due each man, and justice renders it to him. For justice is a virtue, and the prudence of law is a science." This is the true sense of jurisprudence; and yet some modern positivists wish to exclude justice from jurisprudence. This would be juris-imprudence rather than jurisprudence.

Justice Edward S. Dore, in an admirable address on "Human Rights and the Law," has said some words which bear out perfectly the point that Bracton was driving at:

> In one of Juvenal's satires we see a wilful wife commanding her Roman husband to crucify a slave for no reason. When he asks why he should do so, she answers in a sentence that has become the classical expression of law as will: *"Hoc volo; sic jubeo; sit pro ratione voluntas."*[33] What a depth of revealing meaning is packed into that little clause *sit pro ratione voluntas!* Those four words perfectly express any idea of law not based on reason but on will or force.[34]

In the *Year Books* of Edward III there is a very interesting dialogue bearing on the nature of law. The counsel in his argument was saying that the judges should do as others had done in similar cases, "otherwise we should not know what the law is." Justice Hillary interrupted him by saying, "The will of the judges." Chief Justice Stonore responded. "No, law is reason."[35]

Of course, both will and reason enter into the making of a law. Will is not to be despised, because it is given by God to man and belongs to his spiritual nature. As St. Thomas has said, "All law proceeds from the reason and will of the lawgiver; the Divine and natural laws from the reasonable will of God; the human law from the will of man, regulated by reason."[36] In other words, "in order that the volition of what is commanded may have the nature of law, it needs to be in accord with some rule of reason."[37]

It is to the credit of Bracton that, although he apparently did not have the chance of reading St. Thomas's *Treatise on Law*, his ideas came very close to those of Aquinas. His definition of law is embodied in the following passage:

Now let us see what is law; and we should know that law is the common precept of prudent men in council, the coercive prohibition of offenses which are committed intentionally or by ignorance, the impartial bulwark of the common interests. Also God is the author of justice, because justice is in the Creator. And accordingly, rightness and law (*ius et lex*) signify the same thing, and while in the widest sense everything that can be read is called law, strictly it signifies *just sanction*, enjoining what is fair and decent and forbidding the contrary.[38]

As Dr. Miriam T. Rooney has justly remarked, Bracton's definition of law and principles of sanction "are a masterly synthesis of what had gone on before his time in the development of the common law and in the growth of Christian thought."[39]

His influence on later jurists such as Coke, Holt and Blackstone, and on some of our contemporaries, has been salutary and profound.

Bracton's contributions to "case law" and to the idea of the supremacy of law are contributions not only to the common law but also to the philosophy of the natural law. In his book *The Spirit of the Common Law*, Roscoe Pound has pointed out that the two most salient characteristics of the common law are the doctrine of precedents and the doctrine of the supremacy of law. He has further pointed out that there is a common element in these two doctrines, that is, *reason*.

The same spirit is behind each. The doctrine of precedents means that causes are to be judged by principles reached inductively from the judicial experience of the past, not by deduction from rules established arbitrarily by the sovereign will. In other words, reason, not arbitrary will, is to be the ultimate ground of decision. The doctrine of the supremacy of law is reducible to the same idea. It is a doctrine that the sovereign and all its agencies are bound to act upon principles, not according to arbitrary will; are obliged to follow reason instead of being free to follow caprice. Both represent the Germanic idea of law as a quest for the justice and truth of the Creator. The common-law doctrine is one of reason applied to experience.[40]

In this Dean Pound has shown a very keen insight into the spirit of the common law. My only reservation is that he did not seem at the time of his writing to have an adequate knowledge of the Scholasticism of the thirteenth century to trace this spirit to its true source.

In fact, both the idea of the supremacy of law and the practical, concrete way of dealing with cases, which are so characteristic of the common law, came from the wisdom of the Catholic Church. The modern speculative, rationalistic philosophies of natural law are aberrations from the highroad of the scholastic tradition. In this connection, I cannot resist the urge to quote some very sensible words from one of the contemporary authorities on Canon Law, Professor Stephan Kuttner:

> The science of Natural Law, like all knowledge in the realm of practical reason, deals with human acts and cannot be construed, *more geometrico,* in an abstract, speculative fashion, i.e., without the empirical data of actual human relations and social compounds. The *concept* of Natural Law, it is true, taken in its strict sense as the principles which are immediately given by the rational and social nature of man, has its own reality, "exists" in the intellectual order in the manner of Universals; yet in the practical order it can exercise a normative function as *regula et mensura* only by some relation to the contingencies of man's social existence here and now: and these contingencies are many and changeable. They are the subject matter of *positive* law in all its variety and relativity, and it bespeaks the wisdom of medieval schoolmen that they are satisfied with philosophizing about the essential relations of all positive law to the natural, rather than dreaming of a Natural Law which would rule human social behavior once for all as a perfect code in minute detail, and thus make all positive law superfluous by absorption; or rather than removing Natural Law to the ever unattainable rarefied sphere of a transcendental ideal.[41]

This describes the method of St. Thomas. It describes also the method of Bracton and, therefore, the common-law tradition. It is most regrettable that practically all of the seventeenth-, eighteenth-

and nineteenth-century philosophers of natural law departed from this great tradition. They proceeded *more geometrico;* they wove whole systems of so-called natural law just as a spider would weave a net out of its own belly. To mention a few, Hobbes, Spinoza, Locke, Pufendorf, Christian Wolff, Thomasius, Burlamaqui, Kant, Hegel, and even Bentham with his felicific calculus, all belong to the speculative group.[42] Many of the nineteenth-century judges in America abused the name of natural law by identifying it with their individualistic bias. Some of them even erected their irrational racial prejudice to the dignity of natural law. But I shall deal with this later.

CHAPTER IV

FROM THE YEAR BOOKS
TO THOMAS MORE

SHORTLY after the death of Bracton appeared the *Year Books*. The earliest of them came out in 1292. They were produced by the lawyers who had been organized in the Inns of Court and Chancery. These Inns were virtually centers of legal study, which carried on and further strengthened the tradition of the common law as a system of case law. Although the fourteenth century is not adorned by outstanding legal luminaries, its anonymous contribution to the continuity of the legal system is not to be minimized. In the fifteenth century came Littleton and Fortescue. I shall not enter into Littleton's classic work on *Tenures*, except to say that it marks a milestone in the law of real property. John Fortescue, as a declared disciple of St. Thomas Aquinas, was opposed to the Roman precept: *Quod principi placuit legis habet vigorem* ("whatever pleases the sovereign has the force of law").[43] He maintains that "a king of England cannot, at his pleasure, make any changes in the laws of the land, for he rules by a government which is not only regal, but political."[44] He can only make such changes with the consent of the people. For him, the natural law, as revealed in the Old Testament and in the Gospel, is supreme. "For no edict or action of a king, even if it has arisen politickly, hath ever escaped the vengeance of divine punishment, if it hath proceeded from him against the rule of Nature's Law."[45]

In fact, the legal philosophy of the fifteenth century is still deeply Christian. In 1468, for instance, the Chancellor told the House of Lords that "justice was ground, well and root of all prosperity, peace and public rule of every realm, whereupon all the laws of the world had been ground and set, which resteth in three; that is to say, the law of God, the law of Nature, and positive law."[46] In 1469, in the Court of Common Pleas, Yelverton, J., addressing counsel, declared: "We are to act as the canonists and civilians do when a case comes before them for which they find no law—they resort to the Law of Nature which is the ground of all laws."[46a] In a *Year Book* of the reign of Henry VI is found the significant remark that "the law is the highest inheritance which the King has; for by the law he and all his subjects are ruled, and if there was no law, there would be no King and no inheritance."[47] This again reminds us of Bracton.

At the opening of the sixteenth century, there arose a very intesting case, *The Prior of Castleacre v. The Dean of St. Stephens.*[48] A priory had been dissolved and its property vested in the Crown by an Act of Parliament. The question in that case was, did the Crown thereby become "parson" of the church? If so, the King would be entitled to tithes. The Court of Common Pleas was unanimous in holding that the King did not become parson. In the words of Chief Justice Frowicke, "I have not seen that any temporal man can be parson without the agreement of the supreme head." The supreme head was of course the Pope. Justice Kingsmill likewise said, "The act of Parliament cannot make any temporal man to have spiritual jurisdiction; for nothing can do that except the supreme head." So Justice Fisher: "And the king cannot be parson by this act of Parliament, nor can any temporal man through this act be called parson." Not a single dissenting voice appears on record. Who could have expected then that in twenty-eight years' time an Act of Parliament was to transfer the title of "Supreme Head" to Henry VIII? That Act was not only contrary to the law of God and the law of nature, but to the common law itself.

It was under that Act that Thomas More, the most illustrious sage and saint of the common law, was indicted for and convicted of treason. A servile Parliament and a servile Court conspired with

a lawless tyrant to murder a just man. The glorious martyrdom of
St. Thomas More is too well-known to call for a detailed treatment.
All that I want to say is that the common law itself suffered in his
death a fatal wound, from which it has not recovered even now,
at least in England. It does not take a Catholic lawyer to see this.
Maitland, who was neither a Catholic nor even an Anglican, has
this to say:

> In 1535, the year in which More was done to death, the
> *Year Books* come to an end; in other words the great stream of
> Law Reports that has been flowing for near two centuries and
> a half, ever since the days of Edward I, becomes discontinuous
> and then runs dry. The exact significance of this ominous
> event has never yet been fully explored, but ominous it surely
> is. Some words that fell from Edmund Burke occur to us: "to
> put an end to the Reports is to put an end to the law of Eng-
> land."[49]

In the Prologue to his excellent biography of Thomas More,
R. W. Chambers, another non-Catholic, has written: "This book
attempts to depict More not only as a martyr (which he was) but
also as a great European statesman; More's far-sighted outlook was
neglected amid the selfish despotisms of his age; yet his words, his
acts, and his sufferings were consistently, throughout life, based
upon principles which have survived him. More was killed, but
these principles must, in the end, triumph. If they do not, the civilization of Europe is doomed."[50] What are these principles? Chambers quotes the words of one of the greatest Catholic lawyers of
contemporary England, Richard O'Sullivan, K.C.: "The life and
death of Thomas More are witness to the principle of limitation of
the power of the King or of Parliament, and the writings and the
judgments of a constellation of Catholic and non-Catholic historians and lawyers in our own time have led to a reaffirmation of the
principles of Natural and Divine Law for which he lived and
died."[51]

About Henry VIII, Maitland has written: "If Henry were
minded to be 'the Pope, the whole Pope, and something more than
the Pope,' he might trust the civilians to place the triple and every

other crown upon his head. . . . The Civilian would, if he were true to his Code and his Novels, find his ideas realized when and only when the Church had become a department of State."[52] In other words, they might have identified law with the will of the sovereign.

CHAPTER V

CHRISTOPHER ST. GERMAIN

IN 1518 there appeared a remarkable book on equity, written by Christopher St. Germain, a barrister of the Inner Temple, who was at the same time a Doctor of Divinity. *The Doctor and Student*, as the book was called, expounded the laws and customs of England, in the form of dialogues, from the standpoint of conscience. It was the earliest treatise on equity jurisprudence in the English language, and its influence on the later development of equity has been amply treated by historians of English law.[53] But what is of particular interest for our present purpose is a passage which presents the philosophy of equity from the standpoint of the natural law, or, as the author preferred to call it, the law of reason. We often speak of natural law and equity as synonyms without reflecting upon the intricate connections, on the one hand, and the distinctions, on the other, between these terms. The passage which I am going to quote here will clarify the matter, if you attend to it carefully and do some thinking for yourself:

> Equity is a right wiseness that considereth all the particular circumstances of the deed, the which also is tempered with the sweetness of mercy. And such an equity must always be observed in every law of man, and in every general rule thereof: and that knew he well that said thus, *Laws covet to be ruled by equity*. And the wise man saith, *Be not overmuch right wise*; for the extreme right wiseness is extreme wrong: as who saith, If thou take all that the words of the law giveth thee

thou shalt sometime do against the law. And for the plainer
declaration what equity is, thou shalt understand, that sith the
deeds and acts of men, for which laws have been ordained,
happen in divers manners infinitely, it is not possible to make
any general rule of the law, but that it shall fail in some case:
and therefore makers of law take heed to such things as may
often come, and not to every particular case, for they could
not though they would. And therefore, to follow the words
of the law were in some case both against justice and the commonwealth. Wherefore in some cases it is necessary to [leave]
the words of the law, and to follow that reason and justice requireth, and to that intent, equity is ordained; that is to say, to
temper and mitigate the rigour of the law. And it is called also
by some men *epieikeia;* the which is no other thing but an
exception of the law of God, or the law of reason, from the
general rules of the law of men, when they by reason of their
generality, would in any particular case judge against the law
of God or the law of reason: the which exception is secretly
understood in every general rule of every positive law. And
so it appeareth, that equity taketh not away the very right, but
only that that seemeth to be right by the general words of the
law. Nor it is not ordained against the cruelness of the law,
for the law in such case generally taken is good in himself; but
equity followeth the law in all particular cases where right and
justice requireth, notwithstanding the general rule of the law
be to the contrary. Wherefore it appeareth, that if any laws
were made by man without any such exception expressed or
implied, it were manifestly unreasonable, and were not to be
suffered: for such causes might come, that he that would observe the law should break both the law of God and the law of
reason. As if a man make a vow that he will never eat white-
meat, and after it happeneth him to come there where he can
get no other meat: in this case it behoveth him to break his
avow, for the particular case is excepted secretly from his general avow by his equity or *epieikeia*, as it is said before. Also
if a law were made in a city, that no man under the pain of
death should open the gates of the city before the sun-rising;
yet if the citizens before that hour flying from their enemies,
come to the gates of the city, and one for saving of the citizens openeth the gates before the hour appointed by the law,

he offendeth not the law, for that case is excepted from the
said general law by equity, as is said before. And so it appeareth that equity rather followeth the intent of the law, than
the words of the law. And I suppose that there be in like wise
some like equities grounded on the general rules of the law of
the realm.[54]

Thus, equity is the agency by which the law of God and the law
of reason control the operation of the general rules of positive law.
The function of equity does not extend to cases where the general
rules are in themselves void as against the principles of natural law,
for in such cases it is not equity but natural law itself which vitiates
the rules. Its function is limited to those cases where the general
rules are not intrinsically bad, but would work injustice under the
particular circumstances. There equity steps in to stop the operation of a general rule, by introducing an exception to it.

But what makes Christopher's viewpoint philosophically significant is that he does not regard the exception as a human invention
introduced as occasion arises to correct the rule; he considers the
exception as "secretly understood in every general rule of every
positive law." So, according to his view, the exceptions, though
introduced later, really serve only to confine the operation of a
general rule to its inherent limits. In other words, equity does not
change the rule, but only defines its proper scope of application,
and it does it in the name of the law of reason. Both equity and
positive law are subordinate to the law of reason, which delegates
to positive law the authority to make rules and at the same time
entrusts equity with the power of seeing to it that those general
rules are not extended to situations where their application would
defeat their original purpose, or at least is quite irrelevant to the
original purpose.

The historians of English law have invariably noted that the
Doctor and Student made its appearance at a most opportune time.
It will be recalled that Thomas More was the first layman to be
entrusted with the Great Seal, but he knew the scholastic philosophy of law as well as, if not better than, Christopher, who, by the
way, was opposed to More in some theological problems, which
need not detain us here. For the later Chancellors, however, the

Doctor and Student did serve to secure the continuity of the natural-law tradition in equity jurisprudence. But it should be noted that Christopher's explanation of equity is inclined somewhat toward rationalism. He seems to have departed from the Aristotelian position that equity is a *correction* of the general rules of law.[55] *Formally*, his position may be tenable, but *materially* or *functionally* it would be unrealistic to say that all the exceptions that equity has introduced into the law are "secretly understood" in the law itself. Equity, like positive law, derives its authority from the natural law, but the *concrete* measures it adopts are not necessarily parts of the natural law. Equity, as Aristotle and St. Thomas conceived it, would seem to be much less absolute and more human than Christopher made it out to be when he said that it "is no other thing but the exception of the law of God, or the law of reason, from the general rules of the law of men." Thus, Christopher's position does not seem to me to represent the scholastic tradition in its pure form.

My own position can be summed up in a few words. Equity does *correct* the positive law by excluding its application from a particular case; and equity performs this function by the *authority* of the natural law. On the other hand, the actual corrections that equity introduces are not necessarily parts of the natural law. In most instances, they are arrived at by a process of weighing and balancing of the values involved, and this process is far from infallible. The results of such a process cannot be attributed directly to the law of reason, still less to the law of God.

CHAPTER VI

NATURAL LAW IN SHAKESPEARE

EVEN after the Reformation, the scholastic philosophy of law was too deeply implanted in English soil to be entirely uprooted. Shakespeare, for instance, seems to know his common law and natural law pretty well. He knows the psychological reason of case law. He makes Portia say:

> . . . there is no power in Venice
> Can alter a decree established:
> 'Twill be recorded for a precedent;
> And many an error by the same example
> Will rush into the state. . . .[56]

He knows the importance of tempering the rigors of the law with equity:

> And earthly power doth then show likest God's
> When mercy seasons justice.[57]

He knows the importance of observing degree, proportion, form and order, which to him are objective standards of right and wrong because they have an ontological basis:

> Take but degree away, untune that string,
> And, hark, what discord follows; each thing meets
> In mere opugnancy: the bounded waters
> Should lift their bosoms higher than the shores,
> And make a sop of all this solid globe:
> Strength should be lord of imbecility,

And the rude son should strike his father dead:
Force should be right; or rather, right and wrong,
Between whose endless jar justice resides,
Should lose their names, and so should justice too.
Then every thing includes itself in power,
Power into will, will into appetite;
And appetite, an universal wolf,
So doubly seconded with will and power,
Must make perforce an universal prey,
And last eat up himself. . . .[58]

Shakespeare has such a profound respect for the dictates of natural reason that even a solemn oath is held to be of no binding force whatever if the pledge is to do a thing contrary to the basic principles of justice. In *Henry VI, Second Part*, he makes the Earl of Salisbury declare:

It is great sin to swear unto a sin,
But greater sin to keep a sinful oath.
Who can be bound by any solemn vow
To do a murderous deed, to rob a man,
To force a spotless virgin's chastity,
To reave the orphan of his patrimony,
To wring the widow from her custom'd right,
And have no other reason for this wrong,
But that he was bound by a solemn oath? (v, 1)

No one has painted more vividly "the majesty and power of law and justice." In *Henry IV, Second Part*, we find a dialogue[59] between Henry V and the Lord Chief Justice, who had sent him to prison for some offense during the reign of his father. Newly become king, he still felt resentful towards the Chief Justice. The first words the new king addressed to him were: "You are, I think, assur'd I love you not." The Chief Justice answered: "I am assur'd, if I be measur'd rightly, your majesty hath no just cause to hate me." "What!" said Henry V, "rate, rebuke, and roughly send to prison the immediate heir of England! Was this easy? May this be wash'd in Lethe, and forgotten?" The Chief Justice replied quietly to the effect that he was merely upholding the majesty of the law and administering justice on behalf of his father, and then added some reasons particularly appealing to the psychology of the new king:

> Be now the father and propose a son,
> Hear your own dignity so much profan'd,
> See your most dreadful laws so loosely slighted,
> Behold yourself so by a son disdain'd;
> And then imagine me taking your part,
> And, in your power, soft silencing your son:
> After this cold considerance, sentence me;
> And, as you are a king, speak in your state,—
> What I have done that misbecame my place,
> My person, or my liege's sov'reignty. (v, 2)

Henry V's answer to this is worth quoting, as showing how considerations of policy support, if extrinsically, the intrinsic demands of justice:

> You are right, justice; and you weigh this well;
> Therefore still bear the balance and the sword:
> And I do wish your honours may increase
> Till you do live to see a son of mine
> Offend you and obey you, as I did.
> So shall I live to speak my father's words:
> "Happy am I, that have a man so bold
> That dares do justice on my proper son;
> And not less happy, having such a son,
> That would deliver up his greatness so
> Into the hands of justice." You did commit me:
> For which, I do commit into your hand
> The unstained sword that you have us'd to bear;
> With this remembrance, that you use the same
> With the like bold, just, and impartial spirit
> As you have done 'gainst me. There is my hand. (v, 2)

An idealist is liable to be shocked to find that the majestic reign of the law should be founded on such a homely basis as utility. Yet this is how nature works in order to attain her ends. She has her eyes principally on virtue, but she has a way of sweetening its practice. Who, for instance, would procreate and bring up the young if nature had not sugar-coated her pills?

The works of Shakespeare are strewn with grains of legal wisdom, of which many a prominent jurist, notably Josef Kohler of Germany, has treated in learned monographs. Here we must be contented with these little snapshots. But I cannot dismiss him without pointing to his integral humanism. Like the common law itself, he does not expect man to be more than human, nor does he allow him to be less. For him, the ordinary man has a dignity which inheres in his God-given nature. What makes Shakespeare such a supreme artist is that he always holds the mirror up to nature. He makes Hamlet declare:

> . . . What is a man,
> If his chief good and market of his time
> Be but to sleep and feed? a beast, no more.
> Sure, he that made us with such large discourse,
> Looking before and after, gave us not
> That capability and god-like reason
> To fust in us unus'd. . . . (iv, 4)

It is the rational nature of man that makes him "The beauty of the world, the paragon of animals."[60] But when his reason is corrupted by passion, he loses his proper nature and becomes worse than a beast.

In *Troilus and Cressida*, he makes Hector cite Aristotle to the effect that the hot passion of distempered blood does not conduce to a free determination between right and wrong; "for pleasure and revenge have ears more deaf than adders to the voice of any true decision." Then Hector continues to expound a philosophy of law, which is in the true tradition of Aristotle:

> . . . Nature craves
> All dues to be render'd to their owners: now,
> What nearer debt in all humanity
> Than wife is to the husband? If this law
> Of nature be corrupted through affection,
> And that great minds, of partial indulgence
> To their benumbed wills, resist the same;
> There is a law in each well-order'd nation
> To curb those raging appetites that are
> Most disobedient and refractory.

> If Helen then be wife to Sparta's king,
> As it is known she is, these moral laws
> Of nature, and of nations, speak aloud
> To have her back return'd: thus to persist
> In doing wrong extenuates not wrong,
> But makes it much more heavy. . . . (ii, 2)

This philosophy springs directly from the natural reason and conscience of Hector, but, curiously enough, Hector resolved "to keep Helen still," and tried to rationalize this irrational resolution by introducing the conventional philosophy of glory and posthumous fame!

This reminds me of an interesting discussion that Shakespeare introduced in *As You Like It* between Touchstone, the conventional philosopher, and Corin, the natural philosopher. There is no question that Shakespeare's sympathies are with the latter, for he makes him talk sense rather than, as in the case of Touchstone, nonsense:

> Sir, I am a true labourer, I earn that I eat, get that I wear, owe no man hate, envy no man's happiness, glad of other men's good, content with my harm; and the greatest of my pride is to see my ewes graze and my lambs suck.

Incidentally, this sheds a light on the social conditions of the English people. By the time of Shakespeare, everyman had long become a freeman. Evidently, Corin the shepherd was a copyholder.

CHAPTER VII

COKE

THIS leads us to Sir Edward Coke, of whom Holdsworth has said: "What Shakespeare has been to literature . . . Coke has been to the public and private law of England."[61] At a time when political speculation was tending to exalt a sovereign person or body above the law, Coke had the insight and the courage to resort to the law of God and the law of nature, thus preserving the medieval idea of the supremacy of the law. In *Calvin's Case*,[62] he declared that "the law of nature is part of the law of England," that "the law of nature was before any judicial or municipal law," and that "the law of nature is immutable." He identified the law of nature with the *eternal law*.[63] He said, "The law of nature is that which God at the time of creation of the nature of man infused into his heart, for his preservation and direction; and this is *lex aeterna*, the moral law, called also the law of nature. And by this law written with the finger of God in the heart of man, were the people of God a long time governed, before the law was written by Moses, who was the first reporter or writer of law in the world." Again, in *Dr. Bonham's Case*,[64] he laid down the principle of judicial review: "And it appears in our books, that in many cases, the common law will controul Acts of Parliament, and sometimes adjudge them to be utterly void: for when an Act of Parliament is against common right and reason, or repugnant, or impossible to be performed, the common law will controul it, and adjudge such an Act to be void." This seminal thought did not germinate in England, but, as we shall see, it was later transplanted to America and there flowered.[65]

But even in England, this doctrine of judicial review of Parliamentary acts had some later echoes. In the case of *Day v. Savadge*,[66] Chief Justice Hobart declared that "even an act of Parliament, made against natural equity, as to make a man Judge in his own case, is void in itself; for *Jura naturae sunt immutabilia*,[67] and they are *leges legum*."[68] The influence of Bracton on Hobart and Coke is manifest.

In fact, in his struggle with King James I, Coke cited Bracton as an authority. He maintained in the presence of the king that by the law of England the king in person could not judge any cause, and that all cases, civil and criminal, were to be determined in some court of justice according to the law and custom of the realm. Natural reason dictates that the adjudication of legal controversies should resort to "artificial" reason. Natural law must be supplemented by human law, for art perfects nature; and this too is a precept of the natural law.

The momentous encounter between Coke and King James furnishes much food for thought. We will let Coke tell his own story:[69]

A controversy of land between parties was heard by the King, and sentence given, which was repealed for this, that it did not belong to the common law: then the King said, that he thought the law was founded upon reason, and that he and others had reason as well as the Judges: to which it was answered by me, that true it was, that God had endowed His Majesty with excellent science, and great endowments of nature; but His Majesty was not learned in the laws of his realm of England, and causes which concern the life, or inheritance, or goods or fortunes of his subjects, are not to be decided by natural reason but by the artificial reason and judgment of law, which law is an act which requires long study and experience before that a man can attain to the cognizance of it; and that the law was the golden met-wand and measure to try the causes of the subjects: and which protected His Majesty in safety and peace: with which the King was greatly offended, and said, that then he should be under the law, which was treason to affirm, as he said; to which I said that Bracton saith, *quod Rex non debet esse sub homine, sed sub Deo et lege* [that the king must not be under any man, but under God and the law].

This is perfectly in line with the Thomistic position that while there is necessity in the general principles of natural law, the remoter conclusions and the particular determinations of the natural law are a matter for human law, which, as Coke has pointed out, must depend upon experience and study, and which must vary according to the conditions of mankind and circumstances of the time. In fact, St. Thomas envisions the eternal law, the natural law and the human law as a continuous series. He even holds that the natural law can be changed by way of addition. It grows by recognizing new values emerging in the process of civilization.[70]

For Coke, too, the law of God, the law of nature or reason, and the law of the land form a continuous series. For him the common law is a tree rooted firmly in God and nature, and growing into an evergreen. No one seems to know the spirit of the common law more intimately than Coke. It is not for nothing that Maitland calls him "the incarnate common law."[71]

CHAPTER VIII

HOLT

THE idea of Coke that the king and even Parliament are under God and under the law is a tough idea. Even as late as the eighteenth century, we find Lord Holt supporting Coke's ideas in the case of *City of London v. Wood*:[72] "And what my Lord Coke says in *Dr. Bonham's Case* in his 8 Co. is far from any extravagancy, for it is a very reasonable and true saying, that if an act of Parliament should ordain that the same person should be party and Judge, or, which is the same thing, Judge in his own cause, it would be a void Act of Parliament; for it is impossible that one should be Judge and party, for the Judge is to determine between party and party, or between the Government and the party. . . ." He says further that, though an act of parliament may do certain things that "look pretty odd," yet obviously there are limits. For example, it "may not make adultery lawful."

In *R. v Knollys*,[73] Holt held that the House of Lords could not extend its privilege at will. In *Ashby v. White et al.*,[74] and *Paty's Case*,[75] he denied a similar claim by the House of Commons. Yes, there are things which even Parliament could not do. It is significant that the decision of *Ashby v. White et al.* was followed in 1839 in the case of *Stockdale v. Hansard*.[76]

In view of this, it is, indeed, strange to hear a judge of the Court of Common Pleas declare in 1871: "It was once said,—I think in Hobart,—that, if an Act of Parliament were to create a man judge in his own case, the Court might disregard it. That dictum, however, stands as a warning, rather than an authority to be followed. We sit here as servants of the Queen and the legislature. Are we to act as regents over what is done by parliament with the consent of the Queen, lords, and commons? I deny that any such authority exists."[77] I do not question the particular judgment in that case. It might possibly have been reached on some other grounds. But when you hear a judge speak in such a servile tone, you have reason to fear that the common law is beginning to lose its soul.

Now to return to Holt. Steeped in the spirit of the common law, Holt had the greatest respect for the dignity and liberty of the human person. In several cases, he held that no one could be a slave on English soil. He said in one case that "By the common law no man can have a property in another. . . ."[78] In another case he declared that "as soon as a negro comes to England he is free; and one may be a villein in England, but not a slave."[79]

In many of his decisions one senses a gentle reasonableness so characteristic of the common law. For instance, in the case of *Blankard v. Galdy*,[80] he distinguished settled colonies from conquered colonies. In the settled colonies "all laws in force in England are in force there. . . ." On the other hand, in the conquered colonies, "the laws of England do not take place there, until declared so by the conqueror. . . ." If a pagan country is conquered, "their laws by conquest do not entirely cease, but only such as are against the law of God; and . . . in such cases, where the laws are rejected or silent, the conquered country shall be governed according to the rule of natural equity." This consideration for the habits and customs of a people is one of the greatest qualities that the common law assimilated from the mellow and moderate wisdom of the Scholastics, whose philosophy of the natural law leaves much room for diversities.

In the world of practical lawyers, the best-known case that Holt decided is *Coggs v. Bernard*.[81] In that case, Lord Holt, relying on the authority of Bracton, distinguished no less than six kinds of bailments, and tried, with the patience of a scholar and the discernment of an artist, to determine the degree of care which the bailee in each category should exercise. This case has jurisprudential significance, for here you see the judicial process at work; you see how the mind of the judge reacts toward different situations; you see a most delicate and sensitive scale telling how much care is required in each case, and the corresponding degree of negligence sufficient for holding the bailee liable. In some situations, the utmost care is required, and therefore the slightest negligence is sufficient to constitute ground for liability. In other cases, fairness requires a slight degree of care, and therefore only gross negligence on the part of the bailee would make him liable. In still other situations, where ordinary care seems to be called for, ordinary negligence is enough. Of course, there is no finality about this classification. In fact, Justice Story has reduced the bailments into three categories, namely, those for the benefit of the bailor, those for the benefit of the bailee, and those for mutual benefit; and he has rationalized further the degrees of care and negligence appropriate to each class. But what I am interested in bringing out is that this is the modality of our common law, very much similar to that of the Roman law in its formative and creative days, before it was codified. The common law is a patient and kindly housewife who knows how to make, stitch by stitch, a seamless tunic for you to wear.

Of course, legal distinctions are seldom matters of black and white. As you know, gross negligence may amount to intentional wrong, and great intentional wrong may merge into malice. In the words of Ulpian, *Magna negligentia culpa est, magna culpa dolus est.*[82] The possibility of a great danger is equivalent to the probability of a small one. And then we must remember that law is not an exact science; and we are not required to weigh the consequences of our actions "with as much exactness as an apothecary would drugs on his scales."[83] On the whole, all that we are required to do is to exercise the reasonable judgment of an ordinary prudent man.

The common law is full of fringes and penumbra, full of shades and nuances; this is what makes it so human, so attractive, and so natural. In the enchanted garden of common law, there are many shady groves which cheer your heart and refresh your spirit at the same time that they lure you on to new vistas. It is not a closed garden, but one which is continuous with the wild fields, hills and rivers on one side, and leads to the streets and market-places on the other. At first you feel all but lost in the labyrinthine ways and paths; you want to discover some design, but you find none. But daily saunterings in the garden familiarize you gradually with the genie of the place, the atmosphere, the ever-changing moods of the garden, with the inevitable result that you are more and more fascinated by it. You begin to divine a certain vague design, but the element of surprise is never lacking, because it seems to change with the weather and assumes a new aspect upon the advent of every new season. Perhaps you find some traces of human designing here and there, but you are not able to tell exactly where nature ends and art begins. You do not find a general design, except perhaps the design of nature or of a mysterious Providence. What you find is not logical consistency arrived at once for all, but an endless series of organic adaptations which must be renewed every day.

CHAPTER IX

MANSFIELD

THE common law is not a closed system but an open system. In its golden days, the winds blow into it from heaven. In its days of expansion, the winds blow in from the oceans, as is the case in the age of Mansfield.

Lord Mansfield was perhaps the most dynamic personality that ever adorned the English bench. I do not regard him as a first-rate legal scholar or philosopher. But he was a man full of practical common sense and profound moral intuitions, with sufficient grounding in the humanities to quote from Cicero. He hardly seems to distinguish the *ius gentium* from the *ius naturale*, any more than Gaius did.[84] But for his practical purposes, *ius gentium* was good enough to be natural law. Anyway, the cosmopolitan usages and customs of the international merchants were nearer to the law of nature than the local laws of a single country. In *Luke et al. v. Lyde*,[85] which involved a claim for freight, he declared that "the maritime law is not the law of a particular country, but the general law of nations. *Non erit alia lex Romae, alia Athenis; alia nunc, alia posthac; sed et apud omnes gentes et omni tempore una eademque lex obtinebit.*"[86] Nowhere was his Scotch common sense and native wit more clearly shown than in his creation of Mercantile Special Juries. As Lord Campbell has told us, "Lord Mansfield reared a body of special jurymen at Guildhall, who were generally returned on all commercial cases to be tried there. He was on terms of the most familiar intercourse with them, not only conversing freely with them in Court, but inviting them to dine with him. From them he learned the usages of trade, and in return he took great pains in explaining to them the principles of jurisprudence by which they were to be guided."[87] When the law keeps its eyes open to the realities of life, the result is growth and development. By adopting and applying the *ius gentium*, Lord Mansfield added a new mansion to the common law, which is a house of many mansions. While theoretically he seems to have confused the idea of natural law with the international usages of trade, yet he was acting in the spirit of the natural law, for one of the precepts of the natural law is precisely that human law should adapt itself constantly to the changing conditions of human civilization. A system of law that does not advance falls back.[88]

His decisions on quasi-contracts have an even closer bearing upon the law of nature. In *Moses v. Macferlan*,[89] which was an action of *indebitatus assumpsit* to recover six pounds which the defendant got and kept from the plaintiff "iniquitously," Lord Mansfield laid down a great principle. "This kind of equitable action," he said, "to recover back money which ought not in justice to be kept, is very beneficial, and therefore much encouraged. It lies only for money which, *ex aequo et bono*, the defendant ought to refund: it does not lie for money paid by the plaintiff, which is claimed of him as payable in point of honor and honesty although it could not have been recovered from him by any course of law." In other words, such an action would not lie where "the defendant may retain it with a safe conscience, though by positive law he was barred from recovering." But it does lie for "money paid by mistake, or upon a consideration which happens to fail, or for money got through imposition (express or implied), or extortion, or oppression, or an undue advantage taken of the plaintiff's situation, contrary to laws made for the protection of persons under those circumstances. . . . *In one word, the gist of this kind of action is, that the defendant, upon the circumstances of the case, is obliged by the ties of natural justice and equity to refund the money.*"

Lord Mansfield was in the great tradition of the common law. He knew how to extend existing forms of action to new situations when "natural justice and equity" called for it. The common law is tough, but it is also elastic. This is the secret of its vitality and its capacity for growth. But in the nineteenth century, under the influence of Bentham and Austin, many English judges looked more and more to Parliament as the sole maker of the law, and, while they still considered themselves bound by the old precedents, they did not dare to create a new precedent. In the meantime, they no longer thought in terms of "the law of God, the law of nature, and the law of the land." For them there was no higher law than the positive law. They no longer saw eye to eye with Thomas More, Christopher St. Germain, Coke, Holt and Mansfield. Their mentality was akin to that of John Austin, to whom the idea of natural law and natural rights was a joke, and who could write: "A sacred or inalienable right is truly and indeed invaluable; for seeing that it means nothing, there is nothing with which it can be measured."[90]

In the present century, positivism seems to have reached its climax with some of the English judges. In 1913, Lord Justice Hamilton, referring to *Moses v. Macferlan*, said, "Whatever may have been the case 146 years ago, we are not free . . . to administer that vague jurisprudence which is sometimes attractively styled 'justice as between man and man.'" In 1923, Lord Justice Scrutton declared that "the whole history of this particular form of action has been what I may call a history of well-meaning sloppiness of thought."[91]

It is to be hoped that this extreme positivism is only a temporary setback to the law of nature and to the equitable spirit which is the very soul of the common law.[92] But one can have a glimpse of the modern judicial temper in England from the thoughtful words of C. K. Allen: "Charles Dickens did not exaggerate the desolation which the cold hand of the old Court of Chancery could spread among those who came to it 'for the love of God and in the way of charity.' All that is gone, and we breathe again a healthy atmosphere; but even today it is not in a spirit of cynicism, but of cold truth, that a modern Chancery Judge is able to say, 'This Court is not a Court of conscience.' Our scepticism of 'conscience' is commensurate with our veneration for prescriptive formula; perhaps both need to find a more tolerant basis of co-existence."[93]

A prophet is not without honor except in his own country. It cheers my heart to see that the spirit of Lord Mansfield has found a congenial home in this country. The seeds which he sowed in the field of quasi-contracts and unjust enrichment were transplanted to this new home of the common law, and have grown into a lovely tree called "Restitution," which may be taken as a symbol of the restoration of the common law to its original vigor. The American Law Institute has produced a restatement on Restitution. Professors Seavey and Scott of Harvard, in a joint article on the subject, after enumerating seven types of situations in which a constructive trust is imposed, come to this conclusion: "In all these situations there is one common element, namely, that a person who holds the title to property would be unjustly enriched at the expense of another if he were permitted to retain it. He is therefore chargeable as constructive trustee of the property."[94] The whole idea was beautifully expressed in the classic opinion of Judge Cardozo in *Beatty v. Guggenheim Exploration Co.*,[95] where he said, "When property has been acquired in such circumstances that the holder of the legal title may not in good conscience retain the beneficial interest, equity converts him into a trustee."

What a catch-all the device of constructive trust has become in American jurisprudence can be gathered from the words of Judge Desmond in a recent case: "A constructive trust will be erected whenever necessary to satisfy the demands of justice. Since a constructive trust is merely 'the formula through which the conscience of equity finds expression,' its applicability is limited only by the inventiveness of men who find new ways to enrich themselves by grasping what should not belong to them" (299 N.Y. at 27). When people are committing "the oldest sins the new kind of ways," the courts are giving the newest remedies the old kind of ways.

CHAPTER X

NATURAL LAW GOES
UNDERGROUND

IN his admirable article, "The Development of American Law and
Its Deviation from the English Law," Dean Pound has remarked
with a justifiable pride, ". . . the widest departure of American
law from English law is in the constitutional law. But in this departure Americans have been thoroughly English. We have continued and developed the doctrine of the English common-law
courts from the Middle Ages to the seventeenth century, where
England, having in 1688 substituted parliamentary absolutism for
the royal absolutism claimed by the Stuarts, departed from the doctrine of the common-law lawyers."[96] This is quite true. But it must
not be imagined that all modern judges in England have been
alienated entirely from the common-law rhythm of the law of God,
the law of nature, and the law of the land. There is a good deal of
truth in Professor Goodhart's remark that "the bark of the English doctrine is worse than its bite."[97] So far as the power of judicial
review of Parliamentary Acts is concerned, they have officially re-
pudiated the overriding authority of the natural law. But where
the question of validity of a Parliamentary Act is not involved, the
natural law, couched in such terms as "natural justice and equity,"
"just and reasonable," or in some other terms, has assumed the
humbler role of a supplementary source for filling the gaps of the
positive law.[98] For instance, in *Cooper v. Wandsworth Board of
Works* (1868), 14 C.B.N.S. 184, Justice Byles announced that "although there are no positive words in a statute requiring that the

party shall be heard, yet the *justice of the common law* will supply the omission of the legislature." It seems that, through the power of interpreting, the court still exercises a *de facto*, if not *de jure*, control over the statutes.[99] In the recent case of *Sir Lindsay Parkinson & Co. v. Commissioner of Works*,[100] the Court of Appeal refused to interpret in a literal manner a provision which on its face allowed the defendants to call on the plaintiffs for an unlimited amount of work, although the sum to be paid in remuneration was fixed at a precise and limited figure. Lord Justice Asquith said, "Only the most compelling language would induce a court to construe the combined instruments as placing one party so completely at the mercy of the other."[101]

This reminds me of my former teacher Rudolf Stammler, of the University of Berlin, who maintained that no man should be subjected to the arbitrary will of another, and that a legal demand can only be maintained in such a manner that the obligor may still remain his own neighbor. Now, Stammler was a Neo-Kantian, who sincerely thought his principles of justice to be universally valid; but he did not believe in the natural law. My present attitude toward Stammler's philosophy of law and justice, and toward the views of all other jurists who are idealistically but not ontologically minded, is very much the same as that expressed by Gilson toward Kantism when he said, "Perhaps Kant's ethics are but a Christian ethic cut loose from the Christian metaphysic that justifies it, the still imposing ruins of a temple with undermined foundations."[102]

It is in family law that the English judges still keep more or less intact the common-law tradition of the natural law. In a case involving the right of a parent to the custody of the child, Lord Justice Bowen actually used the term "natural law." He said, "Now the Court must never forget, and will never forget, first of all, the rights of family life, which are sacred."[103] Then, speaking of the welfare of the child, he said, "It is not the benefit to the infant as conceived by the Court, but it must be the benefit to the infant having regard to the natural law which points out that the father knows far better as a rule what is good for his children than a Court of Justice. . . ."[104] In a more recent case of a similar nature,[105] Lord Justice Slesser makes two citations from St. Thomas's

Summa Theologica. One is IIa IIae Q. 10, a. 12, where St. Thomas says, "It is against natural justice if a child, before coming to the use of reason, were to be taken away from its parents' custody, or anything done to it against its parents' wish, because the child is enfolded in the care of its parents, which is like a spiritual womb." The other is III Q. 68, a. 10, where St. Thomas says that if the children "have not yet the use of free-will, according to the natural law they are under the care of their parents as long as they cannot look after themselves."[106]

It is not only what the common law *does,* but what it *does not do,* that makes it the tender mother of the people, a mother who is wise enough to wink at the minor faults and frailties of her children, a mother who knows the importance of not being fussy. Lord Atkin's opinion in *Balfour v. Balfour*[107] is a good illustration of this quality: "The common law does not regulate the form of agreements between spouses (living in amity). Their promises are not sealed with seals and sealing wax. The consideration that really obtains for them is that natural love and affection which counts for little in these cold Courts. . . . The parties themselves are advocates, judges, Courts, Sheriff's officer and reporter. In respect of these promises each house is a domain into which the King's writ does not seek to run, and to which his officers do not seek to be admitted." Although the natural law is not mentioned, yet I think this is in accordance with it, because it is precisely one of the conclusions of the natural law that human law should know its own limits, and leave ample room to ethics. As Paton says, "In marriage, so long as love persists, there is little need of law to rule the relations of husband and wife—but the solicitor comes in through the door, as love flies out of the window."[108]

Even outside the family law, the law of nature is not altogether banned. For instance, in 1768, in an appeal from a decision of Lord Mansfield, a unanimous judgment of the Court of Exchequer said: "The law of Nature is the law of God. . . . we mean to bottom this judgment upon the law of God, the principles of reason, morality, and the common law. . . ."[109] It is interesting to note how the Court bundles all the terms together, as though they meant the same thing. This seems to be characteristic of the mentality of

English judges.[110] But their hearts are in the right place. They are practical, and they do not care much for names. After all, so they think,

> "What's in a name? That which we call a rose
> By any other name would smell as sweet."[111]

It is in the same spirit that Justice Farwell declared, in *Bradford v. Ferrand*,[112] that "the conception of *aequum et bonum* and the rights flowing therefrom which are included in the *ius naturale* underlie a great part of English Common Law; although it is not usual to find 'the law of nature' or 'natural law' referred to in so many words in English cases."

The common law is too deeply rooted in Christianity to be cut loose entirely from the natural-law tradition. It has a noble idea of man, of the human person. It sets the highest value on human life and human liberty, on the rational and social nature of man. It has not worked out an explicit scale of values; but if we look at it as a whole, we should see that it sets a much higher value on the interests of personality than on the interests of property. For instance, in *Scaramanga v. Stamp*,[113] a case in maritime law, Lord Justice Brett said that "it is contrary to public policy that a ship should not deviate in order to save life: for a vessel to go out of her course with that object is not a violation of the contract that she should proceed direct to the port for which she is bound." In his opinion, Chief Justice Cockburn said that if deviation of a ship were for the sole purpose of saving property, it would not be thus privileged but would entail all the usual consequences of deviation. Then he goes on to do a bit of sound philosophizing:

> The impulsive desire to save human life when in peril is one of the most beneficial instincts of humanity. . . . To all who have to trust themselves to the sea, it is of the utmost importance that the promptings of humanity in this respect should not be checked or interfered with by prudential consideration as to injurious consequences which may result to a ship or cargo from the needed aid. . . . Goods' owners must be taken . . . as acquiescing in the universal practice of the maritime world prompted as it is by the inherent instinct of

human nature and founded on the common interest of all who are exposed to the perils of the sea.[114]

Here we hear the very voice of the common law. It is a judgment just and reasonable and ordained to the common good. A true jurisprudence must at times move beyond prudence, or rather from a lower prudence to a higher. Our lady is never so graceful and true to herself as when she gives spontaneous expression to the dictates of her heart. Chief Justice Beasley was her spokesman when he declared, "The law hedges round the lives and persons of men with much more care than it employs when guarding property."[115]

"Laws," said St. Thomas, "are laid down for human acts dealing with singular and contingent matters which have infinite variations. To make a rule fit every case is impossible."[116] This has been borne out by the juridical experience of all countries, whether they depend mainly on legislation or on case law. As Allen has pointed out, in cases of first impression, that is, cases which are covered neither by statute nor by precedent, the judge simply has to resort "to those principles of reason, morality, and social utility which are the fountainhead not only of English law but of all law. The judge is not embarrassed by the absence of 'authority' in clear cases of this kind, for no authority is needed for the affirmation of the very essence of law."[117] From the modern cases that he cites to substantiate this statement, one may safely conclude that, although the law of nature is deprived of its metaphysical or ontological basis in England, so that it is no longer held to have any power of invalidating a positive law, as in the days of Bracton and of Coke, yet it till holds the residuary power of complementing it. Driven out from the front door, it has returned by the back door. Even in this age of positivism, there can be no way of uprooting the law of nature so long as man remains man. Practically in all modern codes, natural law, by whatever names it may be called, is admitted as one of the sources of the law. I need only give one sample:

In all civil matters, where there is no express law, the judge is bound to proceed and decide according to equity. To decide equitably, an appeal is to be made to natural law and reason, or received usages, where positive law is silent.[118]

NOTES

1. *Omychund v. Barker* (1744) 26 English Reports 15.
2. *Faust, First Part.* The translation is mine.
3. Tennyson, "Aylmer's Field."
4. Maitland, *A Short Sketch of English Legal History* (Putnam, 1915), p. 5.
5. *Collected Legal Papers*, p. 156.
6. Butler, *The Lives of the Saints*, ed. by Herbert Thurston, S.J. (Burns and Oates, 1932), February 25.
7. *Ibid.*, September 19.
8. *Ibid.*, October 13.
9. Rom. 13:8-10.
9ᵃ. It is in this sense that we can say with Prof. Edward F. Barrett, "Natural Law is at the root beginnings of our Common Law and Equity." See *Catholic Lawyer*, Vol. 1 (April, 1955), p. 135.
10. Pollock and Maitland, *History of English Law*, 2d ed. (1905), Vol. I, p. 176.
11. *Ibid.*, p. 184.
12. I mentioned this in a spirit of levity, because I was talking to lawyers. The fact is that this limit of legal memory came to be fixed by an historical fortuity. Very early, a party in a litigation who relied upon a custom would say that it had existed "from time immemorial." In order to give definiteness to this vague standard, statutes in the early part of the thirteenth century fixed the limit of legal memory at 1189, the first year of the reign of Richard I. Any custom that was proved to have existed from that year was deemed to have existed "from time immemorial." Apparently, those statutes were passed at a time when the oldest men living could still remember that year and could therefore testify to the effect that such and such a custom did exist then. The last statute to mention that date was the Statute of Westminster I in 1275. But centuries elapsed, and the limit of legal memory remained the same, because it was never abolished by a later statute. In the twentieth century, this date is certainly absurd, but it is not obsolete. Mr. Keeton has made an interesting observation: "In practice, the difficulty is surmounted by proving that the custom has been continuously followed within living memory—a procedure which places a high premium upon the services of the 'oldest inhabitant'. But if those who deny the validity of the custom can show that at some early date the custom could not have operated, this is fatal to the custom as a source of law; and more than one alleged custom has come to grief on this ground in recent times" (*The Elementary Principles of Jurispru-*

dence, 2d ed. [Pitman, 1949], p. 80). This is one of the idiosyncrasies of the common law. I mentioned it in order to bring a smile to the faces of my readers, and use it as a springboard for plunging into that period.

13. Pollock and Maitland, *op. cit.*, Vol. I, p. 132.
14. *Ibid.*, p. 133.
15. *Ibid.*, p. 173.
16. *Ibid.*, p. 171.
17. Coke, *Compleate Copy-Holder* (1641), sec. 9.
18. *"regardant"* means individually.
19. *Sommersett's* Case (1772), 20 State Trials 1.
20. Powicke, *Stephen Langton* (Oxford, 1928), pp. 47–48. After looking into the evidences and weighing them carefully, Powicke says that "there appears to be no doubt that he, and not King Robert of France, or Pope Innocent III, was the author of one of the greatest hymns, the *Veni Sancte Spiritus*."
21. Pollock and Maitland, *op. cit.*, Vol. I, p. 174.
22. James Kent called Bracton "the father of the English law" (*Commentaries on American Law*, 12th ed. by O. W. Holmes, Jr., Vol. I, p. 499).
23. Pollock and Maitland, *op. cit.*, Vol. I, p. 206.
24. Maitland, *Bracton and Azo* (Selden Society, 1894), *passim*.
25. Bracton, *De legibus et consuetudinibus Angliae*, ed. by Woodbine, 1915, I, 16.
26. In early times, the aggrieved parties applied to the king for justice. The king issued his writ to the sheriff or some other suitable person, ordering him to look into the matter and giving certain directions. Gradually a regular set of writs for judicial proceeding grew up. The forms of the writs became fixed, the directions that the king gave became crystallized into different categories of relief. It was in this practical way that the substantive rights and duties of persons took definite contours. The common law grew mainly through procedural channels. The process whereby the common law develops through procedural channels is like digging a well or gathering water by means of conduits. But at a certain point of its evolution, especially in the seventeenth and eighteenth centuries, the common law became a river which created its own channels. That is, when the judges became aware of the underlying philosophy of the substantive law, they did not hesitate to extend the forms of actions in order to do justice.
27. Ehrlich has brought out some of the analogies between English law and Roman law. "As in Rome, so in England, the material law was chiefly the law of several actions (*actiones*)." See *Fundamental Principles of the Sociology of Law*, trans. by Moll (Harvard, 1936),

p. 275. These actions are the channels in which the principles of justice and natural law are made to flow. While the channels are constructed by what Coke calls "artificial reason and judgment of the law," the principles are derived from "the natural reason." The former are changeable, while the latter are immutable.

28. Pollock and Maitland, *op. cit.*, Vol. II, p. 674. It should be noted that the "new formulary system"—the system of writs—differs from the old in that, while the formula in the Roman law concludes the proceeding before the court, the writ opens it. But the procedural emphasis is the same.

29. See Carlyle and Carlyle, *A History of Mediaeval Political Theory in the West*, 3d ed. (London, 1915), Vol. III, p. 34.

30. Bracton, *De legibus*, III, O. 2 (fol. 107).

31. *Ibid.*, fol. 5b.

32. *Ibid.*, fol. 3b.

33. "As I will, so I judge. That I will it is reason enough."

34. *Fordham Law Review*, Vol. 15 (1946), p. 11.

35. *Year Books* 18–19, Edward III, pl. 378. I am using a modernized text.

36. *S. T.*, I–II, 97. 3. *in corp.*

37. *Ibid.*, 90. 1. *ad* 3.

38. Bracton, *De legibus*, fol. 2.

39. Rooney, *Lawlessness, Law and Sanction*, p. 76. This book contains an excellent exposition of Bracton's philosophy of law (pp. 58–76).

40. Pound, *The Spirit of the Common Law* (Marshall Jones, New Boston, N.H., 1921), pp. 182–3. This book should be read together with his later lectures on "The Church in Legal History," delivered at the Catholic University of America in 1939 and published in *Jubilee Law Lectures* in the same year.

41. "The Natural Law and Canon Law," in *Natural Law Institute Proceedings*, Vol. 3 (1949), p. 85 (Notre Dame, 1950). I do not quite see eye-to-eye with Prof. Kuttner where he says that the concept of the natural law "exists" merely "in the intellectual order in the manner of Universals." Being derived from the eternal law, which is in the Mind of God, I should think that the natural law is rooted in the Reason and the Will of God and therefore possesses a higher degree of reality than the words of Kuttner would seem to indicate. But I am in entire accord with his criticism of the speculative philosophers of natural law, who have proceeded *more geometrico*. A typical instance is Samuel Pufendorf's *Elementa iurisprudentiae universalis*, where, as Coleman Philipson has aptly pointed out, he "adopts the Euclidean method, and professes to establish certain conclusions by the strict process of mathematical demonstration." See *Great Jurists of the World* (Boston, 1914, p.

310). The great difference between these speculative philosophers and the medieval Schoolmen is that, while the former are rationalistic and dogmatic, the latter are rational and experimental.

42. See Mitchell, "Bentham's Felicific Calculus," *Political Science Quarterly*, Vol. 33 (1918), pp. 161–83. Pollock was not far from the truth when he declared that Bentham's works were *Naturrecht* pure and simple. Pollock, *History of the Science of Politics* (London, 1925), pp. 111–12. St. Thomas's philosophy of natural law comprehends the principle of utility, but looks beyond it.

43. See Fortescue, *De Laudibus Legum Angliae*, trans. by Chrime (1942), c. 9. Concerning this precept Bracton had in all fairness pointed out that it should not be isolated from its context so as to appear to justify the arbitrary will of the king, for there is a qualifying clause at the end of the section: "according to the Lex Regia which was passed concerning his power" (Bracton, *De legibus*, fol. 107a). So it is law, not the king's will, which is the ultimate authority. It seems to me that Bracton had a deeper lawyer-like understanding of Roman law than Fortescue or even Maitland. In making comparisons between legal systems, we must avoid the setting up of violent contrasts.

44. *Ibid.*

45. Fortescue, *De Natura Legis Naturae*, trans. by Gregor (1874), Pt. I, c. 27.

46. See O'Sullivan, *Under God and the Law* (Newman, 1949), p. xvi.

46ᵃ. *Y.B.* 3 Edward IV, p. 9 (Mich. pl. 9).

47. *Year Books* 19, Henry VI, pl. 1 (1504).

48. *Year Books* 21, Henry VII, pl. 1 (1506).

49. Maitland, "English Law and Renaissance" in *Select Essays in Anglo-American Legal History* (Boston, 1907), Vol. I, pp. 192–3.

50. Chambers, *Thomas More* (Harcourt, 1936), p. 15.

51. *Ibid.*, p. 383.

52. Maitland, *Canon Law in the Church of England*, p. 90.

53. The full title of the book is: *The Doctor and Student: or Dialogues between a Doctor of Divinity and a Student in the Laws of England.* I am using the edition of William Mutchall, printed in 1874 by Robert Clarke & Co., Cincinnati.

   The historical significance of St. Germain's work is summed up by Plucknett: "The new school of lay chancellors learned from it the doctrine of conscience, and so were able to continue the work of their predecessors in the same spirit" (*A Concise History of the Common Law*, 2d ed. [The Lawyers Co-operative Publishing Co., Rochester, N.Y., 1936], p. 248). (New edition Little, Brown & Company, Boston, 1956.)

54. Dialogue I, Chap. 16. The word "leave" which is put in brackets is

my substitution for "love" in the Cincinnati edition I am using (p. 44). The reader will agree with me that "love" does not make sense in the particular context, and that it is almost certainly a misprint for "leave."

55. Aristotle: "What creates the problem is that the equitable is just, but not the legally just but a correction of legal justice." See Max Hamburger, *Morals and Law: The Growth of Aristotle's Legal Theory* (Yale, 1951), p. 98.

56. *Merchant of Venice*, Act IV, Scene 1.

57. *Ibid.*

58. *Troilus and Cressida*, Act I, Scene 3.

59. Act V, Scene 2.

60. *Hamlet*.

61. Holdsworth, *Some Makers of English Law* (Cambridge, 1938), p. 132.

62. 7 Co. Rep. 1, 77 Eng. Rep. 377 (K.B. 1610).

63. In this he departs from the Scholastic tradition.

64. 8 Co. Rep. 113 b, 77 Eng. Rep. 646 (K.B. 1610). See Plucknett, "Bonham's Case and Judicial Review," *Harvard Law Review*, Vol. 40 (1927), p. 30. The influence of Coke upon American jurists has been tremendous. Even as late as 1831, in *Bank of State v. Cooper*, Justice Green declared, "There are eternal principles of justice which no government has a right to disregard. . . . Some acts, although not expressly forbidden, may be against the plain and obvious dictates of reason. 'The common law,' says Lord Coke, 'adjudgeth a statute so far void.' "—2 Yerg. 599, at 603 (Tenn.). Thus, judicial review was not only based on the Constitution, but on what Corwin has called "a Higher Law."

65. The fact that there is a written constitution in America has something to do with this. See John Marshall's opinion in *Marbury v. Madison* (1803), 1 Cranch 137.

66. Hobart 85 (K.B. 1614).

67. "Natural laws are immutable."

68. "The Law of laws."

69. Prohibitions Del Roy, 12 Co. Rep. 63 (K.B. 1612).

70. See, for instance, on the modern recognition of the right of privacy, Patterson, *Jurisprudence: Men and Ideas of the Law* (Foundation Press, 1953), p. 374.

71. *A Short Sketch of English Legal History*, p. 113, where Maitland writes, "Sir Edward Coke, the incarnate common law, shovels out his enormous learning in vast disorderly heaps."

72. 12 Mod. 669, 687, 688 (K.B. 1701).

73. 1 Ld. Raym. 10 (K.B. 1695).

74. 2 Ld. Raym. 938, 3 Ld. Raym. 320 (K.B. 1703). This case was relied

upon as an authority by Justice Holmes in *Nixon v. Hearndon*, 273
U.S. 536 (1927) for holding that private damage caused by political action may be recovered in a suit at law. This is but one instance
to show the tenacity of the common-law tradition.

75. 2 Ld. Raym. 1105 (K.B. 1705).
76. 9 A. & E. 1 (K.B. 1839).
77. *Lee et al. v. The Bude and Torrington Junction Ry. Co.*, 6 L.R.
    C.P. 576. See also Hall, *Readings in Jurisprudence* (Bobbs-Merrill,
    1938), p. 289.
78. *Smith v. Gould*, 2 Ld. Raym. 1274 (K.B. 1706).
79. *Smith v. Browne and Cooper*, Holt, K.B. 495 (K.B. 1703).
80. 2 Salk, 411 (1694).
81. 2 Ld. Raym. 909 (K.B. 1704).
82. "Great carelessness amounts to intentional fault, and great inten-
    tional fault amounts to fraud."
83. See *Sikes v. Commonwealth*, 304 Ky. 429, 200 S. W.2d 956 (1947).
    There Commissioner Stanley quotes these words. He also writes,
    "Man-made law is not blind to human nature; at least self-preserva-
    tion."
84. Gaius, *Institutes*, 1, 1.
85. 2 Burr. 887 (K.B. 1759).
86. The quotation is from Cicero, *De Re Publica*. See Keyes's transla-
    tion in Loeb Classical Library (Putnam, 1928), p. 211. "And there
    will not be different laws at Rome and at Athens, or different laws
    now and in the future, but one eternal and unchangeable law will
    be valid for all nations and all times."
87. Campbell, *Lives of the Lord Chief Justices*, Vol. II, p. 407, note.
88. No doubt it is a fixed principle that all laws are ordained to the
    common good. But the idea of the common good grows in the
    course of history. See, for instance, what Chief Justice Vanderbilt
    has written about the "successive goals" of American jurisprudence
    from the pioneer days to the present (*Law and Government in the
    Development of the American Way of Life*, p. 19). As St. Thomas
    has said, "It seems natural to human reason to advance from the
    imperfect to the perfect" (*S. T.*, Ia IIae, Q. 97, a. 1, in corp). We
    may add that human reason advances in two ways: first, in recog-
    nizing new values emerging in the process of civilization; secondly,
    in inventing new means for implementing the values. But in no
    case must it act against the fundamental principles of the natural
    law.
89. 2 Burr. 1005 (K.B. 1760). *Indebitatus assumpsit* is the name of an
    action in which the plaintiff declares that the defendant owed him
    a debt or obligation which he had assumed to pay. Two elements
    are essential: an obligation or debt and a promise. But in the present

case, there was really no promise. It was the law that implied a
promise on the part of the defendant. So such cases are called quasi
contracts rather than contracts proper. This is an instance of judges
extending an existing form of action to a new situation in answer
to the demands of justice.

90. Austin, *Province of Jurisprudence*, p. 48. For an appropriate comment on this attitude see LeBuffe and Hayes, *Jurisprudence* (Fordham University Press, 1938), pp. 57–8.

91. *Baylis v. Bishop of London*, 1 Ch. D. 127, 140 (1913); *Holt v.
Markham*, 1 K.B. 504, 513 (1923).

92. I do not maintain that England should adopt the doctrine of judicial review. The public opinion in the English community concerning law-making is homogeneous, and there is little likelihood
of violent divergences of views between Parliament and the judges.
What I do like to see is a frank recognition of natural law and
justice, as a necessary source of law in the adjudication of cases
where the positive law (statutes, customs and precedents) is silent,
or when it is ambiguous and inadequate and stands in need of interpretation and supplementation. The least that we can expect
from the judges and lawyers is that they shall not go out of their
way to announce officiously that Parliament can do all things—a
liberty which, as a matter of fact, Parliament would not assume.
One Attorney-general is reported to have said, "Parliament is
sovereign; it can make any laws. It could ordain that all blue-eyed
babies should be destroyed at birth." (See O'Sullivan, *The King's
Good Servant*, Newman, 1948, p. 18.) One wonders if Parliament
would appreciate the gratuitous conferring of such extraordinary
powers upon it. The *reasonable man* is the hero of the common
law; and certainly it is not for law-officers to suppose that the members of Parliament would lose their reason. To indulge in an
imaginative defence of those lovely blue-eyed babies is academic
enough; but to kill the innocent imaginatively is worse.

93. Allen, *Law in the Making*, 5th ed. (Oxford, 1951), p. 396.

94. *Law Quarterly Review*, Vol. 29 (1938), p. 213.

95. 225 N.Y. 380, 386, 122 N.E. 378 (1919).

96. *Law Quarterly Review*, Vol. 40 (1951), p. 67. *Id.* at 59.

97. A. L. Goodhart, *English Law and the Moral Law* (London, Stevens,
1953), p. 79.

98. As Messner says, "Natural law prevails in all cases where human
law is deficient: it is complementary. By its very nature a deficiency
is found in all human law" (*Social Ethics*, p. 209). This is true in
code countries as well as in case-law countries. See Gutteridge,
Comparative Law, 2d ed. (Cambridge, 1949), p. 88; Paton, *A Text-
Book of Jurisprudence*, 2d ed. (Oxford, 1951), p. 96; Friedman,

Legal Theory, 2d ed. (London, 1949), p. 49; Goodhart, *English Law and the Moral Law* (London, 1953).

99. See Wade, "The Twilight of Natural Justice?", *Law Quarterly Review*, Vol. 67 (1951), p. 103.

100. 2 K.B. 632 (1949).

101. *Id.* at 662.

102. Gilson, *The Spirit of Mediaeval Philosophy* (New York, Scribner, 1936), p. 342.

103. *Agar-Ellis v. Lascelles*, 24 Ch.D. 317, 337 (1883).

104. *Ibid.*

105. *In Re S.M. Carroll*, 1 K.B. 317, 354 (1931).

106. There is a good biographical sketch of Sir Henry Slesser in Hoehn, *Catholic Authors*, (Newark, 1952), p. 557.

107. 2. K.B. 571, 579 (1919).

108. Paton, *A Text-Book of Jurisprudence*, 2nd ed. (Oxford, 1951), p. 53.

109. *Low v. Peers*, Wilmot's Reports, 364, 371, 374 (1770).

110. Laski has described the English mind as one which "is full of real insights, can never concentrate on any subject, never argue about it abstractly, is always driven to the use of a concrete illustration, is rarely logical and about eight times out of ten patently in the right" (Howe, *Holmes-Laski Letters* [Harvard, 1953], p. 303). This is borne out by many of the typical sayings one comes across in English decisions and other writings. For instance, "Ratiocination is good, but common sense is necessary" (Evatt J. in *R. v. Connare*, 61 C.L.R. 620). Sir Thomas Browne: "States are not governed by ergotisms. Many have ruled well, who could not perhaps define a commonwealth. . . . When natural logic prevails not, artificial logic too often faileth" (*Christian Morals, Works of Sir Thomas Browne*, Bohn's ed., Vol. III, p. 111).

111. This does not make Shakespeare a nominalist, for he is not dealing with universals.

112. 2 Ch. D. 655, 662 (1902).

113. 5 C.P.D. 298 (1880). See an interesting article by Richard O'Sullivan on "A Scale of Values in the Common Law," *Modern Law Review*, Vol. 1 (1938), p. 27.

114. *Id.* at 304.

115. (1890) 19 Atlantic 472.

116. Gilby, *St. Thomas Aquinas: Philosophical Texts* (Oxford, 1951), p. 364.

117. Allen, *Law in the Making*, p. 277, note 79. See also a recent book by Sir Alfred Denning, *The Changing Law* (London, 1953), containing an excellent chapter on "The Influence of Religion."

118. Dart's *La. Civil Code*, Art. 21.

SECTION II

THE COMMON LAW IN ITS NEW HOME

CHAPTER XI

THE RECEPTION OF THE COMMON
LAW IN AMERICA

WHEN the common law came to the New World, its youth and vigor were renewed and its horizons broadened. English jurisprudence had depth, but on the whole it was insular in outlook. In the hands of American jurists, the common law grew in breadth while retaining its original depth. The reception of the common law in America was the most momentous event in its evolution since its formation in the thirteenth century. Its fundamental principles were articulated and reaffirmed, while some of its anachronisms were pruned away. Great jurists like James Wilson, Marshall, Story and Kent worked upon their inexhaustible heritage and gave it a new orientation, so as to adapt it to new social conditions and new political institutions. These great lawyers were also statesmen and men of broad culture. They were not rabid reformers. In them a bold creative spirit was combined with a profound sense of historical continuity. They were at once idealistic and practical. If they struck out into new paths, it was with a lawyer-like prudence and cautiousness.

But there was a newness of spirit, a dynamic vim, an open-minded cosmopolitanism, an open-hearted good will toward all, a consciousness of unlimited potentialities coupled with a humility that sprang from the realization of how much was still to be accomplished, an immense self-confidence combined with an eagerness to learn from all sources; and underlying it all was a deep faith in God and His justice. For the common law it was a veritable second Spring, whose beauties defy description in words but evoke profound emotions in the soul. All that I can say is that in contemplating the common law in its new home I often recall some lines in Emerson's *May-Day:*

> When the trellised grapes their flowers unmask,
> And the new-born tendrils twine,
> The old wine darkling in the cask
> Feels the bloom on the living vine,
> And burst the hoops at hint of spring.

"The common law of England," Justice Story declared in *Van Ness v. Pacard* (1829),[1] "is not to be taken in all respects to be that of America. Our ancestors brought with them its general principles, and claimed it as their birthright: but they brought with them and adopted only that portion which was applicable to their situation." This set the tone for the later jurists.

Chief Justice Shaw of Massachusetts, in *Norway Plains Co. v. Boston & Maine Railroad* (1845),[2] had this to say: "It is one of the great merits and advantages of the common law, that, instead of a series of detailed practical rules, established by positive provisions, and adapted to the precise circumstances of particular cases, which would become obsolete and fail, when the practice and course of business, to which they apply, should cease or change, the common law consists of a few broad and comprehensive principles, founded on reason, natural justice, and enlightened public policy, modified and adapted to the circumstances of all the particular cases which fall within it." While these principles are bound, to some extent, to solidify into precise and certain rules in the course of judicial decisions, they can never be totally reduced to rules. There is always some residual mother liquor for the formation of new crystals "when new practices spring up," and "new combinations of facts arise."

In 1890, Chief Justice Comegys of Delaware, in *State v. Williams*,[3] uttered a statement which may be regarded as the American philosophy of the common law. "While the great body of the English common law," he said, "is in force here, yet it is because it, and such statute law as is virtually a part of it, are suited to our condition and circumstances." But what is the criterion of suitability? Are we to be contented with mere expediency and opportunism? So the judge proceeded to say, "In a free government, such as our own, and that of the mother country as well, the object of all law, common or statutory, is the establishment of 'justice,'—that comprehensive term in which are included the three great objects for which, according to our declaration of independence, governments among men are instituted. Whatever rule of the unwritten law, therefore, is at variance with this great purpose of justice,—the security of life, liberty, and the pursuit of happiness,—is one not suited to our condition and circumstances; we having entered upon and hitherto pursued with entire satisfaction and success a career of government for ourselves which admits of no injustice to any individual, however circumstanced or humble in social rank he may be."

In the present century, the dynamic and expansive nature of the common law has been stressed time and again in American jurisprudence. In *Oppenheim v. Kridel* (1923),[4] Judge Crane said, "The common law is not rigid and inflexible, a thing dead to all surrounding and changing conditions, it does expand with reason. The common law is not a compendium of mechanical rules, written in fixed and indelible characters, but a living organism which grows and moves in response to the larger and fuller development of the nation."

Only recently Judge Moore of California declared, ". . . the genius of the law does not encourage stagnation. On the contrary, it demands expansion; in every field of endeavor it provides new rules and new remedies to meet new situations. The lone and forlorn cry that 'it's never been done before' is not sufficient to reverse a new, wholesome trend."[5]

So, too, Judge Crossland of Ohio: "The law looks forward, not backward, to the future, not to the past, to serve the living while honoring the dead, to respect the past for its contribution to the present and future, but not to corrode and die in the forward march of program, progress and purpose. For law was designed

and intended to serve the organized society of mankind, not stifle
or cripple man's effort to grow, advance and prosper."[6]

Similarly, in the famous case of *United States v. Morgan*, 118
Fed. Supp. 621, at p. 688, Judge Medina wrote, "No court can turn
back the hand of time. . . . The eggs cannot be unscrambled. And
if they could, *cui bono?* We must not forget that the law is a living
dynamic force at all times responsive to the needs of society, and
not a mere game in the playing of which judges move about quotations from earlier cases as one would shift kings and queens on a
chess-board."

Perhaps no one has expressed this dynamic quality more poeti-
cally than Justice Cardozo: "The inn that shelters for the night is
not the journey's end. The law, like the traveller, must be ready for
the morrow."[7]

Here let us pause a moment and see where we are. There can be
no question that the dynamic quality of American jurisprudence
is one of its glories. But is there not another quality which gives
meaning and sense of direction to the dynamism? (Because dynamism is, after all, not dynamite.) I am not thinking of the brakes,
which are a necessary part of any dynamism. I am thinking of the
ends of life, which the dynamism is supposed to serve and promote.
Does the law view the ends of life as being confined to the development of material civilization? As I survey contemporary American
decisions, I see some signs that many judges of federal and state
courts are becoming more and more sensitive to the spiritual and
moral interests of man.

In *Bruker v. Burgess and Town Council* (1954),[8] Justice Bell, in
his dissenting opinion, wrote a magnificent passage warning against
the philosophy of change for change's sake. Now, I am not quite
sure whether his position in that particular case was right, but
nonetheless the passage which I am going to quote is a very far-
sighted criticism of a philosophy of life which seems to prevail
among a large, unthinking section of the population. At the present moment, many people are no longer living, but are merely
drifting aimlessly. Now, true progress does not consist in going
along with the currents. Living fish swim against the current; only
dead fish float unresistingly with it. During the present crisis of

Western civilization, we have to lay a great deal of emphasis on the spiritual part of our nature, "without which," as Justice Holmes said, "we are but snails and tigers."[9] It is in this light that we should regard the words of Justice Bell:

> We are living in exciting and rapidly changing times. We rode from the horse and buggy age to the automobile age and then flew too rapidly to the airplane age and the atomic age. The tremendous changes which have occurred and are still daily occurring have necessarily produced uncertainty, unrest and confusion—not only in the minds of men, but in many phases of man's life. As a consequence, "change" is on every man's lips, and unrest and uncertainty in many a man's heart. In the craving for change, in the restless quest for a Utopia of riches and ease, haven't we too often forgotten the things of the spirit, as well as the history of our Country and the immemorial customs of our people? Haven't we rushed frantically and heedlessly after false goods—material prosperity and political panaceas? Should not our wonderful farm people be allowed to preserve in a farming community a few of their ancient privileges, customs and practices, even though more income would be produced by a different (public or private) use?

The more open-minded judges are beginning to be alert to the dangers of the disintegration of the family. In a divorce case which involved the question of "constructive desertion" the Supreme Court of South Carolina deliberately declined to follow the so-called "liberal rule," and did not hesitate to subscribe consciously to the "conservative doctrine," although the former is favored by a majority of jurisdictions. Speaking for a unanimous court, Judge G. Badger Baker said that, although there has been in the recent past some shift in the public policy of the state relating to matrimony, "Nevertheless, marriage still remains an institution in the maintenance of which in its purity the public is deeply interested. . . ." "A recognition of the liberal view would be directly against the interest of society, the obligations of the conjugal relation, and the welfare of families."[10]

In a similar case, which smelled of collusion, the Appellate Court of Indiana, speaking through Judge Royse, said, "Even in this modern atomic age adultery is regarded by most people as a serious offense. It cannot be proved by the kind of evidence we have here. To affirm this judgment . . . would be a 'go sign' for easy divorce. We are not ready to go 'Hollywood.' "[11]

Of course, family integrity is a question that cannot be solved by law alone. Religion, education and social economy have to cooperate in preventing the awful phenomenon of broken homes. But law must do what it can in the work of salvaging. As a result of broken homes, the courts have had to deal with an endless number of child-custody cases. It is particularly in these cases that the Christian humanism of American jurisprudence is to be seen in its fullness. The solicitude of the judges for the welfare of the innocent victims of family discords is more than paternal; it is maternal. In making their decisions, they must consider with infinite tenderness and patience the welfare of the child from all angles, physical, intellectual, moral and spiritual. In such cases, law merges into equity, and equity merges into social case work. The heart and the head, nature and art, work in perfect harmony.

Let a few instances suffice. What a practical and down-to-earth thing the law of nature is can be gathered from cases dealing with the natural relations of men. For instance, Justice Brace of Missouri said:[12]

> In all civilized countries in which the family is regarded as the unit of social organization, its minor members must and ought to be subject to the custody and control of those who are immediately responsible for their being; for the reason that by nature there has been implanted in the human heart those seeds of parental and filial affection that will assure to the infant care and protection in the years of its helplessness, to be returned to the parents again when they in their turn may need protection in their years of helplessness, and their child's strength and maturity. The law at the birth of an infant imposes upon the parent the duty of care and protection, to the performance of which the instincts of nature so readily prompt, and clothes him with the right of custody that he may perform it effectually, upon the presumption that such cus-

tody, being in harmony with nature, is best for the interest, not only of the parent and child, but also of society.

Similarly, Judge Holtzoff has said in a recent case, "The family is the foundation of society. The duty of a married man to support and protect his wife and children is inherent in human nature. It is a part of Natural Law, as well as a requirement of the law of every civilized country. It is not an ordinary indebtedness, such as a contractual obligation or a judgment for damages arising out of a tort." (*Seidenberg v. Seidenberg*, 1954. 126 F. Supp. 19, at p. 23.)

In the famous case of *Pierce v. Sisters of the Holy Names of Jesus and Mary*,[13] the Supreme Court of the United States declared unanimously, "The fundamental theory of liberty upon which all governments in this Union repose excludes any general power of the state to standardize its children by forcing them to accept instruction from public teachers only. The child is not the mere creature of the state; those who nurture him and direct his destiny have the right, coupled with the high duty, to recognize and prepare him for additional obligations."

In *Ramon v. Ramon* (1942),[14] the Domestic Relations Court of New York City, upholding an ante-nuptial agreement that the children to be born were to be brought up in the Catholic faith, said, "The court will take judicial notice of the religious and moral obligations of the parties." The court made several references to Canon Law, but what interests me most is its quotation from the *International Encyclopedia:* "The elevated condition of woman is due to the Canon Law prescriptions which the church enforced in all nations converted to Christianity."

In a recent New Jersey case, *Leith v. Horgan*,[15] where the question was whether the parents of a married woman have the right to visit her against the wishes of her husband, the Supreme Court, while conceding that under the present circumstances it would be wiser not to exercise that right for fear of aggravating "the stresses and strains of her paralysing illness," nevertheless upheld the right in principle. Speaking for a unanimous court, Justice Heher said:

> The marital state is in its very nature superior, but not so exclusive and forbidding as to work a severance, unreasonably

and arbitrarily, of all communion between the wife and her next of kin. Nature's laws are not so amenable to human decree. Neither spouse may allow filial love and affection, commendable as it is, to override conjugal duty. But marital unity would not be served by capricious restrictions upon the natural freedom of either spouse; quite the contrary.

If the Court did not permit the parents to exercise their natural right for the time being, it was because "The welfare of the stricken wife is the determining consideration."

Now, this case is of particular importance from the standpoint of the philosophy of natural law. It views natural rights, not absolutely and abstractly, but as limited intrinsically by reason and as correlative to natural duties. Here no fewer than three natural rights are involved: the natural right of the parents to visit their married daughter, the natural right of the spouses to each other's exclusive conjugal companionship, and the natural right of a person to life. As interpreted by the Court, all these natural rights are to be regulated and evaluated by reason in the light of circumstances and with a view to fairness to all parties involved. They are viewed, as they should be, in the living context of human relations. This way of looking at natural rights has more in common with the Christian tradition of the natural law than with the absolutist, speculative philosophies of modern times. The underlying Christian philosophy of the Court is manifest in the following passage:

> Without mutual forbearance in the interest of the afflicted, as well as the peace of mind and soul that is dearer than all, the deep bitterness engendered by a family tragedy will intensify its grievousness and poignancy and dim the light of faith and hope in a crisis that calls for the finest spiritual qualities. It is indeed a time for charity that suffereth long and is kind, and beareth and endureth all things.

Where natural law and natural rights are understood in the living context of Christian love, they serve to fulfill the glorious destiny of man. Even in the nineteenth century, the judges were never purely individualistic in outlook when they were dealing with family relations and fiduciary relations, because in such cases their natural-law philosophy was kept perfectly sane and healthy by their holding of the mirror to the Gospel. It was only when they were dealing with property rights that they forgot their Christianity and succumbed to the false economic gospel of *laissez-faire*. But of this later.

At any rate, where American jurisprudence is at its best, you find a perfect co-operation of nature and art, of the basic principles of justice and the ingenious methods of juristic thinking, and this can be seen in all fields of the law, literally from "abandonment" to "zoning." American jurisprudence is heading toward a real synthesis between unity and diversity. The end is one, but the means are many. The end is always justice, while the means are flexible. For instance, Judge Moore said, "The interpretation of a contract, like all other facts to be found, should be achieved with an eye to doing justice between the parties to the controversy."[16] Now interpretation is a highly complicated art, but the end that this serves is justice. As Justice Hale says in *Simmons v. Wilson*,[17] "Constructive trusts are purely creatures of equity. Their forms and varieties are practically without limit. Their classification is dependent upon the circumstances surrounding the acquisition of the legal title to property in each particular case. Being remedial in character, their broad function in all of their varied forms and classifications is to redress wrong or unjust enrichment, in keeping with established principles of equity and justice."

All legal doctrines, which the juristic art has formulated, must be applied with an eye to justice. Even the time-honored concept of *stare decisis* must not be blindly followed. As Chief Justice Vanderbilt has put it, "The doctrine of *stare decisis* tends to produce certainty in our law, but it is important to realize that certainty *per se* is but a means to an end, and not an end in itself. Certainty is desirable only insofar as it operates to produce the maximum good and minimum harm and thereby to advance justice."[18]

Where fundamental principles and the great ends of justice are involved, however, the law becomes as immovable as the everlasting hills, and the proper attitude of the judge should be hard as steel.

Fiat justitia, ruat coelum. (Let justice be done, though the heavens may fall.)[19] In *State v. Dryman*,[20] a recent Montana case, the defendant, charged with murder in the first degree, petitioned for change of venue on the ground that an impartial jury could not be formed in Toole County, where feelings were running high against him. Justice Freebourn of the Supreme Court of Montana, in granting the motion, wrote words which reveal the immutable aspect of the law:

> Our Government is one of law which is no mere empty formality to be followed in one case and overlooked in another. Courts are sworn to see that our laws and the provisions of our Constitution are carried out, and that every right accorded thereby to a defendant be given him, regardless of expediency, dissatisfaction of others, or benefit to be gained or lost. If this were not so, the will of man would prevail. Then, like the seasons of the year one following the other, as the wheel of time turned and men changed, what would be just today would be unjust tomorrow. No rule to guide or measure man's conduct would exist.

In its flexible aspect, the common law is like a beautiful river "whose moving surface glides away at one's feet, meandering in and out in endless curves, now seeming to disappear in a whirlpool, now almost lost to sight in the verdure."[21] But the source of this river lies in the higher regions, in a mountain whose immovability and immensity make it a perfect symbol of sublimity.

It was Confucius who said, "The wise take pleasure in the waters; the good take pleasure in the mountains."[22] But jurisprudence, which is the science of justice and the art of what is good and equitable, takes pleasure both in the waters and in the mountains.

CHAPTER XII

THE NATURAL-LAW PHILOSOPHY
OF THE FOUNDING FATHERS

So far we have studied the general physiognomy of American jurisprudence. We have looked at it primarily from the standpoint of the common law. Now we shall consider it from the standpoint of the natural law.

It does not take deep study to discover that the natural law has received a much warmer reception in America than in any other country in the world. The truth is that the vitality of the natural-law tradition depends ultimately upon religion, and no one could ever take religion more seriously and earnestly than the Puritans and their compatriots who founded this nation. To them "the laws of nature and of nature's God" were no products of fancy, nor even mere ideals; they were absolutely *real*, infinitely more real than any human laws. Nor were Americans indulging in rhetoric when they declared, "We hold these truths to be self-evident, that all men are created equal, that they are endowed by their Creator with certain unalienable Rights, that among these are Life, Liberty and the pursuit of Happiness." They meant exactly what they said. They were a generous, sincere, freedom-loving and God-fearing people. They saw these truths so clearly and felt so deeply about them that they were willing to stake their lives upon them. Even in the late 1830's, Alexis de Tocqueville could truthfully testify:

In the United States the sovereign authority is religious, and consequently hypocrisy must be common; but there is no country in the whole world in which the Christian religion retains a greater influence over the souls of men than in America; and there can be no greater proof of its utility, and of its conformity to human nature, than that its influence is most powerfully felt over the most enlightened and free nation of the earth.[23]

The formative days of American jurisprudence are reminiscent of the great days of the Magna Carta, and also of the later struggles of Coke for the supremacy of the law of nature over man-made laws. Coke's efforts had been frustrated in England, but his influence on American lawyers of the eighteenth century was immense. Before the Declaration of Independence, all that the colonists wanted was to be the inheritors of the common law, the common law as Bracton, Coke, Holt, Mansfield and Blackstone understood it. In his pamphlet on *The Right of the Inhabitants of Maryland to the Benefit of the English Laws*, published in the 1760's, Daniel Dulaney, Attorney-General of Maryland, argued for the right of the Americans to the natural and legal liberties, privileges, and rights of Englishmen in the realm. But what is of special bearing on our theme is the way Dulaney conceived the common law. According to him, the common law "takes in the Law of Nature, the Law of Reason, and the revealed Law of God."[24] These are equally binding, at all times, in all places, and on all persons. Besides these universal principles, the common law also embodies such usages and customs as have been experimentally found to suit the order and engagements of society, and to contain nothing inconsistent with honesty, decency, and good manners.[25] These, he said, have obtained the force of law by consent and long use. This conception of the common law is in the grand tradition of Bracton and Coke.

The religious foundations of law are brought out even more clearly and forcibly in the writings of the famous Boston lawyer James Otis. I want to quote a passage which seems to me to be the cornerstone of the orthodox American philosophy of the natural law:

To say the parliament is absolute and arbitrary, is a contradiction. The parliament cannot make 2 and 2, 5: Omnipotency cannot do it. The supreme power in a state, is *jus dicere* only: —*jus dare*, strictly speaking, belongs alone to God. Parliaments are in all cases to *declare* what is for the good of the whole; but it is not the *declaration* of parliament that makes it so: There must be in every instance, a higher authority, viz. *God*. Should an act of parliament be against any of *His* natural laws, which are *immutably* true, *their* declaration would be contrary to eternal truth, equity and justice, and consequently void: and so it would be adjudged by the parliament itself, when convinced of their mistake.[26]

When you hear people talk with such clear vision and true conviction, you feel that the world is beginning again. Like Adam and Eve, they were so close to God. So was Jefferson, who said that "the God who gave us life gave us liberty at the same time." So was John Adams, when he wrote: "I would ask, by what law the parliament has authority over America? By the law of God, in the Old and New Testment, it has none; . . . by the common law of England, it has none. . . ."[27] So was Alexander Hamilton, who wrote: "The sacred rights of mankind are not to be rummaged for among old parchments or musty records. They are written, as with a sunbeam, in the whole volume of human nature, by the hand of Divinity Itself, and can never be erased or obscured by mortal power."[28]

It must be pointed out that, although these great men drew their inspiration mainly from the Bible and the common law, they also absorbed to a degree some rationalistic ideas from such authors as John Locke, Grotius, Pufendorf, Rousseau, Montesquieu, and Burlamaqui. With a few exceptions, they were not too well acquainted with the scholastic tradition. Because, no doubt, of their historical situation, they were inclined to think more of the natural liberties and rights of man than of the natural law and natural duties. They talked more about individual rights than about the common good. Perhaps, in their time, the very establishment and maintenance of individual freedom constituted the chief part of the common good. As Blackstone had put it, "the public good is in nothing more essentially interested than in the protection of every individual's private rights."[29]

Nothing shows the soundness of the Founding Fathers more clearly than in their use of the phrase "life, liberty and the pursuit of happiness." In spite of the influence on them of John Locke, they did not adopt the Lockean rhythm of "lives, liberties and estates." As Bishop Sheen has pointed out in his *Philosophy of Religion*,[30] it was Jefferson who caused the words "pursuit of happiness" to be substituted for the word "property" emphasized by Samuel Adams, who was a follower of Locke. Property may be one element of happiness, but it is not all.

When some of the later judges came to identify "happiness" with "property," they actually departed from the spirit of an overwhelming majority of the early Americans. Justice Brewer was right in maintaining that the Constitution should be read in the light of the Declaration of Independence, but I doubt very much whether his reading of the Declaration was right, when he spoke of the inalienable rights in terms of "the sacredness of life, of liberty, and of property."[31]

Property is, in a derivative sense, a natural right, but there is a hierarchy of values even among natural rights. Important as it is, it does not belong to the same level as life and liberty. Life and liberty are ends in themselves, while property is only an instrumental value. I think many of the erroneous decisions rendered by the Supreme Court of the United States in the last quarter of the nineteenth century and the first decades of the present century can be traced to an overemphasis on the rights of property at the expense of the personal rights of men and the legitimate demands of the common good. Many such decisions have, happily, been overruled by the same Court.

Nothing is so fascinating as to follow the fortunes of the natural-law philosophy in this country. Its chief glory lies in its confirmation of the idea that there is a Law higher than positive laws. In its early days, the American philosophy of the natural law did not separate itself from religion, and it became the rock on which a true democracy was built. The genuine tradition of the natural law is essentially theistic and democratic.[32] As Cardinal Spellman has said, "The role of religion in a democracy is crystal clear from a consideration of the basic meaning of Democracy. The prime function of Democracy, which distinguishes it from and elevates it above every other form of government, is its regard and concern for the dignity and the rights of the individual, inalienable rights derived from the natural law. . . . This great natural law, antecedent to all human enactment and contrivance, is the only foundation on which the structure of Democracy can rest secure. For not by mutual consent or by covenant, not by warrant or state grant are these rights established. They are the gifts of God and the bestowal of God."[33] So long as we remember this, there is no danger of abusing the concept of natural law for justifying a materialistic individualism; because we know that God, who gave us liberty, gave us also reason and a supernatural destiny. In other words, we receive our natural rights together with our natural duties, such as the love of God and of our neighbor.

CHAPTER XIII

THE INDIVIDUALISM OF THE NINETEENTH CENTURY

INDIVIDUALISM, in the sense that every individual person, being made in the image of God, is an end in himself, springs from the Christian ideology, but in this sense it should properly be called *personalism*. Every creature is an individual, but only a rational creature can be a *person*. If individualism is taken in the sense that no one is his brother's keeper, that one is an absolute master of one's property, that one may do whatever one likes with one's own property, even if others are starving to death, it is utterly alien to Christianity. But it cannot be denied that this form of individualism dominated American legal thought for over half a century, so far as the law had to do with commercial and industrial transactions. When such an unchristian tendency was cloaked in the sacred terminology of natural law and natural rights, the inevitable result was legal Phariseeism.

The fact is that many judges of the last century imbibed the thought of speculative and rationalistic philosophers of the eighteenth century who treated the natural law as if it were geometry. If the English judges of the last century were too timid to assert the supremacy and absoluteness of even the primary precepts of the natural law, the American judges were too bold in exalting matters of opinion to the level of the natural law, and even in establishing their prejudices as immutable precepts. Thus they fell into a barren conceptualism and a mechanical jurisprudence.

When personal speculations about the natural law were separated from the life-giving and moderating Christian tradition, the result inevitably was subjective, unhistorical, unrealistic, and sometimes even fantastic. Human nature is so weak and wicked that, if left to itself without the uplifting influence and unerring light of Revelation, it is liable to rationalize pride, cupidity, ignorance and cruelty in the name of the natural law.

Take, for instance, *State v. Bell*,[34] decided by the Supreme Court of Tennessee in 1872. There a white man and a colored woman were married in the State of Mississippi, where such marriage was lawful. Afterwards they went to live in Tennessee, where miscegenation was a crime under a statute. The man was indicted, but judgment was in his favor in the lower court, on the ground that they were legally married in Mississippi. The State appealed, and the judgment was reversed. The court conceded the general rule that a marriage good in one State should be recognized as good in another; but it held that this general rule had to do only with differences in formalities and was not applicable where the marriage was against the public policy and good morals of the State. Justice Turney, who spoke for the court, waxed rhetorical at the end of his opinion:

> Extend the rule to the width asked for by the defendant, and we might have in Tennessee the father living with his daughter, the son with the mother, the brother with the sister, in lawful wedlock, because they had formed such relations in a State or country where they were not prohibited. The Turk or Mohammedan, with his numerous wives, may establish his harem at the doors of the capitol, and we are without remedy. Yet none of these are more revolting, more to be avoided, or more unnatural than the case before us.
>
> Chancellor Kent says the contract of marriage is a stable and sound contract, of natural as well as municipal law. This is neither.

I am not questioning the judgment as such. It might possibly have been justified on grounds of the peace and order of the community. One cannot root out deep-seated popular prejudices violently or expect people to become truly civilized overnight. But to compare such a marriage to polygamy and incestuous unions is absurd, and to justify the position of the court in the name of the natural law is shocking.

When one remembers how the term "natural law" was being bandied about so freely, with a view to lending a cosmic sanction to all kinds of silly ideas, one can understand why jurists of strong moral intuitions became so hostile to any mention of the natural law. To Bentham, for instance, all appeal to the natural law is "but a womanish scolding and childish altercation, which is sure to irritate and which never can persuade,—*I* say that the legislature *cannot* do this—*I* say it *can. I* say that to do this, exceeds the bounds of its authority—*I* say that it does *not*. It is evident that a pair of disputants setting out in this manner may go on perplexing and irritating one another for everlasting, without the smallest chance of ever coming to an agreement. It is no more than announcing, and that in an obscure and at the same time, a peremptory and captious manner, their opposite persuasions, or rather affections, on a question of which neither of them sets himself to discuss the grounds."[35]

I need not dwell upon all the caustic gibes against the natural law. Professor H. Lauterpacht has made a fair observation on this point: "The abuse of the idea of natural law in the defence of causes both paltry and iniquitous has caused many to reject it with impatience. This is perhaps the principal reason why a practical reformer like Jeremy Bentham, a great judge like Mr. Justice Holmes, and a legal philosopher like Hans Kelsen—all believers in social progress—have treated the law of nature with little respect. However, the rejection of an actually or potentially beneficent notion for the reason that it may be and has been abused savours of a kind of realism which has often led mankind to defeat."[36] Sir Frederick Pollock had put his finger on the real cause of this misunderstanding when he wrote: "If Bentham had known what the Law of Nature was really like in the Middle Ages, he would have had to speak of it with more respect."[37] However, the ignorant advocates of the natural law were even more responsible for its eclipse.

The fact is that modern thought since the Reformation has been moving farther and farther from the scholastic tradition. The very word scholasticism became a term of reproach—in the absence, of course, of the slightest understanding of what it actually meant and stood for. In the eighteenth century, the so-called "age of enlightenment," rationalism became the order of the day. Now the fundamental doctrine of rationalism is, as Pope Leo XIII has described it, "the supremacy of the human reason, which, refusing due submission to the divine and eternal reason, proclaims its own independence, and constitutes itself the supreme principle and source and judge of truth."[38]

Human reason, having declared independence from the divine reason, sought after the ultimate basis of legal institutions and found it in the popular will in the form of a social contract. So rationalism was in reality only a rationalization of an underlying voluntarism.

Perhaps the doctrine of *"volonté générale"* (or general will) and the social contract served as an antidote to the autocratic will of the king. It also stands to reason that a plurality of wills working together could check and moderate one another and thus neutralize one another's idiosyncrasies and caprices. This empirical fact is the rational kernel of the doctrine. But when the doctrine of the general will assumes an absolutist aspect, it tends to blind us to the indispensability of reason as the ultimate criterion of rightness in human affairs. For, after all, a multiplication of individual wills can never transmute will into reason. Even the collective will of a community is not *necessarily* more consonant with reason than the will of a single individual.

Rationalism, which had begun by raising human reason to the throne of God, ended by abdicating unconditionally in favor of will, whether it be the will of the State, of the dictator, of the bourgeois individual or of the proletarian class. For the past few centuries the world has been like a very sick man restlessly rolling in his bed, from right to left and from left to right, without any alleviation of his pain. The whole civilization of the modern world is a magnificent edifice built upon sand. It will not save itself by continuing to build still higher, but only by going back to the foundations and humbly begging the Son of God to be its cornerstone.

American jurisprudence could not but be influenced by this general current of European thought. At first this worked well in encouraging the free development of a sparsely populated continent by emphasizing the spirit of free enterprise to the utmost. The ideas of absolute security of property rights and absolute liberty of contract could do little harm at a time when the harvests were full and laborers few. In order to reclaim wastelands from nature, there was nothing wrong in adopting

> "The simple plan,
> That they should take who have the power,
> And they should keep who can."[39]

It was in the second half of the nineteenth century, when industrialism was already well developed and the population had grown immensely, that such a plan became a prolific source of conflicts and hardships, and it should then have been dropped for a more rational scheme. But unfortunately it was re-enforced by the tremendous influence that Darwinism and Spencerian individualism had begun to exercise on the American mind.

In their joint work, *The Age of Enterprise,* Cochran and Miller had this to say:

> Worked out most thoroughly by the Englishman Herbert Spencer, this philosophy [of progress] won America as no philosophy had ever won a nation before. To a generation singularly engrossed in the competitive pursuit of industrial wealth it gave cosmic sanction to free competition. In an age of science, it "scientifically" justified ceaseless exploitation. Precisely attuned to the aspirations of American businessmen, it afforded them a guide to faith and thought perfectly in keeping with the pattern of their workaday lives. When they were hopeful, it was infinitely optimistic; when they were harsh, it "proved" that harshness was the only road to progress; when they had doubts, it allayed these with a show of evidence that apparently was irrefutable. Their cupidity, it defended as part of the universal struggle for existence; their wealth it hallowed as the sign of the "fittest."[40]

This pernicious version of the natural law dominated the minds of the judges to such an extent that all social legislation aimed at ameliorating the conditions of the poor was held unconstitutional by the courts, as against the due process of law.

Father Benjamin L. Masse, S.J., commenting on the enormous influence of the individualistic philosophy of Spencer in the America of those days, has made a very interesting observation which I want to quote:

> This was the heady potion, brewed from Liberal Economics and Darwinian Evolution, which intoxicated many an influential American during the decades between 1870 and 1890. Educational circles drank deeply of the new elixir and furnished some of the most persuasive apostles—among them Eliot of Harvard and Butler of Columbia—of the Evangel according to Spencer. Senator Henry Cabot Lodge struggled to stem the popular tide of Woodrow Wilson's "New Freedom" with arguments borrowed unblushingly from *Man Versus the State*, one of the Prophet's principal works. On first reading Spencer, Andrew Carnegie exclaimed: "Light came as in a flood and all was clear." And, as Justice Holmes testified, even the Supreme Court lost its judicial calm and practically placed the English philosopher among the Founding Fathers.[41]

Of course, America was not alone in this tendency. The dominant classes of the whole of Western Christendom were running after strange gods, the most prominent being the golden calf. I can hardly imagine a worse creature than one who pays lip-service to God while worshipping mammon at heart. By sanctioning ruthless competition in the name of natural law and natural rights, the law was tending to intensify economic and social inequalities under the cloak of maintaining an abstract and formal equality for all!

Taking the theories of Adam Smith and Ricardo for the natural laws governing economic relations of man, the judges buried their heads in the sand of legal technicalities, in complete oblivion of social realities, with the result that law degenerated into an unwitting accomplice to the cupidity of man. In the words of Anatole France, "The law in its majestic equality forbids the rich as well as the poor to sleep under bridges, to beg in the streets, and to steal bread."[42] They did not realize, as Lord Northington did, that "necessitous men are not, truly speaking, free men, but, to answer a present exigency, will submit to any terms that the crafty may impose upon them."[43]

Occasionally, one comes across a judge who was acutely aware of the unrealistic nature of the prevailing law and gave vent to his pent-up sense of justice. In an English case around the middle of the last century, Justice Maule was reported to have said these words:

> Prisoner at the bar, you have been convicted of the offense of bigamy, that is to say, of marrying a woman while you have a wife still alive, though it is true she has deserted you, and is still living in adultery with another man. You have, therefore, committed a crime against the laws of your country, and you have also acted under a very serious misapprehension of the course which you ought to have pursued. You should have gone to the ecclesiastical court and there obtained against your wife a decree *a mensa et thoro*. You should then have brought an action in the courts of common law and recovered, as no doubt you would have recovered, damages against your wife's paramour. Armed with these decrees you should have approached the legislature, and obtained an Act of Parliament, which would have rendered you free, and legally competent to marry the person whom you have taken on yourself to marry with no such sanction. It is quite true that these proceedings would have cost you many hundreds of pounds, whereas you probably have not as many pence. But the law knows no distinction between rich and poor. The sentence of the court upon you therefore is that you be imprisoned for one day, which period has already been exceeded, as you have been in custody since the commencement of the assizes.[44]

This quotation is enough to give us a glimpse of the glaring discrepancy between the idea of legal equality and economic equality. But in England Parliament had a freer hand in reforming the law to bring about in a legal manner a greater degree of social justice; so much so that A. V. Dicey, in his *Law and Public Opinion in England during the Nineteenth Century*, published in 1905, could already speak of the second half century as the period of "collectivism."

For the same period, American jurisprudence presented an entirely different picture, for it was the heyday of individualism.

CHAPTER XIV

THE REACTION AGAINST RATIONALISM AND INDIVIDUALISM

NONE of the American judges of the last century was, to my knowledge, acquainted with the Thomistic distinction between speculative reason and practical reason. According to St. Thomas, the physical sciences belong to speculative reason, while law belongs to practical reason. Speculative reason deals with necessary things, which cannot be otherwise than they are, and therefore there is necessity alike in its universal principles and in its particular conclusions. Practical reason, on the other hand, deals with contingent matters, in which human actions are concerned: and consequently, although there is necessity in the general principles, the more we descend to matters of detail, the less necessity we find. Human laws cannot, in the nature of things, have the unerring quality of scientifically demonstrated conclusions. Not every rule need possess final infallibility and certainty; as much as is possible in its class is enough. For instance, it is a precept of the natural law that we should do justice, and that justice consists in giving each one his due. This is an immutable and necessary principle. But, as St. Thomas says, "The obligation of observing justice is indeed perpetual. But the determination of what is just by human or divine enactment, must needs differ, according to the different states of mankind."[45] It must also be remembered that law is essentially an ordinance of reason directed to the common good. It is a teleological, not a mechanical science. It must be rational, but not rationalistic.

The Rationalists, cut loose from the sound tradition of Scholasticism, vied with each other in weaving from their own bellies complete systems of natural law, from general principles to the minutest details. They relied too much on human reason. Paradoxical as it may seem, it was the juridical rationalism of the eighteenth century that gave birth to the juridical positivism of the nineteenth. The adherents of the former believed in the ability of human reason to work out a complete code. The legislators in some European countries took the hint, and attempted to carry the teaching into practice. They were convinced that "a body of enacted rules might be made so complete and so perfect that the judge would have only to select the one made in advance for the case in hand. . . ."[46] The code of Frederick the Great was drawn up on this theory. The intention was to provide for all contingencies with such careful minuteness that no possible doubt could arise in the future. As Schuster says:

> This stereotyping of the law was in accordance with the doctrine of the law of nature according to which a perfect system might be imagined, for which no changes would ever become necessary, and which could therefore be laid down once for all, so as to be available for any possible combination of circumstances.[47]

In America, this rationalistic conception exercised a deep influence. Although there was no Code, the judges conceived of the common law as "a brooding omnipresence in the sky,"[48] rather than as a tree that has to grow from season to season. Every case, however novel and complicated, was, in theory, covered by the common law, and therefore there could only be one logical decision for each case. It was against this kind of mentality that Justice Holmes revolted. He said, "I once heard a very eminent judge say that he never let a decision go until he was absolutely sure that it was right. So judicial dissent often is blamed, as if it meant simply that one side or the other were not doing their sums right, and if they would take more trouble, agreement inevitably would come. . . . But certainty generally is illusion, and repose is not the destiny of man. Behind the logical form lies a judgment as to the relative worth and importance of competing legislative grounds. . . ."[49] In this he was right, because he was speaking of the decision of concrete cases, which depend upon human determinations of the natural law, and these, according to St. Thomas, can seldom, if ever, claim absolute certainty. But when Holmes made a wholesale denial of the natural law, he fell into Charybdis in shunning Scylla. It is a pity that he never studied St. Thomas.[50] If he had, he probably would not have thrown out the baby with the bath water.

But I must point out an ironic situation in modern American jurisprudence. As one studies the cases on social legislation, one will find that, as a general rule, the judges who used the name of the natural law have rendered wrong decisions, while the judges who were sceptical of the natural law have reached results which coincide with conclusions of the two great Encyclicals: *Rerum Novarum* and *Quadragesimo Anno*. What could be the reason for this strange phenomenon? The reasons seem manifold. In the first place, the economic doctrine of *laissez-faire*, while it might have served the purpose and needs of a particular age, and was therefore historically justifiable to a certain extent, can never be regarded as an immutable precept of the natural law. It certainly helped to develop the marvelous industrial civilization of America, but in the meantime industrial civilization has brought with it new problems unknown to the days of handicrafts. New situations require new measures of law to regulate them: but most of the judges knew only the old law and old legal theories, which they had identified with the natural law. In the second place, their conception of justice was inadequate. They knew only one form of justice, namely, commutative justice: they did not seem to know distributive justice. Usually, only commutative justice is involved in the decision of cases. It is not for the judge to go out of his way to administer distributive justice, which is principally the job of the legislator. But the fault of the conservative judges in those days of transition lay in their unwarranted and arbitrary interference with the legislators simply because that form of justice was new to them.

Let us take one instance. In *Ives v. South Buffalo R.R.*,[51] the Court invalidated the New York Workmen's Compensation Act of 1910. Judge Werner said, "One of the inalienable rights of every citizen is to hold and enjoy his property until it is taken from him by due process of law. When our Constitutions were adopted it was the law of the land that no man who was without fault or negligence could be held liable in damages for injuries sustained by another." Judge Cullen added, "It is the physical law of nature, not of government, that imposes upon one meeting with an injury, the suffering occasioned thereby. Human law cannot change that. All it can do is to require pecuniary indemnity to the party injured, and I know of no principle on which one can be compelled to indemnify another for loss unless it is based upon contractual obligation or fault."

Concerning this decision, President Theodore Roosevelt, speaking through the *Outlook*, quoted "an eminent jurist" as saying that it was "one more illustration of the principle that in many American Courts property is more sacred than life."[52] In those days, the legislative and executive branches were alert to the labor problems and to the need of timely measures to improve the conditions of the workman, but many courts were still intoxicated by the attractive doctrines of individual utilitarianism, which they defended by every weapon in the armory of the speculative type of natural-law philosophy. The very name of the natural law came to be anathema to the more advanced jurists, who sneered at the natural law because they did not know the practical, reasonable, human and progressive type of natural-law philosophy expounded by St. Thomas and Suarez. As a matter of fact, the program of social legislation offered by the new sociological jurists was not a whit more radical or progressive than the Catholic natural-law tradition as expressed by the social encyclicals of Leo XIII and Pius XI.

In the early nineteen-twenties, I did not know anything about Thomism or the encyclicals. But somehow I already felt that Justice Holmes's criticism of the law of nature was one-sided. In one of my letters to him (Jan. 8, 1922), I have found this curious passage: "Jurists, in general, are conservative in their use of terms, and they will not yield their 'natural law' unless we show them that they have only visualized the back of Natural Law—as Moses only saw the back of God—and that our vision of Natural Law, which, like the face of God, is ever-glowing, vivid, expressive of internal feelings, responsive to external changes, and looking forward to the welfare of Humanity, is a truer vision of Natural Law."

When I wrote this I thought that was a new idea of the natural law. But thirty years later, when I came to study the legal philosophy of St. Thomas, I felt as though the little acorn in my heart had suddenly grown into a splendid oak!

But to return from this digression, in the early decades of this century, Holmes, Brandeis, Pound and Wigmore were in the vanguard of the new school of legal philosophy; but there were not lacking open-minded judges, even outside the new school, who came to see that labor problems, which involved the question of the livelihood of the masses, belonged to an entirely different category from the contractual relations between two individuals. Justice Pitney, for instance, in a Workman's Compensation case, looked at industry as a co-operative enterprise between employer and employee. He said:[53]

> Employer and employee, by mutual consent, engage in a common operation intended to be advantageous to both; the employee is to contribute his personal services, and for these is to receive wages, and ordinarily, nothing more; the employer is to furnish plant, facilities, organization, capital, credit, is to control and manage the operation, paying the wages and other expenses, disposing of the product at such prices as he can obtain, taking all the profits if any there be, and, of necessity, bearing the entire losses. In the nature of things, there is more or less of a probability that the employee may lose his life through some accidental injury arising out of the employment, leaving his widow or children deprived of their natural support. . . . This is a loss arising out of the business, and, however it may be charged up, is an expense of the operation, as truly as the cost of repairing broken machinery or any other expense that ordinarily is paid by the employer. . . . It is plain that, on grounds of natural justice, it is not unreasonable for the state . . . to require him to contribute a reasonable amount, and according to a reasonable and definite scale, by way of compensation for the loss of earning power incurred in the common enterprise, irrespective of the question of negligence, instead of leaving the entire loss to rest

where it may chance to fall, that is, upon the injured employee or his dependents.

Finally, Justice Pitney points out that liability without fault is not a novelty in the common law. That there should be no liability without fault is a sound general rule. But it does not apply to the field of industry, where the livelihood of the workers is involved. As Justice Brandeis says, some laws attempt to enforce individual justice, while other laws attempt to do social justice. They have different fields of application.[54]

In this connection, it should be noted that during the past three decades social and economic thought in America has gradually arrived at a middle way between individualism and collectivism.

The thirteen "norms" of social-economic life adopted by the recent Conference of Protestant Churches of America[55] seem to me quite representative of the general consensus of opinion in contemporary America. I will select three of the said "norms" for a sample. It will be seen that they fall into line with the Catholic position on the same matter.

1. All ethical demands upon economic institutions must take account of the importance of efficiency and productivity in the satisfying of human needs, as essential marks of a sound economy which seeks the maximum welfare of the greatest number of people.

2. Christians should work for a situation wherein all have access at least to a minimum standard of living. Such a minimum should be sufficient to permit care of the health of all and for suitable protection of the weaker members of society, such as children, the sick, the aged, and the incapacitated. It would protect the able-bodied against hazards beyond their control.

3. Since private ownership of many forms of property is a stimulus to increased production of goods and services and a protection to personal freedom, wider ownership among our people should be encouraged. But there are fundamental moral differences between the ways of acquiring property as well as between the ways of using it. Property, and position, too, which give men great power over the lives and economic situation of others, require constant moral scrutiny.

CHAPTER XV

THE TREND TOWARD PERSONALISM

PERHAPS the most important and difficult problem of jurisprudence is how to strike the golden mean between individual interests and social interests, how to transcend both individualism and collectivism, and bring them into a vital and philosophical synthesis, instead of being contented with makeshift compromises. It is most significant that Dean Pound, who was among the first to protest against the abuses of the dogma of liberty of contract, should have recently uttered a warning against what Josserand calls "contractual dirigism."[56] "May we not have faith that [the common-law] tradition will have continued strength to resist the effects of economic unification of the world and losing sight of the individual in the general bigness of things, and the tendency of the service State to become omnicompetent and totalitarian, and so to secure to the English-speaking world the liberty which it has always claimed as its birthright."[57] But in order to keep the common-law tradition, we have, as a first step, to pass through a spiritual renaissance and go back to the great tradition of Coke, St. Thomas More and Bracton. Finally, we must have a clear grasp of the Scholastic idea of the common good, which lay at the base of the common law from its very beginning.

The common good does not mean merely the collective good of the State. It includes that, but above all it embraces all the personal goods common to men as men. In order to minister to these goods, the law must recognize and protect the fundamental rights of the person, which Pius XII has enumerated as follows:

> . . . the right to maintain and develop physical, intellectual, moral life, and in particular the right to a religious training and education; the right to worship God, both in private and public, including the right to engage in religious works of charity; the right, in principle, to marriage and to the attainment of the purpose of marriage, the right to wedded society and home life; the right to work as an indispensable means for the maintenance of family life; the right to the free choice of a state of life, and therefore of the priestly and religious state; the right to the use of material goods, subject to its duties and social limitations.[58]

It will be seen that this list of fundamental rights of man is comprehensive enough to cover the three main heads of inalienable rights—life, liberty and the pursuit of happiness.

It is worthy of note that in connection with "the right to the use of material goods," the Holy Father hastens to add the words "subject to its duties and social limitations." Material goods have never been regarded by the Church, or by any true Christian, as ends in themselves, but only a means to the higher ends. It is with regard to material goods that St. Thomas said that "The common good takes precedence over the private good, if it be of the same genus; but it may be that the private good is better generically."[59] On the other hand, strictly personal rights, such as the right to worship God, should never be interfered with by the State in the name of the common good, for the simple reason that they belong to a higher order than the material interests with which the State has to do.

It is of prime importance for us to understand the underlying Christian philosophy of the institution of private property. Christianity steers a middle course between communism and capitalism. On the one hand, it holds that private property is not unlawful as against the natural law. On the other hand, it holds that private property, which is constituted by the division of possessions and distribution of material goods to individuals, is not made by the natural law but devised by positive law.

St. Thomas justifies the institution of private property, not by the dictates of natural law, but by the consideration of consequences in the light of experience. He declares that "two elements enter into human competence in appropriating external things, the *administration* and the *enjoyment.*"[60]

On the element of *administration*, he offers the following explanation:

> The first is the power to take care of them and manage them, and here it is lawful for one man to possess property: indeed it is necessary for human living, and on three grounds. First, because each man is more careful in looking after what is in his own charge than what is common to many or to all; in the latter case each would shirk the work and leave to another that which concerns the community, as we see when there is a great number of servants. Secondly, because human affairs are conducted in a more orderly fashion when each man is charged with taking care of some particular thing himself, whereas there would be confusion if anyone took charge of anything indeterminately. Thirdly, because a more peaceful state is preserved when each man is contented with what is his own. Hence we observe that quarrels arise more frequently among people who share in common and without division of goods.[61]

On the element of *enjoyment*, he says:

> The second element in human competence concerns the enjoyment of material things. Here man ought to possess them, not as his own, but as common, to the extent of being ready to communicate them to others in their need. Hence St. Paul says: *Charge the rich of this world to give easily, to communicate to others*, &c.[62]

Christ Himself said, "Take heed and guard yourselves from all covetousness, for a man's life does not consist in the abundance of his possessions." He illustrated this by a parable:

> The land of a certain rich man brought forth plenty of fruits. And he thought within himself, saying: What shall I do, because I have no room where to bestow my fruits? And

he said: This will I do: I will pull down my barns and will build greater; and into them will I gather all things that are grown to me and my goods. And I will say to my soul: Soul, thou hast much goods laid up for many years. Take thy rest: eat, drink, make good cheer. But God said to him: Thou fool, this night do they require thy soul of thee. And whose shall those things be which thou hast provided? So is he that layeth up treasure for himself and is not rich towards God (Luke 12: 15–21).

To the fragmentized and trivialized mind of modern man, all this talk would seem to be utterly irrelevant to jurisprudence. But the Church Fathers did not think so. In a homily on this parable, St Basil comments that the rich who reckon that the common goods they have seized are their own properties are like those who go in advance to the theatre, excluding others and appropriating to themselves what is intended for common use.[63]

Now St. Thomas has offered a very significant explanation of St Basil's ideas. He says, "A man would not act unfairly if he went beforehand to the theatre in order to prepare the way for others; what is unfair is hindering the enjoyment of others who would go. Similarly, a rich man does not act unlawfully if he encloses what was common at the beginning and gives others a share. But he sins if he indiscriminately excludes others from benefit." Hence Basil says, "How can you abound in wealth while another begs, unless it be that you may obtain the merit of good stewardship and he be crowned with the rewards of patience?"[64]

Everyone knows what an important place the idea of stewardship, or trust, occupies in the system of common law. The State itself is regarded as a trustee of public property; there is no reason why we should not consider all private property as charged with a trust for the common good. That this idea is implicit in the Christian philosophy of life will be clear to us if we read the following provision in the will of Thomas J. Kavanagh, which I have come across in a recent New Jersey case:[65]

Any balance still remaining and not set aside for any direct purpose, is to be used to help the poor and unfortunates and relieve or help relieve those in poverty or distress and provide them with as much of the comforts of life as is possible, but must not be used for gain or profits as it is my intention and desire, that all I have had of this world's goods in comfort and pleasure, were given me by God Almighty only as a trust, to be returned back and to help those who in this life have not been so blessed as I.

This expresses perfectly the Christian philosophy of private property. It is a means to an end. The end is twofold: in the first place, it is to fill the reasonable needs of the individual owner himself, and, over and above these needs, it is to be held in trust under God for the common good. In this I am not stating a self-executing rule of law, but only a general philosophy of legislation to be implemented by the art of law-making, whose lodestar is always the ideal of fairness and reasonableness.

Under God and the law, the supreme consideration is the well-being of man, physical, intellectual, moral, and spiritual. All things, corporeal or incorporeal, are held in trust for this ultimate purpose of the law. They belong to the field of distributive justice.

In a recent case, Chief Justice Griffith Smith has put it very well: "The status of the Sovereign is that of a trustee acting for the common good. . . ." (*Parker v. Moore*, 262 S.W. 2d 891, at 193). I submit that this comes near to the Christian idea of stewardship.

The Holy Father has also said, "The original and essential purpose of social life is to preserve, develop, and perfect the human person."[66] Religion and ethics contribute directly to the realization of this purpose. Human law works toward this end in a less direct way; but, in the words of the Holy Father, it can and should effectively contribute toward "the permanent realization of the common good" by providing for ". . . those external conditions which are needful to citizens as a whole for the development of their qualities and the fulfilment of their duties in every sphere of life, material, intellectual, and religious."[67]

Law is made for man, not man for the law. So ultimately the end of law can be nothing short of the end of man. Now what is the end of man? As St. Thomas views it, it is threefold: the practice of virtues, friendship between man and man, and the enjoyment of God. "The end of human life and society is God."[68] The contribution of law toward this end is twofold. Positively, it is most effective in the procuring of those external conditions that are conducive to the end. Negatively, it must leave man free to pursue the threefold end which constitutes his proper happiness.

Bishop John J. Wright describes the common good as "the mutual bond of all who love the good, the true and the beautiful; who seek good things, not evil; who seek the private good of *persons* and the collective good of the *State*, but the good of both in and under and through the Supreme Good which is God."[69] This holds good both for ethics and for jurisprudence. Justice Roger J. Kiley, speaking from the point of view of human law, has said, "Temporal happiness in a well-governed community is not man's final end. Human Law does not presume to take man to his final end. It aims at a subordinate end, a peaceful and orderly community in which men by living virtuously may be happy and thus strive for perfect happiness with God in a life hereafter."[70] In the light of this teleological background, it would be easy to see that a Catholic philosophy of law can neither be collectivistic nor individualistic.

All human laws must be ordained to the love of God and the love of our neighbor. Judging by this standard, I honestly do not find much to criticize in the present conditions of the American common law. Even the advent of the "service State" does not seem to interfere with our freedom arbitrarily, provided that both the government and the people remember that the servant must never turn into a master. The greatest problem in the America of today is not that we are not free enough, but that the way must be found to fill that freedom with spiritual and cultural values and thus turn it into the liberty of the children of God. Man is made in the image of God, and we lawyers have a special way of resembling Him. To resemble the Father, we should cultivate Justice; to resemble the Son, we should follow the law of nature; and to resemble the Holy Ghost, we should practise equity.

In a paper on "Law and the Spirit," Richard Kehoe, O.P., has said, "What should urge a Catholic, then, to urge the doctrine of Natural Law should not be any notion that on its basis an order of life can be founded in which believers and non-believers can live happily together, secluded from Spiritual and Supernatural issues, but the conception of Nature, with all its laws, as being the sphere within which the Supernatural must work, as providing the Body which the Spirit must inform."[71]

This reminds me of what Father Thomas Reardon said in his sermon at a Red Mass for lawyers: "Secularism has confused and destroyed true love because the secularist only views the material end of man, whereas the Christian keeps purpose and destiny in their proper perspective." A Christian philosophy does not aim at a lesser happiness for mankind than positivism does, but a more abundant happiness, which is the natural concomitant to a more abundant justice.

NOTES

1. 2 Pet. 137.
2. 1 Gray 263.
3. 18 Atl. 949.
4. 236 N.Y. 156, 140 N.E. 227.
5. (1953) 263 Pac. 2d 333.
6. (1953) 116 N.E. 2d 54.
7. Cardozo, *The Growth of Law*, p. 20.
8. (1954) 102 Atl. 2d 418. Compare the thoughtful words of Moses J. Aronson: "The recognition of the necessity of a principle of growth entails the obligation of formulating ends or values to mark the stages of progress. For unbridled growth is a meaningless change which spells chaos, precisely as immutable conservatism implies the rigidity of death" (*Journal of Social Philosophy*, Vol. 4, p. 19).
9. *Collected Legal Papers*, p. 246.
10. *Mincey v. Mincey* (1954) 80 S. E. 2d 123.
11. *Nelson v. Nelson* (1954) 116 N.E. 2d 560.
12. (1890) 12 S.W. 798, 99 Mo. 484.
13. (1925) 268 U.S. 510. Justice McReynolds wrote the opinion.
14. (1942) 34 N.Y. Supp. 2d 100.
15. (1953) 100 A. 2d 175.
16. 263 Pac. 2d 333, at 336.
17. (1949) 216 S.W. 2d 847.
18. *Fox v. Snow* (1950) 76 A. 2d 877, at 883. The Chief Justice further said, "The common law would be sapped of its life blood if *stare decisis* were to become a god instead of a guide." Here as else-

where the *via media* is the best. On the one hand, *stare decisis* must not become a fetish. On the other hand, it must remain a guide. Otherwise, as Justice Roberts said, judicial decisions would be like "a restricted railroad ticket, good for this day and train only" (321 U.S. 96, at 113).

19. Lord Mansfield used this maxim. *Rex v. Wilkes*, 4 Burrows Reports 2662.

20. (1954) 269 P. 2d 796.

21. The French publicist Boutmy used this figure in his comparative studies on the constitutional systems of England, France and America. See *Studies in Constitutional Law*, trans. by E. M. Dicey (London, Macmillan, 1891), pp. 3–4.

22. *The Analects of Confucius.*

23. De Tocqueville, *Democracy in America.*

24. See Wright, *American Interpretations of the Natural Law* (Harvard, 1931), p. 59.

25. *Ibid.*

26. Otis, *The Rights of the British Colonies Asserted and Proved* (1764), p. 47.

27. See Wright, *op. cit. supra*, p. 88, note 105.

28. *Ibid.*, pp. 90–91.

29. Pound, *The Spirit of the Common Law*, p. 53.

30. P. 19.

31. Justice Brewer rightly asserted that the Declaration "is the thought and the spirit, and it is always safe to read the letter of the Constitution in the spirit of the Declaration of Independence." *Gulf, Colorado & Santa Fe Ry. v. Ellis*, 165 U.S. 150, 160 (1897).

But see Charles Grove Haines' criticism of Brewer's extreme individualism in his article "The History of the Due Process of Law After the Civil War," in *Selected Essays on Constitutional Law* (Foundation Press, 1938), Vol. I, pp. 268, 295–6.

32. Schmidt, "An Approach to the Natural Law," *Fordham Law Review*, Vol. 19 (1950), p. 25.

33. Address of His Eminence, Francis Cardinal Spellman, at the Military Chaplains' Association Convention Dinner, July 24, 1952 (in mimeograph).

34. (1872) 7 Baxt. 9, 32 Am. Rep. 549.

35. "A Fragment of Government" in Bentham's *Works*, ed. by Bowring (1843), Vol. I, p. 29.

36. Lauterpacht, *International Law and Human Rights* (Praeger, 1950), pp. 108–9.

37. Pollock, "The History of the Law of Nature," *Columbia Law Review*, Vol. I (1901), p. 22.

38. Encyclical Letter *Libertas Praestantissimum.*

39. Quoted by Chancellor Pitney of New Jersey in *Meeker v. City of East Orange* (1909), 77 N.J.L. 623, 74 A. 379, at 385.
40. Quoted by Rev. Benjamin L. Masse, S.J., in his pamphlet *Economic Liberalism and Free Enterprise* (The America Press, 1944), p. 20.
41. *Ibid.*, pp. 20–21. Father Masse quotes with approval the words of Justice Holmes: "The Fourteenth Amendment does not enact Mr. Herbert Spencer's *Social Statics*" (page 20).
42. Quoted by Chief Justice Vanderbilt in *Law and Government in the Development of the American Way of Life*, p. 16.
43. *Vernon v. Bethell* (1762), 2 Eden 110.
44. See Holdsworth, *History of English Law*, 1st ed. (1927), Vol. I, p. 623.
45. *S. T.*, I–II, 104. 3. *ad* 1.
46. Pound, *The Spirit of the Common Law*, p. 178.
47. *Ibid.*, p. 178.
48. Justice Holmes in *Southern Pacific Co. v. Jensen*, 244 U.S. 205, at 222 (1917).
49. *Collected Legal Papers*, pp. 180–1.
50. In a letter to Laski, he wrote that Morris Cohen had advised him against embarking on the study of St. Thomas, and he felt exonerated from doing so. (Letter dated Sept. 15, 1929.) One of the fairest observations on Holmes is to be found in Dr. Peter J. Stanlis's recent article in the *University of Detroit Law Journal* (Vol. 18, p. 163), where, commenting on Holmes' denial of the Natural Law, Dr. Stanlis adds, "Yet the Natural Law refused to be abandoned, and to the end of his life (but without acknowledgment) the corridors of Holmes' legal pragmatism echoed the hushed diction of morality." To my mind, this sums up the whole paradox.
51. (1911) 201 N.Y. 271, 94 N.E. 431.
52. See Kelly and Harbison, *The American Constitution* (Norton, 1948), p. 627.
53. *New York Central R.R. v. White*, 243 U.S. 188, at 203 (1917).
54. *New York Central R.R. v. Winfield*, 244 U. S. 147 (1917).
55. As reported in the *New York Times*, Sept. 16, 1954.
56. Pound's article on "Liberty of Contract," *Yale Law Journal*, Vol. 18 (1904), p. 454, was one of the best criticisms of the *laissez-faire* philosophy of law.
    In 1951, he published an article on "The Development of American Law and Its Deviation from English Law" (*Law Quarterly Review*, Vol. 67), which is one of the best criticisms of too much government. Dean Pound has not changed his point of view. He has maintained his balance.
57. *Law Quarterly Review*, Vol. 67, p. 60.

58. Christmas Broadcast on "The Rights of Man" (1942). The English translation is by Canon Smith.

59. *S. T.*, II–II 152. 4. *ad* 3.

60. *Ibid.*, II–II, 66. 2. *in corp*. I am using here the translation of Thomas Gilby in his *St. Thomas Aquinas: Philosophical Texts*, pp. 345–6.

61. *Ibid.*

62. *Ibid.*

63. *Ibid.*, 66. 2. 2.

64. *Ibid.*, 66. 2. ad 2.

65. *Litcher v. Trust Co. of New Jersey*, (1935) 93 A. 2d 368, at 373. The reader will be interested to know that the idea of trust, which plays such a vital role in the Common Law, originated in the thirteenth century in England when the Franciscan friars positively refused to own any property, so that their benefactors had to resort to the ingenious device of conveying their property to some borough "to the use of" the friars.

66. "The Rights of Man." (See *supra*, note 58.)

67. *Ibid.*

68. *S. T.*, I–II, 100. 6 *in corp.*

69. "Address to St. Thomas More Society," Harvard Law School, November 16, 1952 (in mimeograph).

70. "Human Law," an appendix to the *Summa Theologica* (Benziger, 1948), p. 3266.

71. See O'Sullivan, *Under God and the Law*, pp. 94–5.

PART TWO

IN THE SCHOOL OF CHRIST

Open my eyes, that I may contemplate the wonders of Thy law.

I will run in the way of Thy commandments, when Thou dost enlarge my heart.

Thy laws have become my songs in the place of my pilgrimage.

(Ps. 118:19, 32, 54.)

CHAPTER XVI

CHRIST AND THE LAW

*"In the beginning was the Word, and the Word was with God,
and the Word was God"* (*John 1:1*).

ORDINARILY we think of Christ as the Redeemer of mankind, as the
Shepherd of our souls, and as the Exemplar and Teacher of spiritual
perfection. This is as it ought to be, because He is all these. But one
facet of His infinite Personality is too often neglected, I mean His
intimate relation to Law.

Let us remember that Christ is the Divine Word, the Logos of
God, by whom all things are made and without whom nothing
would have been created. The whole universe, with its endless
riches and with its marvelous order and harmony, hinges on the
Logos. Even before His Incarnation, the Logos was, so to speak,
the ontological bridge between Creator and creation, as He still is
and ever shall be. The Logos is the Self-Expression of God. Speaking of God the Father in connection with the double mystery of
procession and creation, Frank Sheed has summed it up in one
sentence, which seems to me as clear as human language can make
it. "He had expressed Himself once in the uncreated—that is as the
infinite nature could receive the expression of Him—and thereby
produced the Word; He now expressed Himself in the created
order—that is as nothingness can receive the expression of Him—

and thereby produced the universe."[1] Thus, the Logos is at once the Son proceeding from the Father as the Second Person of the Blessed Trinity, and the Way whereby God created heaven and earth and expressed Himself in the created. "And," remarked St. Thomas Aquinas significantly, "*among other things expressed by this Logos, the eternal law itself is expressed thereby.*"[2] While the eternal law is not predicative of a Divine Person, yet it is appropriated with pre-eminent fitness to the Son because of the affinity that reason bears to the Logos.

Now, it may be asked, since Christ Himself is so intimately related to Law, why did He say, Woe to you lawyers! (Luke 11:46, 52)? The popular impression is that Christ has no special love for lawyers. As a German proverb has it, "Good lawyer, bad Christian." The fact, of course, is that Christ did not utter a sweeping denunciation of all lawyers. He was reproving a particular type of lawyers—or, as they were also called, scribes.[3] What He said was: "Woe to you lawyers also, because you load men with burdens which they cannot bear, and you yourselves touch not the packs with one of your fingers" (Luke 11:46). Again He said: "Woe to you lawyers, for you take away the key of knowledge: you yourselves have not entered in, and those that were entering in, you have hindered" (Luke 11:52). It was, then, not because they were lawyers, but because they were such hard-hearted and narrow-minded lawyers that Christ condemned them. Would Christ have condemned a lawyer like St. Ives, who was the "advocate of the poor," a great peacemaker, and above all a man of prayer and penance? The patron of lawyers was so Christlike that it is little wonder he should have become one of the most popular Saints in the Church. Only a few years ago, the Church beatified another lawyer, Contardo Ferrini, once a professor of law at Milan, whose work on the Roman penal law was hailed as a classic by no less a scholar than Mommsen.

In fact, one of the most pleasant conversations that Christ had in his life on earth was the one with a lawyer. When the Pharisees and Sadducees were reasoning together with Christ, the lawyer was listening. Finding that He had answered them well, the doctor of law asked Him which was the first commandment of all. His answer was: "The first commandment of all is, Listen, Israel; there is no God but the Lord thy God; and thou shalt love the Lord thy God with the love of thy whole heart, and thy whole soul, and thy whole mind, and thy whole strength. This is the first commandment, and the second, its like, is this, Thou shalt love thy neighbor as thyself. There is no other commandment greater than these" (Mark 12:29–31). "Truly, Master," the doctor of law commented, "thou hast answered well; there is but one God, and no other beside him; and to love him with the love of the whole heart, and the whole understanding, and the whole soul, and the whole strength, and to love one's neighbor as oneself, is a greater thing than all burnt offerings and sacrifices" (Mark 12:32–33). It is worthy of note how intelligently he paraphrased and developed the meanings of the words of Christ, who, seeing that he understood Him so well, said to him, "Thou art not far from the kingdom of God" (Mark 12:34).

To my mind, this discourse laid the cornerstone of the philosophy of law, of the natural law which is of particular application to the human world. It was no accident that such an important teaching on law should have been delivered to a lawyer. It may be regarded as Christ's special bequest to the profession of law, both for its own benefit and in trust for others.

Speaking to His disciples about the Law of the Old Testament, Christ had made clear His position toward it. "Do not think that I have come to set aside the law and the prophets; I have not come to set them aside, but to bring them to perfection. Believe me, heaven and earth must disappear sooner than one jot, one flourish should disappear from the law; it must all be accomplished. Whoever, then, sets aside one of these commandments, though it were the least, and teaches men to do the like, will be of least account in the kingdom of heaven; but the man who keeps them and teaches others to keep them will be accounted in the kingdom of heaven as the greatest" (Matt. 5:17–19).

Christ elevated the old law of justice by linking it up with the new law of love. Once, after He had expounded the hidden meanings of the parables on the kingdom of heaven to His disciples, He crowned it all with another parable. "So then," He said, "every scribe instructed in the kingdom of heaven is like to a man that is a householder, who brings forth from his storeroom things new and old" (Matt. 13:52). Here He was speaking of Himself and His followers as scribes, or lawyers.

How law-abiding Christ Himself was can be illustrated by His conversation with Peter on the subject of the payment of the didrachma, or the temple pence. When they were in Capharnaum, the collectors of the didrachma asked Peter, "Does not your Master pay the temple pence?" Peter answered, "Yes." When Peter came into the house, Christ forestalled him by asking, "Simon, what do you think? From whom do the earthly kings collect customs and taxes, from their own sons or from others?" "From others," Peter replied. "In that case," said Christ, "the sons should be exempt. However, we must not be a scandal to others . . ." (Matt. 17:23-26). He ordered Peter to pay it.

No less instructive is the example of Our Lady and St. Joseph. Everyone knows how, in obedience to a decree of the emperor Augustus on the taking of the census, they went a long way from Nazareth to Bethlehem to register, in strict compliance with the law of Rome. But what interests me even more is the purification of Our Lady at the temple in Jerusalem. Now, according to the Mosaic Law, the normal requirement for purification of a woman after childbirth included a lamb (Lev. 12:6), but there was a thoughtful proviso at the end that: ". . . if her hand find not sufficiency, and she is not able to offer a lamb, she shall take two turtles, or two young pigeons" (Lev. 12:8). St. Luke was referring to this proviso when he wrote that Mary and Joseph offered a sacrifice according to what is said in the Law of the Lord, "a pair of turtledoves or two young pigeons" (Luke 2:24). He does not make any mention of a lamb. Supernaturally speaking, we may say that the Lamb was there in her arms. Naturally, at any rate, we can infer how poor they were. But poor as they were, they managed to fulfill the Law.

I think that Bracton, "the father of the common law," was probably referring to this and similar incidents when he penned that immortal paragraph in his treatise *De Legibus*, which expounded the philosophy of the supremacy of law over all men, including the king. The passage has been given in English elsewhere in this book; as the reader will recall, Bracton there cited the example of Christ and the Blessed Virgin to re-enforce his doctrine that the king is under God and the law. His logic was that if the King of kings and Queen of queens subjected themselves to the rule of law, there was all the more reason for a servant of God to obey the law.

In this connection, I wish to bring out one of the most ridiculous perversions of medieval teaching. Bracton and other Scholastics persistently taught that the king must not do wrong. But some people have invented the maxim, "The king can do no wrong," and, what is worse, fathered it on the medieval thinkers!

This pernicious maxim has given birth to the doctrine of State immunity from tortious liability. I am happy to note some strong protests against it from some outstanding judges in their dissenting opinions. Judge Jerome Frank calls the doctrine "harsh, undemocratic, and anachronistic" (202 F. 2d 532, at 535). Judge Musmanno of Pennsylvania has likewise denounced it: "It is not consonant with twentieth-century American justice to say that property may be destroyed by anyone, much less the State (the very symbol of correctness in organized society), with legal immunity. The law of nature, compounded of the dictates of the Supreme Lawmaker and reason emanating from untrammeled intellect, rebels against this antiquated doctrine of irresponsibility, no matter by whom or by what exercised" (*Boorse v. Springfield Township*, 1954. 103 A. 2d 708, at p. 713). True, these are but dissenting voices; but one beautiful thing about the common law is that it often happens that today's bark will be tomorrow's bite.

CHAPTER XVII

THE JUDGE OF JUDGES

"To do Thy will, O my God, is my delight, and Thy law is in my inmost heart" (Ps. 39:9).

BRACTON considers Christ not only as the King of kings, but also as the Judge of judges. In the introduction to his treatise, he gives a grave warning to the judges and paints a graphic picture of the Last Judgment. "The seat of judgment,"[4] he begins, "is like the throne of God. Let the unwise and unlearned not presume to ascend it, lest he should confound darkness with light and light with darkness, lest with a sword in the hand, as it were, of a madman he should slay the innocent and set free the guilty, and lest he should tumble down from on high, as from the throne of God, in attempting to fly before he has acquired wings." He seems to think that no human being as such has an inherent right to judge another. The judicial office is a creature of necessity. So he proceeds to say, "Even when a man is obliged to decide cases and to be a judge, still let him beware of the dangers to himself, lest by judging perversely and against the laws, through entreaties or for a price, he should purchase for himself the measureless sorrows of eternal damnation for the momentary enjoyment of a paltry gain. Let him take thought lest in the day of the wrath of the Lord he should incur the vengeance of Him Who has said, *Revenge is Mine: I will repay.* On

162

that day, the kings and princes of the earth shall behold the Son of Man, and shall weep and wail in fear of His punishments; and gold and silver will not avail to set them at liberty. Who, indeed, could think without trembling of that trial, in which the Lord Himself will be the Accuser, the Advocate, and the Judge? From His sentence there could be no possibility of appeal: for the Father has given all judgment to the Son, Who shuts and no one can open, and opens and no one can shut. Oh strict judgment, in which all men must render account, not only for their acts, but for every idle word they have spoken. Who, then, could hide himself from His coming wrath?" Then he presents a most awe-inspiring description of the scenes of the Last Judgment, concluding it with a quotation from St. Augustine: "Oh, how exceedingly great are my sins! Hence, he who has God for the just Judge, with his own conscience as the accuser, has nothing to fear but his own cause."

It was the purpose of Bracton to warn the judges against corruption, prejudice, rashness and ignorance. Therefore, he had to lay particular emphasis on the severity of the Divine Judge. It is not an unprofitable thing for judges and lawyers to be reminded of the eschatological teachings of Christianity, so that they may think of their accountability at the Last Judgment. I have omitted Bracton's terrific description of the terrible scene, not because I want to pander to the sensibilities of modern man. Modern man, by dismissing hell from his mind and losing the sense of sin, has veritably made a hell of the world. But my present purpose is to present other aspects of Christ the Judge. For His wisdom concerning the law reveals itself in many ways even during His life on earth. In judging human relations, in settling thorny problems of the law, in answering the questions of the Pharisees and scribes—everywhere He showed Himself to be the Infallible Judge and Supreme Master of Jurisprudence that He is.

Before I deal with His art of judging, there are some fundamental questions to be thrashed out. To begin with, He did not judge for the pleasure of judging. He repeatedly announced that He had come to save the world, not to pass sentence on the world. He commanded His disciples not to judge, that they might not be judged. He said to the Pharisees, "You judge according to the flesh;

I judge not any man" (John 8:15). But mark what follows, "And if I do judge, my judgment is true; because I am not alone, but I and the Father that sent me" (John 8:16). In this He not only revealed the source of His authority, but the reason why His judgment is true. Paradoxical as it may sound, even in judging He was not judging; because, as He said, "I do nothing of myself, but as the Father has taught me I speak" (John 8:28). On another occasion, He declared, "I cannot of myself do anything. As I hear, so I judge. And my judgment is just: because I seek not my own will, but the will of him that sent me" (John 5:30). It is precisely because the Son does only what He sees the Father doing—that is, He follows the will and the law of the Father—that all judgment has been given to the Son (John 5:22). This establishes an important point in legal philosophy: Law is not what the judge does or will do; on the contrary, whatever the judge does must be based upon the law.

Christ summed up the spirit of the law in the Golden Rule: "Do to other men all that you would have them do to you; that is the law and the prophets" (Matt. 7:12). To put it in terms of modern jurisprudence, the Golden Rule is the natural-law foundation of all human law. It is the meaning and the goal of juridical order. Considered in itself, the principle has a higher reality than all human laws. It is timeless and immutable. But in relation to human laws, which belong to the temporal order and must grow gradually in the process of history, the Golden Rule is an ideal to be realized, a goal to be approached, step by step, through patient struggles and persistent efforts. To say that human laws have already embodied the Golden Rule in all its breadth and depth is to be blind to the actualities and to betray a lack of the historical sense. But to dismiss it from jurisprudence simply because it cannot be realized overnight is to miss the whole meaning and aim of law; it would be like sailing on the open sea without a compass. While the perfect realization of the ideal belongs to the future, yet your aspiration toward it is an ever present reality, which gives you a sense of direction and impels you to progress. If an airplane aims at a high altitude, it cannot reach it like a rocket, but must make many spirals as the eagle does. But even when the airplane is still in the lowest altitude, it must constantly keep an upward slant. However slight and imperceptible the slant may be, it is the indispensable link between a lower level of reality and a higher, and no philosophy can be called realistic if it ignores the upward slant.

Here I wish to bring out my divergence from Mr. Justice Holmes's idea of legal evolution. It is to his credit that he acknowledged the Golden Rule as the criterion of progress. As he said, "The degree of civilization which a people has reached, no doubt, is marked by their anxiety to do as they would be done by. It may be the destiny of man that the social instincts shall grow to control his actions absolutely, even in anti-social situations."[5] "But," he went on to observe, "they have not yet done so, and as the rules of law are or should be based upon a morality which is generally accepted, no rule on a theory of absolute unselfishness can be laid down without a breach between law and working beliefs." In this he seems to have missed the link between the actual and the ideal. The fact that the ideal cannot be perfectly attained by one stroke does not preclude the possibility and the duty to approximate it gradually, nor does it compel the law to a passive acceptance of the popular morality which may happen to prevail in a certain community at a certain time. Law has its own ideal to serve, and an active function to perform as a lever of civilization. While it must not act violently, so as to be out of joint with the prevailing *mores*, it cannot be contented with an entirely horizontal relation with them, but must keep an upward slant all the time. It is only fair to point out that Mr. Justice Holmes showed the upward slant in a number of his decisions and dissents, but I am speaking now of his professed philosophy, which seems to leave a hiatus between the actual and the ideal and therefore tends to be static rather than dynamic.

In this connection, I should like to introduce an interesting case, *Sipp v. Coleman,*[6] decided by the U.S. Circuit, District of New Jersey, in 1910. It was a case of slander. The defendant had said of the plaintiff, "This man has been convicted of beating his mother." The statement was false; but the question was whether it was a slander per se, that is, actionable even without alleging any special damage. The answer to this depended upon the further question whether the beating of one's mother was to be considered as involving moral turpitude. Judge Rellstab held that it did involve moral turpitude, citing the Fifth Commandment, and saying, "Respect and love for parents is written into the love of a normal man's being, and this would prevent him from assaulting them, whatever the provocation." All this is quite sound, but there is nothing extraordinary about it. What strikes me as a lightning-like flash of insight is the following: "Moral standards change with the ages. The changes, however, are upward, and must continue upwards until the standards of Christ shall be universally accepted."

I confess that whenever I see Christ mentioned in the cases, my heart leaps for joy, as when a traveller in a vast forest hears the voice of a friend. But when I came across the above passage, I almost fell into an ecstasy. I imagine that the shepherds of Bethlehem must have experienced the same kind of joy when they saw the Divine Infant lying peacefully in the manger, the Word Eternal made flesh, who was to "advance in wisdom and age and grace before God and men."[7] Eternity was to grow in time! But if the Eternal Himself condescended to enter the realm of Time and to grow with the seasons, we have infinitely more reason to progress without cease. Ever to advance and never to fall back is Time's best tribute to Eternity. A well-guided dynamism bears a genuine affinity to Eternity, while a "jurisprudence of conceptions" aiming at the preservation of the *status quo* is but a poor mimicry of it. Frankly, when I read the first sentence: "Moral standards change with the ages," my immediate reaction was, Oh, there is one more fashionable judge, trying to keep abreast of the times! But when I read the sequel, I said to myself, Here is a great judge (though hidden from the market of fame) who had hit upon a happy synthesis between the immutability of the natural law and the dynamism of American jurisprudence. I began to realize that it is on the immutable principles of the natural law that all progress of human law hinges.

Perhaps Sir Henry Maine had the same idea vaguely in mind when he said, "The tendency to look not to the past but to the future for types of perfection was brought into the world by Christianity."[8] But I am afraid that his vision was limited to empirical effects and did not rise to the transcendent. The only type of perfection that Christianity has set up is Christ, who is ever ancient and ever new. To speak, therefore, of looking to the future for types of perfection does not seem to make sense, unless one subscribes to the extreme forms of the theory of emergent evolution. Maine was keen enough to see that somehow Christianity had made the progress of human civilization and legal institutions possible, but, being at bottom a utilitarian in outlook, he could not but fail to see the reason why. It is not the type of perfection that is in the future, it is we who must grow gradually "to perfect manhood, to the ripe measure of the fullness of Christ."[9] Likewise, the natural law is beyond the old and the new, although the human realization of it must grow fuller and fuller in the course of history.

In calling Maine a utilitarian, I am not unaware of the fact that he was ostensibly opposed to Bentham and Austin. But the opposition was only in method, not in spirit. On this point, Dr. Rooney, with her usual critical acumen, has made some penetrating observations which I would like to quote. "Unlike Bentham," she wrote, "Maine utilized the materials of history for his writings upon law, but nevertheless, he reads into the legal sources he examines, the preconceived notions of Bentham and John Austin, Bentham's follower in jurisprudence. The weaknesses which Maine found in the Bentham-Austin theories, when encountered by actual experience in India, aroused his critical faculties, but he was too much dominated by the philosophical errors of his era to supply valid correctives. . . . His influence in jurisprudence, accordingly, is as inimical to the principles of the common law as Bentham's is."[10] "While highly critical of the Bentham-Austin concept of sanction," she further observed, "Maine does not repudiate it but accepts it conditionally and builds his own upon it, for his own concept is nothing more nor less than the substitution of natural force, which is subconscious instinct and habit, for the externally applied force of punishment imposed by authority."[11] But what impresses me most is a further observation which Dr. Rooney has made: "In logic, his reasoning is circular, if not downright confused, lacking valid premises and achieving ignorance in conclusion. His chief cosmological error is his failure to recognize the place of order in relation to force, in law as well as in the universe, and the implicit denial of any purpose to existence, in consequence. But Maine not only adopts Bentham's errors for his own, he commits others for which he himself is responsible. Primarily he misunderstands authority, and rejects it as an essential of law, instead of correcting the Benthamite notion by showing the creative power of the intellect and the reasonableness of man."[12] This bears out what I have written in the preceding paragraph. But, to be perfectly candid, it was not until I had seen the picture for myself in the light of Christ that I came to appreciate these findings by Dr. Rooney.

CHAPTER XVIII

THE FOUNTAINHEAD OF LEGAL WISDOM

"Give therefore to Thy servant an understanding heart, to judge Thy people, and discern between good and evil" (*3 Kings 3:9*).

NEEDLESS to say, no system of human law can be perfect, or even nearly so. But it is no exaggeration to say that Anglo-American jurisprudence—the common law of England before the nineteenth century and the common law of America since the eighteenth century—is permeated with the spirit of Christianity to a greater degree than any other system of law except Canon Law. You find dark spots here and there; but where the common law is at its best, you feel that Christ Himself would have smiled upon its judgments. It is so because in many cases the judges have not hesitated to draw their inspiration and light from the words of Christ and His Apostles, particularly St. Paul. In American jurisprudence especially, you find traces of the Christian influence wherever you may turn. Let a few random samples suffice here.

In 1948, there arose a famous case before the Supreme Court of California.[13] The Court held unconstitutional a time-honored statute prohibiting miscegenation. In the course of his opinion, Justice Traynor pointed out that marriage is "something more than a civil contract subject to regulation by the State; it is a fundamental right of a free man."[14] In a concurring opinion, Justice Carter quoted from St. Paul that "God . . . hath made of one blood all nations of men. . . ."[15] In the concurring opinion of Justice Edmonds, it is emphasized that marriage "is grounded in the fundamental principles of Christianity."[16]

In 1914, the Supreme Court of Nebraska had to pass upon the question whether a landowner could build a fence on his own land for no other purpose than to annoy his neighbor.[17] In the course of his opinion, Justice Sedgwick said:

> The common law strenuously adhered to the doctrine that the owner of real estate could use it as he pleased, without regard to the convenience or even the interests of his neighbors. Some exceptions were made as to "ancient lights" and perhaps other such considerations. This rule of the common law was not quite in harmony with the theory of the civil law as expressed in the maxim, "Sic utere tuo ut alienum non laedas."[18] The earlier decisions in this country are inclined to the English view, but in recent years there have been some very notable departures from the strict rule of those courts.[19]

In a similar case,[20] Justice Brown of the Supreme Court of North Carolina had, however, referred to the same maxim as belonging to the common law, and given a very remarkable exposition of it:

> The ancient maxim of the common law, Sic utere tuo ut alienum non laedas, is not founded in any human statute, but in that sentiment expressed by Him Who taught good will toward men, and said, *"Love thy neighbor as thyself."* Freely translated, it enjoins that every person in the use of his own property should avoid injury to his neighbor as much as possible. No one ought to have the legal right to make a malicious use of his property for no benefit to himself, but merely to injure his fellow man. To hold otherwise makes the law an engine of oppression with which to destroy the peace and comfort of a neighbor, as well as to damage his property for no useful purpose, but solely to gratify a wicked and debasing passion.[21]

It makes no difference whether the maxim belongs to the common law or the civil law. The common law is as capable of assimilating good things from other systems as it is adaptable to the changing conditions of society. It must not be identified with the specific rules of any particular period. As Judge Johnsen has pointed out, in the initial adoption of the common law rules "there was equally intended to be an adoption of those principles of extension and growth which always had been regarded as being inherent in the common law system and which in fact constituted the genius of that system."[22] Hence, in some cases, American judges have wisely departed from certain common-law rules, and yet this very fact shows that they are in the great tradition of the common law.[23] My impression is that the greatest judges of the common law have been the readiest to draw upon other systems of law, and the most indifferent ones have been the most provincial.[24] The common law is so deeply steeped in the spirit of Christianity that it cannot but possess something of its catholicity. In this respect, as in so many others, the spirit of the common law is akin to that of St. Thomas Aquinas. It is so original that it can afford to borrow, and even to conceal its originality under the cover of quotations. It seems to have understood well the counsel of Christ to keep its sword in the scabbard.[25]

In cases involving fiduciary relations, the influence of Christianity is particularly marked. I need only to introduce one sample here:

The principle upon which public officers are denied the right to make contracts in their official capacity with themselves or to be or become interested in contracts thus made is evolved from the self-evident truth, as trite and impregnable as the law of gravitation, that no person can, at one and the same time, faithfully serve two masters representing diverse or inconsistent interests with respect to the service to be performed. The principle has always been one of the essential attributes of every rational system of positive law, even reaching to private contractual transactions, whereby there are created between individuals trust or fiduciary relations. The voice of divinity, speaking from within the sublimest incarnation known to all history, proclaimed and emphasized the maxim nearly two thousand years ago on occasions of infinite sacredness.[26]

One of the greatest decisions in contemporary England was the "Snail's Case."[27] The plaintiff, a poor woman, and a friend visited a café in Paisley, where her friend ordered for her a bottle of ginger-beer. As she was drinking, a decomposed snail floated out with the ginger-beer. In consequence of her having drunk part of the contaminated contents of the bottle, she contracted a serious illness. She sued the manufacturer for damages. The lower courts dismissed her action on the ground that there was no privity between the manufacturer and the ultimate consumer. In the House of Lords, her appeal was upheld. What interests us here is the very practical application made by Lord Atkin of Christ's teachings. "The rule," he said, "that you are to love your neighbor, becomes in law, you must not injure your neighbor; and the lawyer's question, Who is my neighbor? received a restricted reply. You must take reasonable care to avoid acts or omissions which you can reasonably foresee would be likely to injure your neighbor. Who, then, in law is my neighbor? The answer seems to be—persons who are so closely and directly affected by my act that I ought reasonably to have them in contemplation as being so affected when I am directing my mind to the acts and omissions which are called in question."[28]

This is one of the best statements on the relation between natural law and human law. Natural law is the common fountain of ethics and jurisprudence. The functions of these latter are different. Each has its forte, and each its limits. The differences and interrelations between law and morals present a fascinating subject of study, but we shall not enter upon it here. All that I wish to say now is that if the law does not require everyone to act as the Good Samaritan, it is not because it is not sufficiently Christian to appreciate the beauty of moral goodness, but rather because it is aware of its own limits, and it has to take account of the frailties of human nature and the actual state of civilization. Jurisprudence would not be prudent if it tried to go beyond the limits of practicability. On the other hand, it would not be just if it did not perform its function as fully as it could within those limits. The end of the law is love, and no measure is set to the end, only to the means. In many matters, the law has to choose the lesser evil.

Oftentimes the legislator or the judge finds himself in the delicate position of that householder in the parable who had to refrain from action for fear that "perhaps while you are gathering the tares you will root up the wheat with them" (Matt. 13:29). Some weeds, however, are so poisonous that if you do not uproot them immediately the wheat itself will be infected. In such a case, a good judge would not hesitate to pluck them out carefully, so as not to injure the wheat.

Take, for instance, the "Spring-gun Case," *Bird v. Holbrook* (Court of Common Pleas, 1828. 4 Bingham 628), where the defendant placed in his garden a spring-gun in order to catch anyone who should come to steal the flowers. The plaintiff, who entered the garden not for stealing, but to help a friend to recapture a peafowl which had flown into the garden, accidentally touched one of the wires attached to the spring-gun, which was thereby discharged, causing a severe wound in his knee. Holding the action maintainable, Chief Justice Best said, "It has been argued that the law does not compel every line of conduct which humanity or religion may require; but there is no act which Christianity forbids, that the law will not reach: if it were otherwise, Christianity would not be, as it has always been held to be, part of the law of England. I am, therefore, clearly of the opinion that he who sets spring-guns, without giving notice, is guilty of an inhuman act, and that, if injurious consequences ensue, he is liable to yield redress to the sufferer. But this case stands on grounds distinct from any that have preceded it. In general, spring-guns have been set for the purpose of deterring; the defendant placed his for the express purpose of doing injury; for, when called on to give notice, he said, 'If I give notice, I shall not catch him.' He intended, therefore, that the gun should be discharged, and that contents should be lodged in the body of the victim, for he could not be caught in any other way."

You will note that in such cases Christianity is introduced not as a supernatural religion, but as a vehicle of the precepts of natural law and justice.

Likewise, in the interesting "Queue Case," *Ho Ah Kow v. Nunan* (Circuit Court, D. Calif., 1879, 5 Sawy. 552, 12 Fed. Cas. 253), where the sheriff, in obedience to an ordinance declared unconstitutional by the Court, cut off the queue of a Chinese, and was ordered to pay damages to the amount of ten thousand dollars. Justice Field, who was sitting as Circuit Judge, had this to say in the course of his splendid opinion: "The ordinance is known in the community as the 'Queue Ordinance,' being so designated from its purpose to reach the queues of the Chinese, and it is not enforced against any other persons. The reason advanced for its adoption, and now urged for its continuance, is, that only the dread of the loss of his queue will induce a Chinaman to pay his fine. That is to say, in order to enforce the payment of a fine imposed upon him, it is necessary that torture should be superadded to imprisonment. Then, it is said, the Chinaman will not accept the alternative, which the law allows, of working out his fine by his imprisonment. Probably the bastinado, or the knout, or the thumbscrew, or the rack, would accomplish the same end; and no doubt the Chinaman would prefer either of these modes of torture to that which entails upon him disgrace among his countrymen and carries with it the constant dread of misfortune and suffering after death. It is not creditable to the humanity and civilization of our people, much less to their Christianity, that an ordinance of this character was possible."

It is not possible to cite even a small fraction of the cases where the influence of Christianity reveals itself with sudden, blinding radiance. But the few instances I have given are representative.

Christ does not enter into the courtroom as the Lawgiver whose words are legally binding on the judges. No, His kingdom does not belong to this world. The common-law judges have quoted His words just as the judges of ancient China would quote the words of Confucius. But just as it is impossible to understand the old Chinese jurisprudence without a knowledge of Confucianism, so it is impossible to grasp the spirit of the common law without taking account of the permeating influence of Christianity.

In some cases, the Christian influence is so subtle that you cannot put your finger on any specific precept which the Court is applying, and yet you feel a Christian atmosphere diffused throughout the opinion. Let one specimen suffice. In *McDaniel v. Trent Mills* (1929) 197 N.C. 342, 148 S.E. 440, the question was whether a wife could recover from a third party, who had through negligence injured her husband, the money she had on her own initiative expended out of her personal estate as a result of the injury. The Court held that in spite of the modern doctrine that husband and wife are no longer one person in the eye of the law, a wife is not to be considered in such a case as a complete stranger volunteering to aid the injured party, as she was acting "through the natural and ordinary considerations of family life." One paragraph of Chief Justice Stacy's opinion is so characteristically Christian in tone and American in accent that the reader will not blame me for quoting it here:

> While the common-law principle of unity of husband and wife and the modern doctrine of complete duality of personalities may clash somewhat in yielding to this result, still, we think the conclusion is supported by the logic of life, if not by the logic of syllogism; and it should be remembered that law is bigger than logic, life is bigger than law, and the function of judicial decision is to state, as near as possible, in terms of law, the meaning of life in action. This middle course, as it may be called, is perhaps a hybrid between the old and new doctrines just mentioned, or a mixture of the two, but, if so, it comes from holding fast to that which is good in the old and pressing forward to that which is helpful in the new, a practice heretofore commended by an authority on domestic relations, a great lawyer, and one of the apostles.

Can the reader guess which of the apostles the Chief Justice was referring to? Could it be that interesting man who, though in chains, pleaded his own cause before King Agrippa with such gusto that the prisoner's bar was turned into a pulpit?[29]

CHAPTER XIX

LETTER AND SPIRIT

"For the letter killeth: but the spirit quickeneth" (*2 Cor. 3:6*).

ONE of the greatest decisions in American jurisprudence was rendered by the New York Court of Appeals in 1889 (*Riggs v. Palmer*, 115 N.Y. 506, 22 N.E. 188). It was an ugly case, but a beautiful decision. Palmer had made a will bequeathing his estate to his grandson. Some time later, the testator manifested some intention to revoke it. In order to prevent him from revoking the bequest, and to obtain speedy enjoyment and immediate possession of his property, the grandson, then a boy 16 years of age, murdered him by poisoning. He was found guilty of murder and sent to jail. But the question in the instant case was, could he inherit the property bequested to him? His argument is that the testator is dead, that his will was made in due form, and has been admitted to probate, and that therefore it must have effect according to the letter of the law.

Judge Earl, speaking for the Court, conceded that the case did fall within the letter of the law, and that "It was the intention of the lawmakers that the donees in a will should have the property given to them." "But," he continued, "it never could have been their intention that a donee who murdered the testator to make the will operative should have any benefit under it." He resorted to some analogies in support of his position. "There was a statute in Bologna that whoever drew blood in the streets should be severely punished, and yet it was held not to apply to the case of a barber who opened a vein in the street. It is commanded in the decalogue that no work shall be done upon the Sabbath, and yet giving the command a rational interpretation founded upon its design the Infallible Judge held that it did not prohibit works of necessity, charity, or benevolence on that day."

This is a clear instance of the wise saying of St. Paul that the letter kills while the spirit gives life. But even in such a clear case, there was a dissenting opinion by Judge Gray, who veritably made a fetish of the letter: "But the matter," he wrote, "does not lie within the domain of conscience. We are bound by the rigid rules of law, which have been established by the legislature, and within the limits of which the determination of this question is confined." However, this is not merely a matter of conscience, it is a matter of plain common sense. The Judge was right in deferring to the will of the legislature and of the testator; but by interpreting their will the way he did he was actually taking them to be irrational beings. The leaven of the Pharisees never ceases to work; but it is encouraging to see that the leaven of the Spirit is, on the whole, even stronger in American jurisprudence.

I am happy to find that Mr. Justice Cardozo, whom many have come to regard as the greatest judge of this century, had the highest admiration for the decision of *Riggs v. Palmer*. Commenting upon it, he said, "Conflicting principles were there in competition for mastery. One of them prevailed, and vanquished all the others. There was the principle of the binding effect of a will disposing of the estate of a testator in conformity with law. That principle pushed to the limit of its logic, seemed to uphold the title of the murderer. There was the principle that civil courts may not add to the pains and penalties of crimes. That, pushed to the limit of its logic, seemed again to uphold his title. But over against these was another principle, of greater generality, its roots deeply fastened in universal sentiments of justice, the principle that no man should profit from his own inequity or take advantage of his own wrong. The logic of this principle prevailed over the logic of the others. . . . The judicial process is there in microcosm."[30]

With his usual mellowness Cardozo called all these different lines of thinking by the name of logic. Not being half as mellow, I am inclined to think that a sheer literalism which would lead to a result "abhorrent to even the most rudimentary sense of justice"[31]— to borrow the words of Chief Justice Vanderbilt in a similar case —is anything but logical, at least from the standpoint of the science of law, whose purpose is to serve the ends of justice. For instance, according to Dean Pound, a statute was enacted not so long ago in one of the states as follows: "Be it enacted that it shall be unlawful for any person or persons to discharge any loaded firearm or firearms in, along or upon any public road or highway in this state except for the purpose of killing some noxious or dangerous animal or an officer in the pursuit of his duty."[32] Would you call a judge logical if he follows the literal, grammatical sense of the statute and draws the conclusion that the killing of a policeman is as lawful as the killing of a noxious animal? Of course, you may say that this is a perfect example of a good syllogism, which may be formulated as follows:

> It is lawful to discharge firearms for the purpose of killing a noxious animal or an officer in pursuit of his duty,
> Now, the policeman who was killed by the prisoner at the bar was clearly an officer in pursuit of his duty,
> *Ergo,* the act of the defendant was lawful.

Granted that it is a good syllogism; but the syllogism is the least important part of juristic logic. The important part in juristic logic lies in the determination of the major premise, which depends upon a weighing of the values involved, because the law is not a speculative science but an axiological science. For the most part, the judge must use inductive logic, a logic of probabilities and balance shading off imperceptibly into the realms of art and ethics. Law, as the great German jurist Ihering said, is a means to an end. If, therefore, a judge is not teleological, he is not logical.

How inseparable law is from ethics and even natural theology is brought to the fore, negatively, by the case of *Oleff v. Hodapp*[33] decided by the Supreme Court of Ohio in 1935. In that case a man named Tego Miovanis had a joint bank account with his uncle, Apostol Miovanis. Each depositor had unlimited authority to withdraw funds, and in the event of death of one party, the survivor would be the sole owner. Afraid that this unlimited authority might be abused by his uncle, and in order to be the sole owner, Tego sent someone to murder the uncle, and succeeded in removing him from the mortal scene. The Ohio Court had to decide whether, as a result of the murder, the joint deposit now belonged exclusively to the murderer, or whether the heirs or representatives of the murderee continued to have an interest in the joint deposit. The court decided, by a majority vote, that after the murder the bank account belonged completely and exclusively to the murderer. In the course of his opinion, Judge Stephenson said:

> We are not subscribing to the righteousness of Tego's legal status; but this is a court of law and not a theological institution. . . . Property cannot be taken from an individual who is legally entitled to it because he violates a public policy. Property rights are too sacred to be subjected to a danger of that character. We experience no satisfaction in holding that Tego is entitled to this account; but that is the law, and we must so find.

This opinion has been severely criticized by many prominent jurists, but Felix Cohen has gone to the root of the matter. He writes: [34]

> There are two things about this opinion that are particularly interesting. One is the Court's statement that "this is a court of law and not a theological institution." The second is the Court's statement that "property rights are too sacred" to be subjected to certain dangers that would follow if the courts allowed considerations of "righteousness" or "public policy" to influence decisions on property rights. Property rights, we are told, are too sacred. Apparently, if property rights were less sacred, or if the right of life were more sacred, the court might have decided the case against the murderer Tego and in favor of the representatives of the murdered uncle.
> This question of the comparative sacredness or holiness of different rights is, I think, one of the most important questions that theological institutions have been considering for a good many years. It seems to me that this question of whether one

property right, or civil right, or human right is more or less sacred than another is a very important part of theology. Why, then, should the Ohio Supreme Court insist that it is not a theological institution when it passes upon the relative sacredness of different rights?

To my mind, this case is one of the instances of the legal maxim: *Summa lex summa crux.* A law pushed to the extreme becomes a cross.

When we remember that Felix Cohen is one of the most ruthless of modern "realists," we shall see that if only one is realistic enough, one cannot be very far from the kingdom of heaven. Judge Jerome Frank has testified that "Most intelligent Americans, if the 'basic principles' of scholastic natural law are described to them, will find them completely acceptable."[35] And one of such "basic principles" was stated in the simplest words by Chief Justice Beasley, who was by no means a Schoolman: "The law hedges round the lives and persons of men with much more care than it employs when guarding property."[36] But do the judges always find the law?

CHAPTER XX

THE HIERARCHY OF VALUES

"Let the counsel of the Holy One of Israel come, that we may know it!" (Isaias 5:19).

Now we are in a position to study the teleology and axiology of Christ. To my mind, the most outstanding quality of Christ's art of judgment is His infallible sense of values. Being the Light of the world, He had a clear and undistorted vision of which things are of greater importance and which are of lesser importance, and He never confused means with ends. He reproved, above all, those "blind guides who strain out a gnat and swallow a camel" (Matt. 23:24). He denounced the scribes and Pharisees because, meticulous as they were in tithing mint, anise and cummin, they forgot about the weightier things of the law—justice, mercy and faith. He did not blame them for attending to those minor items of the law; what He was warning against was exclusive attention to them, to the neglect of the basic principles of justice and equity. (See Matt. 23:23.)

Closely related to their perverted sense of values was their distorted conception of the law. To Christ, laws are made for man, not man for the laws. The end of all laws is to help man in realizing his full humanity. But those legalists took the laws as ends in themselves. They were sticklers for form and made a fetish of the letter; they mistook their narrow ideas for the immutable law of

181

nature. If we pitch all their controversies with Christ against this background, we shall be in a better position to perceive what it was all about. Fundamentally, the clash was between a teleological jurisprudence and a mechanical jurisprudence.

One sabbath day, Christ went into their synagogue and saw a man with a withered hand. Knowing what was going to happen, they asked Him, "Is it lawful to heal on the sabbath days?" Note carefully how He answered them. "What man of you," He said, "if he shall have but one sheep; and this fall into a pit on the sabbath, will he not lay hold and lift it out? Well, how much greater the worth of a man than of a sheep! So it is lawful to do good on the sabbath" (Matt. 12:10–12). When He had healed the withered hand, the Pharisees went out and took counsel together against Him, in order to destroy the great "law breaker." As a matter of fact, He was so far from breaking the law that the healing of the withered hand was but a symbol of the restoration of the law to its pristine vigor and essential function.

Nothing reveals Christ's teleological philosophy of law more than His teaching about the sabbath "The sabbath was made for man, not man for the sabbath" (Mark 2:27). It is understood that the sabbath was meant to give rest to man, and for the praise of God. But to heal the sick and to save life was within the purpose of the law. It brings relief to man, and glory to God. As St. Paul says, "The law is good, if a man use it lawfully" (1 Tim. 1:8). It was precisely the purpose of Christ to show by example how to use the law lawfully, and not to use it so as to defeat its end, as some of the Pharisees were doing.

A very clear presentation of His position is found in the Gospel according to St. Luke:

> There was a sabbath day on which he was preaching in one of their synagogues. Here there was a woman who for eighteen years had suffered under some influence that disabled her; she was bent down, and could not lift her head straight. Jesus saw her and called her to him; Woman, he said, thou art rid of thy infirmity. Then he laid hands on her, and immediately she was raised upright, and gave praise to God. But the ruler of the synagogue, indignant that Jesus should heal

on the sabbath day, turned and said to the multitude, You
have six days on which work is allowed; you should come and
be healed on those days, not on the sabbath. And the Lord
gave him this answer, What, you hypocrites, is there any one
of you that will not untie his ox or his ass from the stall and
take them down to water, when it is the sabbath? And here is
this daughter of Abraham, whom Satan had kept bound these
eighteen years past; was it wrong that she should be delivered
on the sabbath day from bonds like these? (Luke 13:10–16).

St. Luke then goes on to narrate: "All his adversaries were put
to shame by this saying of his, and the whole multitude rejoiced
over the marvellous works he did." Now, this brings out a paradox.
The Pharisees were supposed to be learned in the law, while the
multitude were simple folk. Yet, the reasonableness of Christ's
teaching and action was seen clearly by the simple folk, but it was a
scandal to the Pharisees. This shows that there are no fools like
learned fools. As Confucius said, "Where art overrides nature,
you get the pedantry of a scribe." In the case of the Pharisees,
their conscience and natural reason were encrusted and distorted
beyond recognition by the false teachings and traditions of men.
Miseducation is much worse than no education.

St. John has recorded for us another significant incident. At
the feast of the tabernacles Christ was teaching in the temple, and
the Jews were astonished by His learning. "How does this man
know how to read?" they asked; "he has never studied." Jesus answered, "The learning which I impart is not my own, it comes
from him who sent me. Anyone who is prepared to do his will, can
tell for himself whether such learning comes from God, or whether
I am delivering a message of my own. The man who delivers a
message of his own seeks to win credit for himself; when a man
seeks credit for one who has sent him, he tells the truth, there is no
dishonesty in him" (John 7:15–18).

Christ went on to justify His healing on the sabbath by an
argument which should be of special interest to students of law.
"There is one action of mine," He said, "which has astounded you
all. Listen to this; because Moses prescribed circumcision for you
(not that it comes from Moses, it comes from the patriarchs), you

are ready to circumcise a man on the sabbath day; and if a man
receives circumcision on the sabbath, so that the law of Moses
may not be broken, have you any right to be indignant with me,
for restoring a man's whole strength to him on the sabbath? Be
honest in your judgments, instead of judging by appearances"
(John 7:21-24).

What is of particular importance for the art of judging is the
method of analogy that Christ so skillfully employed, not only on
this particular occasion, but everywhere in His discourses. If
His reasoning was logical, His imagination was poetic. I have
found that those philosophers and jurists who have studied His
teachings closely have not failed to imbibe something of His supreme aptitude for uncovering hidden affinities between things apparently wide apart. Speaking of the works of St. Thomas Aquinas,
Thomas Gilby has observed: "His discourse is a rhythmic response
to things striving to ends, rather than gravely resting in their appointed places. . . . A sense of analogy pervades the whole, and
the terms he uses flicker with internal variations of meaning according to their context." There is a pulse of life and a flavor of
wisdom in his writings even when he is dealing with the most abstract of ideas. To quote Father Gilby again, "The feel for physical
closeness rarely abates; the logical is rooted in the prelogical; ratiocination derives from one intuition and leads to another; scientific
introspection is based on an immediate, if muddled awareness."
Now, this is what I myself have felt about St. Thomas, but I know
of no one, in modern times, who has recaptured the atmosphere as
well as this English Dominican.

But the reason I have dwelt so long upon St. Thomas is that I
have found exactly the same atmosphere in the common law. Here
too a sense of analogy pervades the whole. From the day of Bracton
to contemporary America, the best judges and jurists have shown
the same responsiveness to the rhythms of life, the same philosophy of values, the same "feel for physical closeness," the same
supple sense of analogy and proportion, the same unconscious inter-
action between logic and intuition, the same subtle naïveté, the
same homespun beauty—I would almost say, the same profound
mysticism under the cover of a happy phrase—that have character-

ized the common law throughout the ages and made it such a be-witching subject of study. The common law never ceases to shed "the gladsome light of jurisprudence." It continues to "work itself pure by rules drawn from the fountain of justice."

With regard to the role of analogical reasoning in the judicial development of the common law, no one has written better than Bracton. "The laws," he said, "once they have been approved by the consent of those who use them and made permanent by the oath of kings, can no longer be changed or repealed without the consent of all those by whose common consent and counsel they were promulgated. They may, however, be converted into some-thing better, even without such consent; for that is not destroyed which is transmuted into something better. Thus, should there emerge any new and unwonted cases, and cases which have never before been dealt with in the realm, if there have been any cases of similar nature, these should be decided by analogy (*per simile*), for it is a good occasion to proceed from like to like."[37]

This is one of the most original insights that Bracton contributed to jurisprudence, and it is also most typical of the genius of the common law, which seems to specialize in bringing out new corn from old fields. Like St. Thomas, Bracton was a scribe instructed in the kingdom of heaven by the Divine Master Himself. No won-der that he became the first householder of the common law who was able to bring out of his treasure things new and old, and trans-mute them into a living system.

Justice Lusk of Oregon is in the great tradition of Bracton when he declares that, "The common law's capacity to discover and apply remedies for acknowledged wrongs without waiting on legislation is one of its cardinal virtues." (*Hinish v. Meyer & Frank Co.*, 166 Or. 482, 113 P. 2d 438 at 447.) So is Chief Justice Vander-bilt of New Jersey when he says, "Every change in the law by judicial decision necessarily creates rights in one party to the litiga-tion and imposes corresponding duties on the other party. This is the process by which the law grows and adjusts itself to the chang-ing needs of the times. The process is necessarily used not only to create new rights and corresponding duties but, where necessary, to strike down old ones. *Cessante ratione legis, cessat et ipsa lex* (the reason for a law ceasing, the law itself ceases), is one of the most ancient maxims known to our law and it is constantly followed by our courts."[38] So also Judge Desmond of New York writes, "We act in the finest common-law tradition when we adapt and alter decisional law to produce common-sense justice."[39] But Professor Seavey has summed up the dynamic aspect of the common law in an illuminating passage which, whether he was aware of it or not, is a twentieth-century exposition of the Bractonian doctrine of transmutation: "The judicial advocates of progress have not intended to change principles of English law. They have merely sought to accord more nearly with the fundamental conceptions of justice which underlie the specific rules. To preserve archaic individual rules in a modern society, to fail to respond to changing ideals and needs, necessarily saps the vitality of the law. Without change, the law must obey the order of all living things and die. It is one of the glories of the common law that its capacity for change enables it to remain human and vital. The common law was and should remain as the response of the judges to the civilization of the times in view of its history. There is no principle of common law which prevents the weeding out of historical anachronisms or the correction of judicial errors, and this without resort to Parliament."[40]

Dealing with one of these historical anachronisms, Lord Atkin made a very interesting remark: "When these ghosts of the past stand in the path of justice clanking their medieval chains the proper course for the judge is to pass them undeterred."[41] And yet he too is a worthy descendant of Bracton, who represents medievalism at its best. There are ghosts and ghosts, and some ghosts belong to the family of the Holy Ghost. The truth is that the great principles underlying the common law, unlike its specific rules, are beyond the old and the new. What makes the common law so perennially young and forward-looking is that, in the absence of positive law, or where the authorities are balanced, the best judges have not hesitated for a moment in tilting the beam of the scale of justice by resorting to "that naked and changeless equity . . . which is natural—which savages understand—which cultivated reason approves, and which Christianity not only sanctions, but in a thousand forms has ordained" (Justice Nisbet in *Culbreath v. Culbreath*, Supreme Court of Georgia, 1849. 7 Ga. 64, 67).

The common law, like life itself, flows continuously from the muddy to the clear. It undergoes purification in the very process of muddling through. It has a way of blundering into wisdom. But it is very important to remember that this has been possible not because the common law possesses a mysterious quality in itself, but because it has its source in the wellsprings of Christian prudence and justice, wisdom and love. Once it was separated from these pure springs and gathered volume solely from the surface waters, it would flow from the muddy to the muddier. There is no virtue in following a human tradition if it is not founded on the "laws of nature and of nature's God." This reminds me of another encounter between Christ and the Pharisees, in which Christ upheld natural law and reason against a tradition of men.

As is well known, the Pharisees never ate their meals without first washing their fingers, and there were many other practices, such as the washing of cups and bowls and pans, all in strict accordance with time-honored customs to which they adhered religiously. So when they saw some of His disciples eat their bread with unwashed hands, they came to ask Him, "How is it that thy disciples do not walk according to the tradition of the elders, but eat their bread with defiled hands?" In His answer Christ said, "Well did Isaias prophesy of you hypocrites, as it is written, *This people honoreth me with their lips, but their heart is far from me; and in vain do they worship me, teaching as doctrine the precepts of men.* For, abandoning the commandment of God, you cling to the tradition of men, such as the washing of pots and cups, and many other things of that sort." "And with what skill," He continued, "you evade the law of God, that you may observe the conventions of men! For Moses said, *Honor thy father and thy mother*, and *Let him who curses father or mother be condemned and put to death.* But you say that if a man should tell his father or his mother, 'What you are entitled to receive from me is *Corban* (that is, offered to God),' he is no longer allowed or required to do anything for his father or mother. This is how you make void the commandment of

God by setting up a tradition of your own; and many such-like things you do" (Mark 7:1–13).

Not all human laws are bad, but in this particular instance we have an ingenious device for evading the natural duty to support one's parents by using the artificial formula of "Corban" to defraud the parents of their rightful portion by introducing God as an excuse. To offer a gift to God meant, of course, to contribute to the treasury of the temple. That in itself is not a bad thing. But to do it at the expense of one's parents is a grave injustice. One has to be just before one can be generous. But I cannot help suspecting that in most cases it was not generosity but greed that motivated the son in resorting to such a procedure. The son, it is true, had declared that whatever his parents could get from him was set apart for the temple; but, to quote the great scriptural scholar Father Lagrange, "It goes without saying that one did not consider oneself bound for all that to give to the temple the whole of the parental portion."[42] The whole thing looks pretty shoddy. The parents were robbed, and the spoils were divided between the treasury of the temple and the son.

Apparently, by the time of Christ this was already an old tradition, grown respectable, so that those who followed the custom were probably not even conscious of its rotten core. The familiar had become natural to them. Christ alone could pierce the overgrowth of ingenious theories and rationalizations and see the principle of the convention for what it was.

CHAPTER XXI

NATURAL LAW AND POSITIVE LAW

"I will implant My law in their innermost thoughts, engrave it in their hearts; I will be their God, and they shall be My people" (*Jer. 31:31*).

To my mind, the "Corban" case is of supreme importance for modern students of jurisprudence. There Christ affirms the fundamental distinction between the natural law and positive law. The natural law, as Sir Edward Coke, following the teachings of Christ and St. Paul, has declared in Calvin's Case,[48] is "written with the finger of God in the heart of man"; it existed "before any judicial or municipal law." Being made by God, it is universal and immutable, and of higher authority than man-made or positive laws. If positive laws have a necessary function to perform in regulating the affairs of men, their function is to supplement and implement the natural law by carrying out its fundamental purpose in matters of detail.

For instance, the natural law enjoins the duty of filial piety; so it is for positive or conventional law to prescribe, within the limits of practicability, some of the ways and means of expressing our filial piety, and forbid at least the graver breaches of it. These prescriptions and prohibitions can and must vary with the ever-changing conditions of human society. They must grow with the growth of civilization.

But however they vary and however they grow, they must never be divorced from the original end to which the natural law has ordained them. As soon as the positive laws have become deflected from their natural end and lost their status as a means to that end, they are perverted and, properly speaking, are no longer to be called "laws," because they play false to their essential nature. When this happens, they impede and frustrate the humanity of man. Instead of setting up a social order under which men may freely develop the moral and spiritual nature God has endowed them with, the so-called laws become tyrannical masters who fetter men's hands and feet and even enslave their minds by striking terror and instilling false reasons and motives into them. The Pharisees, who were themselves victims of this abysmal delusion, were in turn deluding others by teaching as sacred canons the mere conventions of men. Having dethroned the truly absolute law of God, they came to exalt what was essentially relative to the pedestal of the absolute.

This is exactly what has been happening in modern jurisprudence, in some countries more and in others less. Positivism began with the denial of the natural law, and has ended by creating strange gods, such as the totalitarian state, class-dictatorship, the Fuehrer, and, the subtlest of all, scientism or worship of facts. Even in America, there have not been lacking legal Pharisees who tended to think of the natural law exclusively in terms of natural rights, to the total neglect of the natural duties; to think of natural rights exclusively in terms of "vested interests," to the total neglect of the weightier interests of humanity; and to find the sanction of law in will and power, whether of the state or of the individual, rather than in reason and justice. If they talked in terms of reason, it was only to justify will, so that theirs was a legal philosophy with voluntarism as the kernel and rationalism as the protecting shell, a sheer *fiat* masquerading as an angel of light. At their worst, they used the names of God and the natural law to canonize their materialistic preoccupations and racial prejudices. I do not mean that they were in bad faith. No, they were just deluded, as the Pharisees had been. In mistaking human doctrines for the law of God, they might have thought that they were doing honor to Him.

At the turn of the century, or thereabouts, there arose a strong reaction against the absolutism of the modern legal Pharisees. A new school of jurists began to preach a kind of "enlightened scepticism"[44] and relativism. They stressed the importance of flexibility of the law as against the rigidity of legal conceptualism; they taught that the law must keep abreast of the times, and as life was moving on, so should the law. No law, therefore, was absolute and immutable. "There are no absolutes," and "all concepts are relative."[45] These words by Chief Justice Vinson summed up the spirit of the whole reaction.

Now the crux of the matter is this: the older school had exalted certain human and intrinsically relative doctrines to the pedestal of the divine and absolute. The new school played the part of the iconoclasts, and, with formidable intellectual weapons drawn from the arsenal of modern psychology and science, threw down every-thing from the pedestal, leaving it as empty and clean as the newly shaven head of a bonze. But when the demon of muddle-headed-ness found the pedestal so empty, he came with seven other spirits, at once more intellectual and more evil than himself, and turned it into their throne, from which they are ruling and ruining millions of human beings.

At present, American jurisprudence is going through a crucial phase of its evolution. There is a visible trend toward the revival of natural-law philosophy, centered on the dignity of the human person. The historical situation which has made this movement not only possible but inevitable has been very ably described by Chief Justice Vanderbilt: "There has been a marked tendency to think of man merely as a cog in the economic machine. Happily, how-ever, this tendency seems to have been checked, in part because of a postwar resurgence of interest in religion which is fostering a militant faith in the worth of the individual and his capacity for good, and in part because of our alarm over the spread of totali-tarian government and its effect on the individual."[46] As I survey the judicial decisions of contemporary courts in America, I have grounds for hoping that this resurgence of spiritual idealism is more than a temporary fashion, that it is the beginning of a truly glorious age in the history of jurisprudence. In this age, we have to steer, with as much moral courage as prudent caution, between the Scylla of extreme dogmatism and the Charybdis of extreme scepticism.

A certain amount of dogmatism is unavoidable in moral sciences as in physical sciences; but dogmatism should be reserved for the really fundamental principles which no normal human being can deny. Take, for instance, this proposition: You should not bear false witness against another so as to convict him of a crime, say, of murder, of which he is entirely innocent. No matter whether you are white or black, yellow or brown, unless you are morally insane, you would admit this to be absolutely true. I confess that to my mind this and other propositions of a similar nature are as absolutely certain as the proposition that one plus one equals two. But if you want me to prove its truth, I have to admit that I cannot, because self-evident truths neither can nor need to be proved. I can illustrate the proposition by some concrete and picturesque examples, just as I can illustrate the proposition that one plus one equals two by adding one apple to another, in the hope that what you cannot conceive abstractly may be plain to see. If you should still deny the proposition, I would say that there is something wrong with your mind, just as I would say there is something wrong with your philosophy of life if you should think it a very honorable thing to falsely charge an innocent person with the crime of murder and send him to the electric chair in order that you may marry his wife. The point I am driving at is that not everything human is relative, for there are things which are absolutely wrong. Such is my dogmatism.

On the other hand, a certain amount of scepticism is a necessary and desirable equipment of a judge. The law has to cope with endless variations and permutations of the circumstances of life, and very often an unexpected situation presents itself for your judgment. As Bracton so candidly pointed out, there are cases where "nothing similar has ever happened before, and their adjudication is beset by obscurity and difficulties."[47] In such cases Bracton strongly advised the judge to ponder carefully and take counsel.

"And yet," he lamented, "there are some persons who, presuming on their own knowledge, as if in the matters of law they could be ignorant of nothing, are unwilling to seek counsel of anyone. In fact, in such a case, it would be more honest and more prudent for them to seek counsel than to decide anything with temerity, for it is not an unsalutary thing to be doubtful about contingent things."[48] If you are intellectually honest and humble, you will not be cocksure of everything, but rather sceptical of your own opinions. If the Pharisees had been more sceptical of the traditions of men, they would probably have been more faithful to the laws of God.

CHAPTER XXII

LAW AND EQUITY

"I will show thee the way of wisdom, I will lead thee by the paths of equity" (Prov. 4:11).

LET us now study another encounter between Christ and the Pharisees, which took place again on a sabbath. As Christ and His disciples were walking through a field of standing grain, the disciples were hungry, and they began to pluck ears of grain and eat them, rubbing them with their hands. Some of the Pharisees said to them, "Why are you doing what it is not lawful to do on the sabbath? Whereupon Jesus answered them, Why, have you never read what David did, when he and his followers were hungry? How he went into the tabernacle, and ate the loaves set forth there before God, and gave them to his followers, although it is not lawful for anyone except the priests to eat them?" (Luke 6:2–4).

Christ cited the example of King David not in the spirit of *stare decisis*, or adherence to precedent, but because it happened to be a precedent which embodied an important principle of law. It was a rule of the Divine positive law that only priests could eat the loaves of proposition; but this, like all other rules of positive law, should be understood in the context of the normal conditions of life, and does not apply to the exceptional situation in which David and his companions found themselves. The rule was made for protecting the interests of priests, and normally it should be observed; for although it does not belong to the law of nature, it is in harmony with it. Preservation of life, on the other hand, belongs to the law of nature. When you are confronted with a situation which compels you to choose between breaking a positive law and violating the natural law, you would be justified, or at least excused, in choosing the former. To every rule of positive law there are exceptions, which are based either directly upon a precept of natural law or upon the presence of higher equities.

This brings us to the intimate relations between "law" and "equity," and their respective roles in the development of a legal system. Whether they are administered by two separate courts or by one and the same court makes not much difference. What is important is that the judge should know that both "law" and "equity" are integral parts of a whole, that each has a necessary function to fill in the administration of justice, and that the perfect development of the law depends largely upon their harmonious co-operation.

In the evolution of legal systems, "law" as represented by strict rules came first, and "equity" was born in the judicial process, slowly and not without labors and pangs. Some rules had to be laid down to introduce some sort of order into the social relations of men. At first the judges would not think of allowing any exception to the rules, however hard they might work on certain individuals, because to relax the rules might easily wreck the newly achieved order. But when social order was more or less stabilized, the judges became less preoccupied with the maintenance of peace and order, and had more time to think of justice and equity as between the parties. In the meantime, most judges, being steeped in a legal tradition and inured to those mental habits suited only to a bygone situation, found it difficult to respond freely to the new demands. At this juncture, a great deal depends upon the advent of men of legal genius who were more clear-visioned and sensitive to the demands of justice than the rank and file of judges, and knew how to introduce timely exceptions to the hard-and-fast rules in such a way as to win over at least some of the less stubborn brethren. Christ's citing the precedent of David is to be understood in this light.

This is no place to enter into the details of this interesting phase of legal evolution. I shall content myself with one or two examples. In Justinian's *Institutes,* we read:

> Exceptions are intended for the protection of the defendant, who is often in this position, that though the plaintiff's case is a good one in the abstract, yet as against him, the particular defendant, his contention is inequitable. For instance, if you are induced by duress, fraud, or mistake to promise Titius by stipulation what you did not owe him, it is clear that by the civil law you are bound, and that the action on your promise is well grounded; yet it is inequitable that you should be condemned, and therefore in order to defeat the action you are allowed to plead the exception of duress, or of fraud, or one framed to suit the circumstances of the case. So too, if, as a preliminary to an advance of money, one gets a stipulation from you for its repayment, and he never advances it after all, it is clear that he can sue you for the money, and you are bound by your promise to give it; but it would be iniquitous that you should be compelled to fulfill such an engagement, and therefore you are permitted to defend yourself by the exception that the money in point of fact was never advanced.[49]

Logically, rules and exceptions are simultaneous; they are, as it were, on a horizontal plane. But historically, the rules came first and the exceptions arose later as new situations, not anticipated when the rules were made, presented themselves to the judgment of the court. And it is to be noted that in Roman law as in the common law the exceptions were introduced, not as direct modifications of the substantive law, but through the channels of procedure, whether as defenses or as petitions for special relief.

Equity is to law what poetry is to prose. The beauty of "law" consists in its clarity and orderliness. The beauty of equity lies in its flexibility and plasticity, in its untrammeled response to values and delicate sense of proportion. Joseph Story, one of the very greatest of American jurists, wrote, "The beautiful character—

pervading excellence, if one may say so—of equity jurisprudence is that it varies its adjustments and proportions so as to meet the very form and pressure of each particular case in all its complex habitudes."[50]

Needless to say, both legal rules and equity are necessary to the art of law, although a layman or even a judge who had not gone deep into the law is prone to think of the law exclusively in terms of rules. The insight of Aristotle is still worth repeating that the function of equity is to correct the defects of a legal rule which arise inevitably from its necessary generality. How true this is can be illustrated by an interesting discussion which took place between Mencius,[51] a Chinese contemporary of Aristotle, and one of his pupils. At that time it was a rule of social etiquette that in the giving and receiving of things between a man and a woman, aside from husband and wife or parents and children, there must be no physical contact. For instance, if a male guest came to visit, the housewife in serving him with a cup of tea should place the cup on a table or a mat, from which the guest was to take it. In no case must she place it directly into his hands. Now, the pupil of Mencius asked the master whether there was such a rule of propriety. Mencius answered, "Yes." The pupil then asked, "If my sister-in-law is drowning in a river, shall I not use my hands to rescue her?" The master replied, "If you did not, you would not be a man but a beast. That there must be no physical touch between a man and a woman is a rule applicable to the normal circumstances of social life. It has no application when your sister-in-law is drowning. There must be a sense of balance."[52]

Now, equity is nothing else than just this sense of balance, for the exercise of which there could be no hard-and-fast rules. Like taste, it can only be cultivated and refined through experience, reading, observation and reflection. Some rudiments of it are a part of man's natural endowment; but their development depends upon a proper kind of education, mostly self-education. This is why some great jurists have advised their younger brethren that in order to know the law adequately one needs to know more than the law. Sir Henry Finch, in his *Monotechnia* (1613), taught that legal knowledge consists of two elements, one proper to the law itself—

that is, the knowledge of statutory and decisional law—and the other drawn from outside sources. It is drawn, to quote his unforgettable language, "out of the best and very bowels of Divinity, Grammar, Logic; also from Philosophy, Natural, Political, Economic, Moral, though in our Reports and Year Books they come not under the same terms, yet the things which you find are the same; for the sparks of all sciences are raked up in the ashes of the law."[53]

Of course, the important thing is to keep the fire of justice burning intensely in your heart; otherwise so much fuel, and some wet logs too, would quench it, and instead of light there would be only smoke. On the other hand, when the sparks are raked up, you need more fuel to feed them; otherwise they would burn themselves out.

Bracton calls law a moral science, and places it under ethics. I agree that law is a moral science, but I would put it parallel with ethics, the two being twin sisters under the common ancestry of the natural law. But in any case they are of kindred blood. How closely related they are is clearly brought out by a passage which I have come across in Manson's excellent, though little-known, book, *The Builders of Our Law:*

> Lord Mansfield advises the student of English law with the intention of practising at the Bar to begin with Tully's Offices—the title then given to Cicero in three books, "De Officiis." The advice may sound strange to some, but in truth it is sound advice, because all law has a moral foundation. A clear understanding of the duties of men in society is the true basis of legal science. Denman was a pupil of Tidd, the author of the famous Practice, and this was the lesson he learnt from him. "I well remember," says Denman, "the advice he gave to a pupil who was about to commence practice: 'When you are called upon for your opinion, make yourself perfect master of the facts, and then consider what is right. You may be pretty sure that is the law, without looking much into the cases.' " This advice—especially as to cases—must be received with discretion, but it is substantially sound.[54]

Everyone knows how well-read Thomas More was in the humanities. I have always admired his sense of balance, which he kept up to the very moment of his martyrdom. "I die the king's good servant, but God's first."[55] In his case I think the fire of justice and the water of wisdom worked together in perfect harmony to make him the great Chancellor that he was.

What impresses me most is the encounter he had with the judges of the King's Bench. Himself an accomplished student of the common law, he suggested to the judges of the law courts that they ameliorate the rigors of the law by their own initiative. His advice was not accepted, because it was far ahead of the time. But it has become a reality both in England and in America where law and equity have been fused.[56] More's views are of jurisprudential significance, because they go to prove that law and equity are intrinsically interrelated, and while equity presupposes law, law stands in need of equity for its own fulfillment. "Adjudication," as Plucknett says, "like any other questions of human conduct, depends upon a nice balance between law and equity, rule and exception, tradition and innovation."[57]

But in More's time there was a great deal of friction between the chancery and the law courts, chiefly arising from the fact that More's predecessor Wolsey had issued many injunctions staying the execution of judgments of the law courts. The law judges were mostly conservative and technically minded. They adhered to the law strictly, even at the expense of substantial justice. For instance, if I pay you my debt but forget to get back from you a document which I have signed, you can still bring an action at law against me on the strength of the written document, and the judge would give judgment against me. In such a case, I can complain to the Chancellor, and after hearing both parties he would enjoin you not to put in force your judgment, because it would be unconscionable for you to be paid twice. If you disregard the injunction and go ahead to enforce the judgment, the Chancellor can send you to prison. Although the injunction is addressed to the party and not to the court, the effect is practically the same. As Maitland says, "You in breach of trust have obtained a judgment—the Chancellor does not say that this judgment was wrongly granted, he does not annul it, he tells you that for reasons personal to yourself it will be inequitable for you to enforce the judgment, and that you are not to enforce it. For all this, however, it was natural that the judges should take umbrage at this treatment of their judgment."[58]

More did not issue as many injunctions as Wolsey, but still there were some complaints on the part of the judges. When his son-in-law, Roper, informed him that the judges did not like his injunctions, More ordered his clerks to make a docket of the whole number of injunctions both past and pending, and invited the judges to dine with him in the council chamber at Westminister. I shall let his son-in-law tell the rest of the story.

> After dinner, when he had broken with them what complaints he had heard of his injunctions, and moreover showed them both the number and causes of every one of them, in order, so plainly that, upon full debating of those matters, they were all enforced to confess that they, in like case, could have done no other wise themselves, then offered he this unto them: that if the justices of every court (unto whom the reformation of the rigour of the law, by reason of their office, most especially appertained) would, upon reasonable considerations, by their own discretions (as they were, as he thought, in conscience bound) mitigate and reform the rigour of the law themselves, there should from thenceforth by him no more injunctions be granted. Whereunto when they refused to condescend, then said he unto them: "Forasmuch as yourselves, my Lords, drive me to that necessity for awarding out injunctions to relieve the people's injury, you cannot hereafter any more justly blame me." After that he said secretly unto me, "I perceive, son, why they like not so to do, for they see that they may by the verdict of the jury cast off all quarrels from themselves upon them, which they account their chief defence; and therefore am I compelled to abide the adventure of all such reports."[59]

It is a pity that More's decisions as Chancellor have not been handed down in the reports. But there is an anecdotal account of a Solomonic judgment which he delivered in his own home. The story is found in the life by one "Ro. Ba.," written by the end of Elizabeth's reign, and printed in *Ecclesiastical Biography*. The judgment is so characteristic of him that I think the reader cannot afford to miss it. The English is not modern, but its very quaintness has a charm of its own:

> Sir Thomas his last wife loved little dogs to play withal. It happened that she was presented with one, which had been stolen from a poor beggar woman. The poor beggar challenged her dog, having spied it in the arms of one of the serving men, that gave attendance upon my lady. The dog was denied her; so there was great hold and keep about it. At length Sir Thomas had notice of it; so caused both his wife and the beggar to come before him in his hall; and said, "Wife, stand you here, at the upper end of the hall, because you are a gentlewoman; and goodwife, stand there beneath, for you shall have no wrong." He placed himself in the midst, and held the dog in his hands, saying to them, "Are you content, that I shall decide this controversy that is between you concerning this dog?" "Yes," quoth they. "Then," said he, "each of you call the dog by his name, and to whom the dog cometh, she shall have it." The dog came to the poor woman; so he caused the dog to be given her, and gave her besides a French crown, and desired her that she would bestow the dog upon his lady. The poor woman was well apaid with his fair speeches, and his alms, and so delivered the dog to my lady.[60]

I should think that Christ Himself would have smiled at this decision. Most Chancellors, one would imagine, are cherubic, but this one is seraphic like St. Francis. Or is More a kindred of Chesterton, a Cherub in build but a Seraph in spirit? But I wonder if the Puritans could ever approve of such a jolly Saint.

CHAPTER XXIII

THE ALPHA AND THE OMEGA

"I am Alpha and Omega, the beginning and the end. To him that thirsteth I will give of the fountain of the water of life freely" (*Apoc. 21:6*).

IT is an undeniable fact that the Americans are, on the whole, a religious people. All foreign writers on America who have probed at all beneath her material civilization have been struck by the profound and pervading undertone of faith and confidence in God and good will toward all men.[61] Public men from the earliest days to President Eisenhower have been unanimous in their emphasis on religion as the foundation of national welfare.

George Washington set the tone. I need only quote a few sentences from his Farewell Address to illustrate the sobriety and matter-of-factness so characteristic of the American way of looking at morality and religion. "Let it simply be asked," he said, "where is the security for property, for reputation, for life, if the sense of religious obligation desert the oaths, which are the instruments of investigation in courts of justice? And let us with caution indulge the supposition that morality can be maintained without religion. Whatever may be conceded to the influence of refined education on minds of peculiar structure, reason and experience both forbid us to expect, that national morality can prevail in exclusion of religious principles."

That this was no mere political shrewdness, but sprang from a deep faith and implicit trust in God, is revealed unmistakably in a passage dealing with international relations. "Observe good faith and justice," he admonished, "towards all nations; cultivate peace and harmony with all; religion and morality enjoin this conduct; and can it be that good policy does not equally enjoin it? It will be worthy of a free, enlightened, and, at no distant future, a great nation, to give to mankind the magnanimous and too novel example of a people always guided by an exalted justice and benevolence."

This may sound too idealistic, but, on the whole, it has been the persistent tradition of American diplomacy, which is being continued even in this atomic age of ours. The cynics have taken it amiss. The utilitarian jurist, T. E. Holland, for instance, wrote, "The appeals to 'natural law' in modern diplomacy, perhaps most frequently made on behalf of the United States, have been little more than rhetorical."[62] But Washington and his followers are neither hypocrites nor fools. A utilitarian positivist like Holland simply could not understand the sincerity, much less the wisdom, of an idealism which is based on a higher reality. If the positivists would, in the fashion of Pilate, ask "What is the law of nature?", without waiting for an answer, Washington asked another question which challenges a definite answer from every decent man. "Can it be," he said, "that Providence has not connected the permanent felicity of a nation with its virtue? The experiment, at least, is recommended by every sentiment which ennobles human nature. Alas! is it rendered impossible by its vices?"

These last words reflect the deep Christian faith of the American pioneers. The pioneers had come to this continent principally for religious freedom. They were mostly conscientious dissenters in England. They were sincere Christians. Independent and self-reliant, they drew their inspiration from the Bible, which was their daily food. Whatever theological errors their private interpretation might have led them to, the central tenet of their philosophy of life was essentially sound. *Seek first the kingdom of God, and everything else will be added unto you.*

Dean Pound has summed up the Puritan influence upon American jurisprudence in these words: "Contract and voluntary culpable conduct were taken to be the solving ideas for all legal problems. When later the exigencies of an urban industrial society called for what we commonly speak of as social legislation, for a time that type of legislation fared hard when it came in conflict with this ideal."[63] While doing justice to its contributions to law in the pioneer days, he took Puritanism to task for its ultra-individualistic bias. "In this the Puritan is the incarnation of the Reformation. Individual freedom of interpretation, individual free association, individual rights were the basis of his religious, political and legal views. But abstract individual free self-assertion and individual interests are by no means all that legal systems have to look to, and in the nineteenth century our law showed on every side the ill effects of taking these for the sole basis."[64] He quoted from Morley a rather severe stricture upon it: "Nowhere has Puritanism done us more harm than in this leading us to take all breadth and color and diversity and fine discrimination out of our judgments of men, reducing them to thin, narrow and superficial pronouncements upon the letter of their morality or the precise conformity of their opinions to accepted standards of truth."[65]

So both Pound, with his keen moral intuitions and Promethean spirit, and Morley, with the refined aesthetical taste of an urban gentleman, were dissatisfied with the "Puritan bed of Procrustes."[66] However, it seems to me that much more is involved than the choice between rusticity and urbanity, between self-reliance and compromise, between individualistic and sociological jurisprudence, or between modern voluntarism and a relationally organized society of the medieval type. To me, the issue lies infinitely deeper; we are confronted with a choice between a narrow Christianity and a full Christianity. If I were compelled to choose between Puritan rusticity and Morleyan urbanity, I would certainly prefer the former to the latter. One ounce of genuine faith is worth more than a ton of dilettantism.[67]

Furthermore, the Founding Fathers of this Republic were not all Puritans. There were many different shades and nuances of religious belief, ranging from Deism to Catholicism. There was nothing particularly Puritanical about the Declaration of Independence and the Bill of Rights. To declare that all men were born equally endowed by God with certain inalienable rights, such as life, liberty and the pursuit of happiness was to assert no more than the common denominator acceptable to all reasonable men.

The fault of the nineteenth-century jurisprudence in America lay not in its assertion of the natural rights of men, but in its failure to think more of the natural duties. Instead of taking the human being in the fullness of his personality and humanity for its ideal, it took the abstract individual for its norm, the merest skeleton of man which easily merged into the "economic man." The "economic man" gave birth to captains of industry on one hand, and mere cogs of the social machine on the other. The world has been divided between individualistic utilitarians and socialistic utilitarians, and at the core of both is a materialistic philosophy of life, which in jurisprudence finds its expression in positivism.

No one has grasped the real situation of modern jurisprudence as clearly as His Holiness Pius XII, who, as a few of us know, is a consummate jurist. "The nineteenth century," he said, "is the one largely responsible for juridical positivism. If its consequences were slow in making themselves felt in all their seriousness in legislation, it is due to the fact that culture was still imbued with the Christian past and that the representatives of Christian thought were still able almost everywhere to make their voice heard in legislative assemblies. It remained for the totalitarian state of the anti-Christian stamp—the state which has deliberately, or at least as a matter of fact, broken every tie with a supreme divine law—to reveal to the world the true countenance of juridical positivism."[68]

The jurisprudence of all countries outside the totalitarian states is forced to choose one of two roads. Either it goes downwards to where they are now, or it takes the upward road and returns wholeheartedly to God. Staying where it is, it would be like a house which is divided against itself and therefore cannot stand.

There can be no return to individualism. But the remedy for individualism is not socialism. For, to borrow a homespun—or rather, home-cooked—figure from Frank Sheed, men are not "eggs with no higher fate than to merge their own personalities in some social omelette."[69] The trouble with individualism is not that it has picked up the wrong entity. In this human world there are no other substantial entities than individuals. The idea that society is a substantial whole is foreign (*pace* Gierke) to Christian thought.[70] Society is no organism. Nor does a people or a nation possess a soul, as Savigny has fancied.[71] The Catholic position is that society is an organization rather than an organism. The organization is for man, not man for the organization.

On the other hand, society is not a mere sum-total of individuals, nor a pure fiction, which is no more than a figment of imagination. It is not artificial, but natural, in the sense that it is rooted in the very nature of man. It has its functions and its laws, although these functions and laws are all ordained to the fullest development of the human person, who is made in the image of God.

The main trouble with individualism is that it lays emphasis on the individuality rather than the personality of man; on *matter*, which is the principle of individuation, rather than on *spirit*, which is the principle of harmony. The self-assertive will of the individual was developed to the full, while the nobler elements of human nature, such as reason, love and affection, consideration for others, sense of family unity and human solidarity were neglected. Individualism is not Christian any more than collectivism. Let us recall the words of St. Paul:

> For you, brethren, have been called unto liberty; only make not liberty an occasion to the flesh, but by charity of spirit serve one another.
> For all the law is fulfilled in one word, *Thou shalt love thy neighbor as thyself*. But if you bite and devour one another: take heed you be not consumed one of another (Gal. 5:13–15).

Dean Pound's righteous indignation over the ill effects of individualism was more than justified; but I respectfully submit that it is not quite fair to attribute individualism entirely to Puritanism. I think that Bentham's utilitarianism, Darwin's theory of natural selection, and Spencer's doctrine of *laissez-faire* were the more immediate and palpable influences in the formation of the individualistic jurisprudence of the nineteenth century, when Puritanism was constantly on the wane. In fact, the earlier judges like Wilson,

Marshall, Kent, Story, Livingston and Shaw were far more humanistic and balanced than many of the later judges.

Whatever one may say of the Puritans, it cannot be denied that their faith in God and in the teachings of Christ was sincere, and that they were not materialistic, but spiritually minded. Dean Pound quoted from Lord Acton that it appeared to the Puritans "that governments and institutions are made to pass away like things of earth, whilst souls are immortal; that there is no more proportion between liberty and power than between eternity and time; that, therefore, the sphere of enforced command ought to be restricted within fixed limits and that which has been done by authority and outward discipline and organized violence, should be attempted by division of power and committed to the intellect and the conscience of free men."[72]

But if all this is true, as I think it is, then they should rather be praised than blamed, for they verily built American democracy upon the rock of Christianity. Puritanism is not to be destroyed, but fulfilled.

It is very significant that during the last two decades Dean Pound has been warning, in season and out of season, against the dangers of too much government and the submergence of the individual in the bigness of things. Equally significant are the words of another sociological jurist, Justice Frankfurter, in the Steel-Seizure Case:[73]

A constitutional democracy like ours is perhaps the most difficult of man's social arrangements to manage successfully. Our scheme of society is more dependent than any other form of government on knowledge and wisdom and self-discipline for the achievement of its aims. For our democracy implies the reign of reason on the most extensive scale. The Founders of this Nation were not imbued with the modern cynicism that the only thing that history teaches is that it teaches nothing. They acted on the conviction that the experience of man sheds a good deal of light on his nature. It sheds a good deal of light not merely on the need for effective power, if a society is to be at once cohesive and civilized, but also on the need for limitations on the power of governors over the governed.

To that end they rested the structure of our central govern-

ment on the system of checks and balances. For them the doctrine of separation of powers was not mere theory; it was a felt
necessity. Not so long ago it was fashionable to find our system of checks and balances obstructive to effective government. It was easy to ridicule that system as outmoded—too
easy. The experience through which the world has passed in
our own day has made vivid the realization that the Framers
of our Constitution were not inexperienced doctrinaires.
These long-headed statesmen had no illusion that our people
enjoyed biological or psychological or sociological immuni-
ties from the hazards of concentrated power.

These spontaneous expressions on the part of two veterans of
the school of sociological jurisprudence show whither the wind is
blowing. It is up to the younger generation of jurists to build up a
truly fundamental philosophy of law by resorting to the very
fountains of the common law, the spirit and teachings of Christ. If
we are teleologically minded, let us not satisfy ourselves with anything short of the end which is also the beginning, the Omega who
is also the Alpha.

CHAPTER XXIV

THE LOGIC OF THE LOGOS

"For the Son of God, Jesus Christ . . . was not now 'Yes' and now 'No,' but only 'Yes' was in Him" (2 Cor. 1:19).

No one, I am sure, would call Christ a mere logician, any more than He was a mere professor of law. But the Logos simply could not help being logical in His thinking. For it is not possible for truth to contradict itself.

On one occasion the Pharisees, after they had witnessed the cure of a possessed man who was blind and dumb, remarked that Jesus was casting out devils by the power of Beelzebub, the prince of devils. That was a sheer contradiction and a blasphemy against the Spirit. So Christ told them, "Every kingdom divided against itself shall be made desolate, and every city or house divided against itself shall not stand. And if Satan cast out Satan, he is divided against himself; how then shall his kingdom stand?" (Matt. 12:25–6). He further said to them, "Either make the tree good and its fruit good; or make the tree bad and its fruit evil. For by the fruit the tree is known" (Matt. 12:33). He had also said to His disciples, "Beware of false prophets, who come to you in the clothing of sheep, but inwardly they are ravening wolves. By their fruits you shall know them. Do men gather grapes of thorns, or figs of thistles? Even so, every good tree bringeth forth good fruit, and the evil tree bringeth forth evil fruit. A good tree cannot bring forth evil fruit; neither can an evil tree bring forth good fruit" (Matt. 7:15–18).

Concerning this passage, I have a confession to make, which is not in my *Beyond East and West*. When I was in my early twenties, with my mind full of new-fangled pragmatism, I wrote to a friend that I had discovered the true founder of pragmatism in the person of Christ, and that the greatest pragmatist was not William James but St. James! Did Christ not judge everything in terms of its fruits or consequences? After many years of reflection, I came to realize that there is a world of difference between the ideas of Christ and pragmatism. To Christ, the tree is the starting point. To William James, the fruit is the tree. As he put it, "the truth of a proposition consists in its utility and satisfactoriness."[74] This is really a form of subjectivism which leads nowhere. Fortunately, James was a profounder man than his philosophy. Like any Irishman he was potentially a poet and full of practical common sense. Whenever he gave rein to his Celtic imagination, not attempting to confine reality within the conceptual ring-fence of a definition, he was capable of breaking through the enchanted circle of a self-imposed subjectivism and solipsism. The fact is that pragmatism, like the "cynical acid" of Justice Holmes, was a reaction against a barren conceptualism. As a dissolvent of conceptualism, it did perform a useful function. For, as Father Garrigou-Lagrange says, "Practical truth can co-exist with speculative error. Pragmatism can claim this partial truth."[75] But if we pay too much attention to the fruits, we shall be likely to forget the tree, and in the end there will be no more fruits. The important thing is take care of the tree, and the fruits will be good. Plant the tree near running waters, and it will bring forth its fruit in due season.[76]

How deeply I myself was steeped in the spirit of pragmatism can be gathered from the fact that I once turned the legal maxim *Ubi ius, ibi remedium* into *Ubi remedium, ibi ius*. Where there is a remedy or redress, there is a right! That is to say, whether you have a right depends upon whether the courts will give you redress against its violation. If they will not, then your right is unenforceable, and an unenforceable right is no more than the ghost of a right. That was my philosophy of law.

Does it not sound realistic to you? But when I myself became a judge, I found that the philosophy did not work! When I decided in favor of a plaintiff, I could not say to him, "You had a right, because I have given you redress"; I could only say to him, "I have given redress because you had a right." Similarly, when I decided against a plaintiff, I could not say, "You had no right because I have given you no redress"; I could only say, "I cannot give you redress because no right of yours was infringed." There is simply no way to get rid of a right antecedent to the remedy. The contours of a right are molded by its remedy, but not its inner kernel. It may not be too far-fetched to say that the right is like the tree, and the remedy is like the fruit. If we applied the logic of Christ, we should be brought back to sanity; for then we should see that both the right and the remedy exist and are important, that a remedy presupposes a right, that the right may be tested by the remedy, and that the remedy should be improved whenever necessary to insure a better protection of a right. Furthermore, just as the tree is rooted in the earth, so a true right is rooted in natural law and justice.

So long as we realize that jurisprudential truth rests on an order higher than itself, we can absorb all the seeds and grains of truth, goodness and beauty found in all systems of law and in all schools of philosophy, and all sciences and arts, without losing touch with Reality. Christ said, "My Father's house has many mansions." Moreover, each mansion has many storeys, infinitely more than the Empire State Building. For under the Supreme Reality, there are countless levels of reality, and a Christian philosopher must never shut his eyes to any level. What is good enough for God to create is good enough for us to study. In the words of His Holiness Pius XII, "Faith cannot but stamp with its seal the truth which the human mind discovers, considers and systematizes."

But of all studies, logic is the basis. So let me give another example of the use of logic by the Divine Logos. "By what authority do you do these things? And who gave you this authority?"[77] Thus did the chief priests and elders challenge His authority, and I do not blame them for that, because He had been cleansing the temple, which should have been a house of prayer, but which they had turned into a den of thieves. But how did He answer the challenge? Just like a great lawyer practising the art of cross-examination. He answered the question with a counter question. "I also will ask you one question," He said, "and if you answer me this, I in turn will tell you by what authority I do these things. Whence was the baptism of John? from heaven, or from men?" This question should have jerked them into an intellectual wakefulness, so that they could do some logical reasoning and think things through. But their minds were long closed and their hearts hardened. Their mental laziness and fear of consequences were too great for them to face the issue. So they consulted with one another, saying, "If we say, 'From heaven,' He will say to us, 'Why then did you not believe him?' If we say, 'From men,' we are afraid of the people, for all regard John as a prophet." Avoiding the logical issue, they took refuge in a "We don't know." One wonders if something of the same psychology is not at the back of modern agnosticism.

There can be no middle ground between God and Satan. You belong either to one or to the other. A different situation presents itself when we consider the relation between God and Caesar. Christ's solution of it is of capital importance for the students of Western political thought. The story is familiar, but it bears repeating. The chief priest and scribes were seeking a pretext for the arrest of Christ; they sent forth spies, who should pretend to be just men, that they might entrap Him in His talk and deliver Him up to the ruling power and to the authority of the procurator. "Master," the spies began, "we know that you speak and teach the truth, that you have no respect of persons, but teach the way of God as it is. Is it lawful for us to give tribute to Caesar, or is it not?" But knowing their craftiness, He said to them, "Why do you test me? Show me a denarius. Whose image and inscription does it bear?" "Caesar's," they answered. So He said to them, "Render, therefore, to Caesar the things that are Caesar's and to God the things that are God's." (See Luke 20:24–25.)

This, then, is the way of God as it is, and because it is the way of God it has produced wonderful fruits of religious liberty and orderly government wherever the plan is adopted. Around this simple precept of Christ, an immense literature has grown throughout the ages. But no one, to my knowledge, has presented its significance and effect better than the great historian Lord Acton:

> After the fourth century the declarations against slavery are earnest and continual. And in a theological but yet pregnant sense, divines of the second century insist on liberty, and divines of the fourth century on equality. There was one essential and inevitable transformation in politics. Popular governments had existed, and also mixed and federal governments, but there had been no limited government, no State the circumference of whose authority had been defined by a force external to its own. That was the great problem which philosophy had raised, and which no statesmanship had been able to solve. Those who proclaimed the existence of a higher authority had indeed drawn a metaphysical barrier before the governments, but they had not known how to make it real. All that Socrates could effect by way of protest against the tyranny of the reformed democracy was to die for his convictions. The Stoics could only advise the wise man to hold aloof from politics, keeping the unwritten law in his heart. But when Christ said: "Render unto Caesar the things that are Caesar's, and unto God the things that are God's," those words, spoken on His last visit to the Temple, three days before His death, gave to the civil power, under the protection of conscience, a sacredness it had never enjoyed, and bounds it had never acknowledged; and they were the repudiation of absolutism and the inauguration of freedom. For our Lord not only delivered the precept, but created the force to execute it. To maintain the necessary immunity in one supreme sphere, to reduce all political authority within defined limits, ceased to be an aspiration of patient reasoners, and was made the perpetual charge and care of the most energetic institution and the most universal association in the world. The new law, the new spirit, the new authority, gave to liberty a meaning and a value it had not possessed in the philosophy or in the constitution of Greece or Rome before the knowledge of the truth that makes us free.[78]

But no nation has carried out the precept of Christ more happily than America. The beginner cannot but note an apparent paradox in American jurisprudence. On the one hand, the population is predominantly Christian. On the other hand, the very first article of the Bill of Rights reads: *Congress shall make no law respecting an establishment of religion, or prohibiting the free exercise thereof.* Similar provisions are found in the state constitutions.

One wonders why these Christians, believing as they did that their Faith is the only salvation of the world, did not attempt to make Christianity the established religion of America.

The explanation is twofold: historical and theological. Historically the pioneers remembered only too well what had happened in England from the days of Henry VIII. Even in the eighteenth century the persecution of the dissenters had not ceased, although it had taken a more subtle form. For instance, according to the Test Act, all persons elected to municipal office must take a definite form of oath, incidentally acknowledging the King to be the Head of the Church of England, and if anyone elected should refuse to accept the office he would be subject to fine. The practice grew of electing wealthy dissenters to office, and when they declined to take the necessary oath, they were heavily fined. This became a substantial source of revenue. In a celebrated speech, Lord Mansfield denounced this vicious practice. "Conscience," he said, "is not controllable by human laws, nor amenable to human tribunals. Persecution, or attempts to force conscience, will never produce conviction, and are only calculated to make hypocrites or martyrs. . . . The common law of England, which is only common reason or usage, knows of no prosecution for mere opinions. . . . There is nothing certainly more unreasonable, more inconsistent with the rights of human nature, more contrary to the spirit and precepts of the Christian religion, more iniquitous and unjust, more impolitic than persecution. It is against Natural Religion, Revealed Religion and Sound Policy."[79]

This leads us to the theological explanation. Faith is a matter addressed to the reason and good will of man. Its life depends upon an inner conviction. To compel people to accept Christianity by the police force of the state would be propagating Christianity by an unchristian means.

There is an extremely significant, though often neglected, incident in one of Christ's journeys to Jerusalem. It came to pass, when the days had come for Him to be taken up, that He steadfastly set His face to go to Jerusalem, and sent messengers before Him. And they went and entered a Samaritan town to make ready for Him; and they did not receive Him, because His face was set for Jerusalem. But when His disciples James and John saw this, they said, "Lord, wilt thou that we bid fire come down from heaven and consume them?" But He turned and rebuked them, saying, "You do not know of what manner of spirit you are; for the Son of Man did not come to destroy men's lives, but to save them." And they turned to another village.[80] James and John became Saints later, but at that time their manner of spirit was anything but Christian, anything but democratic.

Yet, even in America, religious persecutions were rife in the seventeenth century. Religious freedom was not born without pains. All the different sects of Protestantism were at loggerheads with one another. Maryland was the first colony to establish by law an equal freedom for all Christians. To quote an interesting passage from James Kent: "The Catholic planters of Maryland procured for their adopted country the distinguished praise of being the first of the American states in which toleration was established by law; and while the Puritans were persecuting their Protestant brethren in New England, and the Episcopalians retorting the same severity on the Puritans in Virginia, the Catholics, against whom the others were combined, formed in Maryland a sanctuary, where all might worship and none might oppress, and where even Protestants sought refuge from Protestant intolerance."[81]

The question has often been asked if Christianity is a part of the common law. It depends upon what you mean by Christianity. If you mean a revealed religion, a Faith as defined by the Apostles' Creed, it is not a part of the common law in the sense that you are legally bound to believe in it. Christianity as a Faith comes into the courts, not as a law, but as a fact to be taken judicial notice of, on a par with other facts of common knowledge. On the other hand, if you mean by Christianity the fundamental moral precepts embodied in its teachings, it is a part of the common law in the sense that all the universal principles of justice written in the heart of every man are a part thereof. They are not enforced as specific rules of law but are applied as guiding principles whereby laws are made and cases decided.

One of the clearest expositions of the doctrine of separation of church and state is to be found in the majority opinion of Justice Douglas in *Zorach v. Clauson* (1952), 72 S.Ct. 679, the famous "released time" program case. There we shall see that separation of church and state is one thing, while a complete divorce of law from religion is quite another. Not only common sense but logic requires us to keep this important distinction clearly in mind. Let me quote some passages from this remarkable opinion:

> There cannot be the slightest doubt that the First Amendment reflects the philosophy that Church and State be separated. And so far as interference with the "free exercise" of religion and an "establishment" of religion are concerned, the separation must be complete and unequivocal. The First Amendment within the scope of its coverage permits no exception; the prohibition is absolute. The First Amendment, however, does not say that in every and all respects there shall be a separation of Church and State. Rather, it studiously defines the manner, the specific ways, in which there shall be no concert or union or dependency one on the other. That is the common sense of the matter. Otherwise the state and religion would be aliens to each other—hostile, suspicious, and even unfriendly. Churches could not be required to pay even property taxes. Municipalities would not be permitted to render police or fire protection to religious groups. Policemen who helped parishioners into their places of worship would violate the Constitution. Prayers in our legislative halls; the appeals to the Almighty in the messages of the Chief executive; the proclamation making Thanksgiving Day a holiday; "so help me God" in our courtroom oath—these and all other references to the Almighty that run through our laws, our public rituals, our ceremonies would be flouting the First Amendment. A fastidious atheist or agnostic could even object to the supplication with which the Court opens each session: "God save the United States and this Honorable Court. . . ."
>
> We are a religious people whose institutions presuppose a Supreme Being. We guarantee the freedom to worship as one chooses. We make room for as wide a variety of beliefs and

creeds as the spiritual needs of man deem necessary. We sponsor an attitude on the part of government that shows no partiality to any one group and that lets each flourish according to the zeal of its adherents and the appeal of its dogma. When the state encourages religious instruction or cooperates with religious authorities by adjusting the schedule of public events to sectarian needs, it follows the best of our traditions. For it then respects the religious nature of our people and accommodates the public service to their spiritual needs. To hold that it may not would be to find in the Constitution a requirement that the government show a callous indifference to religious groups. That would be preferring those who believe in no religion over those who do believe. Government may not finance religious groups nor undertake religious instruction nor blend secular and sectarian education nor use secular institutions to force one or some religion on any person. But we find no constitutional requirement which makes it necessary for government to be hostile to religion and to throw its weight against efforts to widen the effective scope of religious influence. The government must be neutral when it comes to competition between sects. It may not thrust any sect on any person. It may not make a religious observance compulsory. It may not coerce anyone to attend church, to observe a religious holiday, or to take religious instruction. But it can close its doors or suspend its operations as to those who want to repair to their religious sanctuary for worship or instruction. No more than that is undertaken here.

CHAPTER XXV

NATURE AND GRACE

"For the law was given by Moses, grace and truth came by Jesus Christ" (John 1:17).

So far we have viewed the juridical teachings of Christ almost entirely in the light of natural reason. But a question may arise in the mind of the reader. If it is merely as a body of precepts of natural law that Christianity becomes a constitutive part of human law, and if these precepts are but self-evident principles of justice written in the heart of every human being, wherein, then, is its peculiar contribution to jurisprudence? For, even without Christianity, a philosophy of law based purely on natural reason would serve the purpose just as well. For instance, in that interesting "Queue Case,"[82] where Justice Field denounced an ordinance as being "not creditable to the humanity and civilization of our people, much less to their Christianity," he was evidently thinking of the American ideal of fairness and referring to the golden rule of the Gospel. But he could just as well have cited the golden rule of Confucius: "Whatever you do not desire for yourself must not be inflicted upon another."[83] In fact, this negative form of the golden rule would seem to be of more immediate applicability to questions of human law, which, by reason of its intrinsic limits as well as by considerations of prudence, is more directly concerned with the avoidance of evil than with the pursuit of goodness. The introduction of Christianity into judicial opinions would, therefore, seem more rhetoric than logic, more rhyme than reason.

Now, this question goes very deep. It is true that, theoretically, man can arrive at the notion of the natural law by following the light of natural reason, with which he is endowed by God. Plato, Aristotle and Cicero had expounded the doctrine of natural law with varying degrees of perfection. Confucianism had attained to a vision of the natural law which comes even nearer to that of the Christians. This is no place to write about Confucianism. Let one quotation from the Confucian classic *The Golden Mean* suffice: "What is ordained by Heaven is called essential nature. Conformity to the essential nature is called the natural law. The refinement of the natural law is called culture."[84]

It is remarkable how closely this statement corresponds to St. Thomas' philosophy of law, which sees the eternal law, the natural law and human law as forming a continuous series. "What is ordained by Heaven" is the plan of Divine Providence, which is another name for the eternal law. "Conformity to the essential nature" corresponds to what St. Thomas calls "participation in the eternal law by the rational creature," and this conformity or participation is the natural law. The refinement of the natural law is the task of culture, which includes human law and manners.

The coincidence between Thomist and Confucian ideas shows that St. Thomas, in treating of the law, did not go beyond the sphere of natural reason, because Confucius and his disciples had reached practically the same conclusions about the natural law being the bridge between the eternal law and human law, without the aid of the light of revelation.

The moral precepts of the Old Testament belong to the natural law not because of revelation, but because they can be known through the light of natural reason. Revelation only confirms them more explicitly. This is borne out by an interesting entry in the journals of the famous Jesuit missionary to China, Matthew Ricci. He wrote: "Copies of the Commandments were printed in Chinese and given out to all who asked for them. Many who received them said they would live in the future according to these command-

ments, because, as they claimed, they were in such accord with the
voice of conscience and with the natural law. Their reverence for
the Christian law increased with their admiration for it."[85]

Nothing brings out the essential unity of mankind more clearly
than the fact that in fundamental principles the peoples of all races
and all stages of civilization are in substantial agreement.

But if this is the case, the question of the relevancy of Christianity
to jurisprudence appears all the more challenging. The answer to
the question is twofold: first as regards the intellect and secondly
as regards the will. But it should at once be admitted that the question brings us to the borderland between reason and faith.

It is of faith that, as a consequence of the Fall of man, human
nature has been so damaged that the intellect is darkened by the
passions, and its vision of the natural order and law is not only
limited but blurred and in some points distorted. Moreover, when
certain human conventions have grown into a respectable tradition,
people are apt to consider them as sacred doctrines. What is merely
familiar and customary often appears to the ordinary man as an
integral part of the immutable order of nature. To take an example
from my personal experience, in my childhood days women still
followed the custom of foot-binding. My eyes were so accustomed
to the spectacle of the beautiful, lily-like feet that when occasionally I saw a lady from the country with a pair of natural feet, I
would burst out laughing and tell it as "news." For the natural feet
looked as unnatural as the unnatural feet looked natural. So easily
could one's judgment be warped by conventions!

Moral precepts, it is true, are not so changeable as the fashions
of beauty. The basic principles of justice, such as that it is wrong
to slay the innocent, to sell justice, to give a judgment without an
examination of the facts, to injure another deliberately and without
cause, and so forth, are universally recognized. But other principles,
such as that of the equality of men and that of monogamy, may not
be so clear to all, and yet these too belong to the law of nature. The
function of the moral precepts as embodied in the Old Law is to
readjust man's defective vision to the landscape of the natural order.
Without the light of revelation, even sages like Confucius and Aristotle could not see the whole landscape clearly. Notwithstanding

certain infused lights they might have received from God, their vision was somewhat like that of the man who, after being cured of blindness, lifted his eyes and saw men like trees walking.[86] Here again I want to borrow an observation from Frank Sheed. "If we were supremely good thinkers," he said in his *Communism and Man,* "the result would be true as far as it went. But it would not go all the way, for . . . God has a purpose for man higher than man's nature can of itself attain."[87]

Concerning the need of the Divine law to reaffirm the moral precepts which belong to the natural law, St. Thomas has made the relation crystal-clear. "It was eminently fitting," he said, "that the Divine law should come to man's aid not only in those things which are beyond the reach of reason, but also in those things in which human reason may be impeded. So far as the universal principles of the natural law are concerned, human reason could not go astray in the abstract; but through being habituated to sin, it became obscured when it came to consider what particular things should be done in a concrete situation. Besides, with regard to the other moral precepts, which are, so to speak, conclusions drawn from the universal principles of the natural law, the reason of many men went astray, to the extent of judging certain things lawful which are intrinsically evil. Hence it was important to save man from both these defects by the authority of the Divine law. Thus among the articles of faith are set forth not only those things which are beyond the reach of reason, for instance, that God is Triune; but also those things to which right reason can attain, for instance, that God is One. This is done in order to remove the manifold errors to which reason is liable."[88]

If human reason is weak, human will is weaker. Even if we should know the whole of the natural law, we shall still fall far short of it in action, or even rebel against it as Lucifer did and become Satan, if we do not depend upon sanctifying and actual graces from God. As St. Thomas said, "In the state of corrupted nature man cannot fulfill all the Divine commandments without healing grace."[89] This is why immediately upon the heels of his treatise on law follows the treatise on grace. The two treatises are distinct, but not separate. They must be studied together as parts of the whole picture. For a Christian to be satisfied with a mere philosophy of the natural law and to consider faith as beyond his specialized field is to prefer the old wine to the new, saying, "The old is better." Let him heed the warning of St. Paul: "Take care not to let anyone cheat you with his philosophizings, with empty phantasies drawn from human tradition and worldly principles, which were never the teachings of Christ." Let him remember that faith comprehends reason, while reason does not comprehend faith. Specialization is the bane of modern civilization; and when it is carried into things of the spirit it is simply fatal.

A Christian must not judge others by the measure of his own faith, but he must judge himself by this yardstick, and he need not be ashamed of the Gospel. When a Christian lawyer expounds his philosophy of law to a non-Christian, he should try to confine himself as much as in him lies to natural reason and the facts of experience, and not require the other party to assume his faith; but at the same time he can avail himself of the right of free speech by frankly acknowledging his own faith and, if the listener is willing to hear, expounding his philosophy of law from the standpoint of his faith. He should be careful to steer between the Scylla of imposing his faith upon others, as though it were a matter of logical reasoning so that it would be irrational to reject it, and the Charybdis of refraining altogether from speaking about it, as though faith were entirely irrelevant to the science of law.

The relevance of the Christian faith to law can be proved empirically by the history of jurisprudence. When I compare the jurisprudence of non-Christian nations with the jurisprudence of the Christian nations, I cannot help observing that the latter is decidedly superior in quality. For one thing, there is a far greater respect for the dignity of man as man. Let one example suffice. The historian of English law, Theodore Plucknett, has told us that "the Church brought with it moral ideas which were to revolutionize English law." "Christianity," he continues, "had inherited from Judaism an outlook upon moral questions which was strictly individualistic. The salvation of each separate soul was dependent upon the actions of the individual. This contrasted strongly with the custom of the English tribes which looked not to the individual but the family group of which the individual formed a part. Necessarily such a system had little place for an individualistic sense of morals, for the group can hardly be credited with moral intention in the sense that an individual can. With the spread of Christianity all this slowly changed. First, responsibility for actions gradually shifted from the whole group to the particular individual who did the act; and then the Church (and later the law) will judge that act, if necessary, from the point of view of the party who committed it."[90] Plucknett is using the epithet "individualistic" in a good sense, but in view of its other, not-so-good connotations, I would prefer the word "*personalistic.*"

But there can be no question about the general accuracy of his observation. As Bracton said, "It is the intention that fixes the character of an act."[91] So had the Christian emperor Justinian declared, "*Actus non facit reum nisi mens sit rea.*" (No act can constitute a crime without guilt in the mind.)[92] This personalization and inwardization of criminal responsibility can be traced, at least indirectly, to the influence of the teachings of Christ, "Do you not realize that nothing entering a man from outside can defile him? . . . For it is from within, out of the heart of man, that come evil thoughts, adulteries, immorality, murders, thefts, covetousness, wickedness, deceit, shamelessness, jealousy, blasphemy, pride, foolishness. All these evil things come from within, and defile a man" (Mark 7:18, 21–23). It is truly a marvel to observe that collective responsibility, unreasonable as it is, was such a universal phenomenon in the history of comparative jurisprudence; but wherever Christianity made its advent, this formidable citadel either collapsed suddenly or yielded gradually to its more or less humanizing influence.

As to the doctrine of *mens rea*, although it is more or less known to the legal systems of all civilized nations, yet it has been carried out more effectively in Christian countries. Incidentally I wish to mention that in America there has arisen in the recent past a dangerous tendency of basing criminal responsibility upon public welfare or the balance of interests.[93] But it has been checked by prominent jurists like Francis B. Sayre and Jerome Hall, whose works have been cited by the late Justice Jackson of the Supreme Court of the

United States in an excellent opinion in *Morissette v. U.S.*[94] This case marks one of the strong trends of contemporary jurisprudence —the redoubled emphasis on the element of *mens rea.*

The most remarkable influence of Christianity is to be seen in the attitude of the judges toward the political sovereign. They put the law above the state and the government. They have no respect of persons, because they have equal respect for all persons. They neither look up to their superiors to see what would be their pleasure, nor lord it over the parties before them. Speaking of the Puritans, Justice Holmes had this to say: "Whether they knew it or not, they planted the democratic spirit in the heart of man. It is to them we owe the deepest cause we have to love our country, that instinct, that spark that makes the American unable to meet his fellow man otherwise than simply as a man, eye to eye, hand to hand, foot to foot, wrestling naked on the sand."[95]

If we go a step further, we shall see that those Puritans had drunk in this spirit of true democracy from its very fountainhead. How often they must have pondered the words of their Divine Master: "You know that the rulers of the Gentiles lord it over them, and their great exercise their authority over them. Not so is it among you. On the contrary, whoever wishes to become great among you shall be your servant; and whoever wishes to be first among you shall be your slave; even as the Son of Man has not come to be served, but to serve, and to give his life as a ransom for many" (Matt. 20:25–8).

Starting from the Fatherhood of God and the brotherhood of men, the Christian jurists of all ages have with one voice denounced tyranny, and succeeded in bridling the powers of the political sovereign. True, Mencius had justified the right of revolution by saying that a tyrant is no king, but a mere fellow.[96] But Bracton went even further. For him, the power of the king is a power to do justice, not to do injustice. If he does justice, he is a servant of God. If he deviates into the path of lawlessness, he becomes "a servant of the devil!"[97] No pagan writer, to my knowledge, has ever written in this way about a king. The best jurists and judges in Christendom are in the direct tradition of the Apostles, who said in their matter-of-fact way, "We must obey God rather than men."[98] Without this foundation the reign of law is not possible.

Richard Hooker's words sound perennially fresh to the lovers of the law: "Of law there can be no less acknowledged, than that her seat is the bosom of God, her voice the harmony of the world; all things in heaven and earth do her homage, the very least as feeling her care, and the greatest as not exempted from her power."[99] If this is considered a mere rhetorical flourish, and not a sober statement of one aspect of Reality, then all talk about the Rule of Law would be no more than empty propaganda—if not a bogus check. But it cannot be denied that in the common-law countries the Rule of Law has been realized to a remarkable degree.

One robin does not make a spring; but in America there are countless voices uttering their conviction of the reign of law. There is Magistrate Shapiro, for example, of the City Magistrate's Court of New York,[100] who, in holding that to fall asleep on a subway train was not disorderly conduct, announced some of the greatest principles of American jurisprudence. "If these defendants are vagrants, they should be tried as such . . . but to let them plead guilty to disorderly conduct, when no such offense is involved, merely because they are not protected by counsel and because they are perhaps regarded by some as 'zeros' on the human scale would make a mockery of justice." There are no zeros in American law, nor is there any person who counts for more than one. "These defendants, by all appearances, are derelicts, but they are human souls whose rights may not be trampled on."

I am happy to see the magistrate use the word "souls," because the dignity of man is founded on the immortal soul that he bears within him. Hitler did not believe in the existence of the immortal soul, and under his dictatorship human beings were treated worse than animals are treated in this country. But to return to Magistrate Shapiro, there is a delightful touch of humor and personal candor at one point in his magnificent opinion. "It is common knowledge," he said, "that many persons fall asleep on trains. Would that mean that they are ipso facto guilty of disorderly conduct? If so, many of our citizens who use the rapid transit facilities of our City must at least once in their lives have been guilty of disorderly conduct, and this Court must confess that if sleeping on a train be the test, he is a confirmed violator of the statutes against disorderly conduct."

A Chinese proverb has it, "Although the yamen [Magistrate's Court] is small, the law is great." This is literally true in America. The strength of the judicial system here lies especially in the solid quality of the judges of the lower courts. Even where occasionally a judge does not act up to the standard of the tradition, he is immediately corrected in a higher court.

The artless candor of the American comes from an open mind and a generous heart. As a rule, a Christian has fewer inhibitions than a pagan, because the truth has made him free, and he has nothing to fear except his own sin. While I am on this subject, an interesting witchcraft case decided by Lord Holt swims through my mind. It is well known that Holt was something of an Augustine in the early part of his life. When he was a student at Oxford, so Edward Foss tells us, "he is reputed to have been notorious for his idleness and for his association with dissolute companions, who led him into every kind of licence and extravagance. Some tales that were subsequently related of him give probability to the report of his juvenile delinquency; but he soon saw the error of his ways, deserted his old haunts and associates, left the university without taking a degree, and applied himself diligently, under the tuition of his father, to that profession of which he was destined to be one of the brightest ornaments."[101]

Felix culpa! For Almighty God, who alone could draw good out of evil, made use of that prodigal son to do away with the horrible persecutions and prosecutions of the witches, which were such a black spot on English law. I will let Foss tell the story. "Among the anecdotes that have reference to his early follies is the following, which shows that he did not hesitate to acknowledge them when the confession would serve the ends of justice. In a trial of an old woman for witchcraft, the witness against her declared that she used a 'spell.' 'Let me see it,' said the judge. A scrap of parchment being handed to him, he asked the woman how she came by it, and on her answering, 'A gentleman, my lord, gave it to me to cure my daughter's ague,' enquired whether it cured her. 'Oh! yes, my lord, and many others,' replied the old woman. He then turned to the jury and said, 'Gentlemen, when I was young and thoughtless, and out of money, I and some companions, as unthinking as myself, went to this woman's house, then a public one, and having no money to pay our reckoning, I hit upon the stratagem to get off scot-free. Seeing her daughter ill of an ague, I pretended I had a spell to cure her. I wrote the classic line you see, and gave it to her, so that if any one is punishable, it is I, and not the poor woman.' She was of course acquitted, and did not fail to receive from the judge a compensation for the trouble he had caused her. In none of the trials before him for this supposed crime was a conviction obtained, and prosecutions for it from his time fell into discredit, which was increased by his putting into the pillory one Hathaway, convicted of pretending to be witched by a poor woman whom he had recently indicted for the crime."[102]

I confess I am simply bewitched by this wizard of the common law. At his best he fulfilled almost to perfection Christ's counsel of being wise as a serpent and innocent as a dove.

The other great wizard of the common law is Lord Mansfield, who made a most revealing confession, not from the Bench, but in a private conversation with the famous Shakespearean player Garrick. "My dear Garrick," he said, "a judge on the bench is now and then in your whimsical situation between tragedy and comedy; inclination drawing one way, and a long string of precedents the other."[103]

There is a popular misconception about the legal profession. The layman thinks that to be a legal expert all that one needs is a good head. A good head is important, but a good heart is infinitely more so. In fact, Monsignor John L. McNulty once remarked to me, "A good heart is worth all the brains in the world." Of course, he did not mean that brains are of no use. He was only making an axiological statement. My own view is that the head has been too exclusively emphasized in legal education. The heart too must be cultivated. The hard-hearted are far from justice. I have not known of a great judge or lawyer without a great heart. The head and the heart are like husband and wife. When they live harmoniously together, you have a happy home. When they conflict, or when one of them domineers over the other, it is no home but hell. Normally, the husband is the head of the family, and the wife is the heart. But the heart is the power behind the throne. It cannot take the place of the head, but when the heart is full of love, the head will be full of wisdom. Would Portia have been so ingenious and resourceful if she were not in love?[104] The heart quickens and stimulates the head into activity. Without a good heart, the head works mechanically and weaves out barren concepts unrelated to the purpose of all law, the rendering of justice. The trouble with the legal Pharisees is not that they are not brainy enough, but that certain false theories of law which they have imbibed in youth inhibit the heart to the point of atrophy.

Juridical positivism which attributes all authority to the state and reduces the manifold sources of the law to the one single stream of legislation has placed the law and the judicial function in a false perspective. When the starting point is wrong, everything else is wrong, except when one accidentally forgets about one's theory. Unless the jurist remembers that justice is the sole purpose of law and love is the fulfillment of justice, he may be a master of legal technicalities but he does not really know the law. But on the whole the common law judges have adhered, whether consciously or unconsciously, to the sound tradition. As George Constable has very keenly observed, "The heart's inarticulate feeling for the middle solution of natural law leads to many court decisions which, in the name of equity or reason or natural justice and decency, use the natural law not falsely to rationalize but correctly to justify."[105]

I have said elsewhere in this book that the common law was not only founded on justice but rooted in grace. What I meant was that the judges have been Christians, or at least have imbibed more or less unconsciously the atmosphere of a Christian civilization. In this sense I think it is fairly accurate to say that the common law has its roots in grace. But when I called the Roman law a deathbed convert, I had in mind only the law of ancient Rome as summed up in the *Corpus Juris Civilis*. I did not have in mind the Continental development of it. Recently, I was thrilled to find a very wonderful description, by His Holiness Pius XII himself, of the contact and fructification between the old law and the new spirit. After relating how the Roman law and the Christian Church survived the decline and fall of the Roman Empire, he said:

> Thus it was that in Rome and in the world leavened by its civilization these two vital realities—one the fruit of the legal wisdom of a people and thus of human origin, the other a radiation from the world of revelation announced by the Son of God made Man and as such of transcending and Divine origin —met and fused with an intimate bond; through this bond the law of Rome, penetrated with the new light emanating from the Christian message, was transformed in spirit. It was elevated in its conceptions and perfected in many of its institutions. It was enriched in its dispositions, receiving gradually the principles, ideas and higher requirements of the new doctrine. Legislative works of Christian emperors were born of this fertile union of human knowledge and Divine wisdom, of which there remain traces so indelible that they demonstrate to the modern world how between true juridical science and the teaching of the Christian faith there is no opposition but concord, because Faith cannot but stamp with its seal the truth which the human mind discovers, and considers and systematizes.[106]

Here again we find nature and grace working together. But is it not significant that the two greatest systems of jurisprudence in the world should both have been pupils in the school of Christ? These systems, the common law and the Continental law, furnish the most fascinating subjects for comparison. They are similar in that both nature and grace have co-operated in their making. And yet there is an important difference. With the common law, which I have called a "cradle Christian," natural wisdom and the Christian influence grew hand and hand in the course of the centuries. With the Continental law, on the other hand, natural wisdom had reached a high degree of maturity before grace began to work upon it. This is perhaps why the common law is instinctively Christian, while the Continental law is rationally Christian. Both have their great qualities. One possesses classical beauty, the other romantic charm. But I, being a convert like the Continental law, am especially attracted by the enviable qualities of the cradle Christian who has Christianity running, as it were, in the blood.

I cannot conclude this study of the Judge of judges better than by quoting from His living Vicar a glorious passage expounding Ulpian's definition of jurisprudence ("The knowledge of things human and Divine, the science of what is just and unjust"), and at the same time illuminating and vitalizing it with the light and fire of the Spirit. On the first part of the definition the Holy Father comments:

> What a noble objective he assigns to juridical science in this definition and how high he raises it above all other branches of human knowledge! The gaze of the jurist worthy of the name sweeps over the broadest horizon, whose fullness and variety are indicated by the very things to which he must give his attention and study. He must know, above all, Divine things (*divinarum rerum notitia*), not only because in human social life religion must have first place and direct the practical conduct of the believer, for whom law, too, must prescribe her standards: not only because some of the principal institutions, such as matrimony, have a sacred character which law cannot ignore: but above all because without the higher knowledge of Divine things, the human panorama, which is the second, more immediate object (*humanarum rerum notitia*) which the mind of the jurist must dwell on, would remain without that foundation which is beyond every human vicissitude in time and space and rests in the absolute in God.
>
> No doubt, the jurist is not called upon by his profession to dedicate himself to theological speculation in order to know his subject. But if he is incapable of rising to the vision of the highest transcendent Reality, from Whose will is derived the order of the visible universe and of his own small portion which is the human race with its inherent and morally necessary laws, it will be impossible for him to perceive, in all its marvelous unity and its intimate spiritual depth, the interlacing of social relations (over which law presides) and their regulative norms.[107]

Addressing himself to the second part of the definition, the Holy Father says:

> Justice is not only an abstract concept, an external ideal, to which legal institutions must seek to conform themselves as

far as possible in a given historical moment; it is also and above all something immanent to man, to society, to its fundamental institutions, by virtue of that body of practical principles which it dictates and imposes, and by virtue of those more universal norms of conduct which form part of the objective human and civil order established by the perfect mind of the First Maker.

The science of the just and unjust supposes, therefore, a higher wisdom which consists in knowing the intrinsic order of the thing created and consequently its Ordainer. Law, as Aquinas taught, is the object of justice (*est objectum justitiae*). It is the norm in which the great and fruitful idea of justice becomes concrete and real, and as such leads to God, eternal and immutable Justice in its essence: from God it receives light and clearness, vigor and strength, meaning and content.

The jurist, then, in the exercise of his profession moves between the finite and the Infinite, between the Divine and the human, and in this necessary movement lies the nobility of the science he cultivates.[108]

In other words, the jurist is to be by grace what his Divine Master is by nature!

NOTES

1. *Theology and Sanity*, p. 109.
2. *S. T.*, I–II, 93. 1. *ad* 2.
3. See in *A Commentary on the New Testament* (Catholic Biblical Association, 1942), the comments under Matthew 23:13–39.
4. Bracton, *De legibus et consuetudinibus Angliae*, fols, 1b and 2.
5. Holmes, *The Common Law* (Little & Brown, 1881), p. 44.
6. (1910) 179 Fed. 997.
7. Luke 2:52.
8. Maine, *Ancient Law* (introduction by Pollock, 1920), p. 80.
9. Ephes. 4:13.
10. Rooney, *Lawlessness, Law, and Sanction*, p. 104.
11. *Ibid.*, p. 110.
12. *Ibid.*, p. 111.
13. *Perez v. Lippold* (1948) 198 P. 2d 17.
14. *Ibid.*, at 18–19.
15. *Ibid.*, at 30. See Acts 17:26.

16. *Ibid.*, at 34.
17. *Bush v. Mockett* (1914), 95 Neb. 552, 145 N.W. 1001.
18. "So to use your own as not to injure another."
19. 145 N.W. 1001–1002.
20. *Barger v. Barringer,* 151 C.C. 433, 66 S.E. 439.
21. 66 S.E. 442.
22. 174 F. 2d 838, at 840.
23. It often happens that in departing from a specific rule, the American judges cite English jurists who have criticized it severely.
24. Take, for instance, Judge Story's opinion in *Bright v. Boyd* (1 Story 478), where in the absence of a common-law precedent, Continental authorities were liberally quoted. This is in the tradition of Lord Holt and Lord Mansfield.
25. John 18:11.
26. Judge Hart in *Stockton Plumbing & Supply Co. v. Wheeler,* 68 Cal. App. 592, 229 P. 1020, at 1024.
27. *Donoghue v. Stevenson* (1932) L.R., A.C. 562.
28. *Ibid.*, at 580.
29. Acts 25.
30. Cardozo, *The Nature of the Judicial Process* (Yale, 1921) pp. 41–3.
31. *Neiman v. Hurff,* 93 A. 2d 345, at 347.
32. Pound, "A Hundred Years of American Law," in *Law: A Century of Progress,* Vol. 1, p. 8.
33. 129 Ohio St. 432, 195 N.E. 838.
34. *Ohio State Law Journal,* Vol. 12 (1951), 4.
35. Frank, *Fate and Freedom* (Simon and Schuster, 1945), p. 295.
36. *Van Winkle v. American Steam-Boiler Ins. Co.* (1890), 52 N.J.L. 240, 19 A. 472.
37. *De legibus,* fol. 1b.
38. *Fox v. Snow* (1950), 76 A. 2d 877, at 882.
39. *Woods v. Lancet* (1951), 303 N.Y. 349, 102 N.E. 2d 691 at 694.
40. Seavey, "Candler v. Crane, Christmas & Co.: Negligent Misrepresentation by Accountants," *Law Quarterly Review,* Vol. 67 (1951), p. 468.
41. (1941) A.C. 1, 29.
42. M.-J Lagrange, *Evangile selon Saint Marc* (Paris, 1929), note 11 on pp. 185–6.
43. 7 Co. Rep. 1, 77 Eng. Rep. 377 (K.B. 1610).
44. Holmes, *Collected Legal Papers,* p. 186.
45. *Dennis v. U.S.,* 341 U.S. 494, 508.
46. Vanderbilt, *The Doctrine of the Separation of Powers and Its Present-Day Significance* (University of Nebraska, 1953), p. 49.
47. *De legibus,* fol. 1b.
48. *Ibid.*

49. *The Institutes of Justinian*, trans. by J. B. Moyle, 3d ed. (Oxford, 1896), p. 197.
50. Quoted by Chief Justice Shepherd of the Supreme Court of North Carolina in *Edwards v. Culbertson* (1892).
51. *The Works of Mencius.*
52. The idea of balance occupies a very important place in the Confucian moral philosophy. Confucius himself once said, "Some students are willing to learn with you, but you cannot expect them to stand with you on the principles. Others will stand with you on principles, but do not understand the importance of balance."
53. Quoted by O'Sullivan in his *The King's Good Servant*, pp. 18–19.
54. Manson, *Builders of Our Law During the Reign of Queen Victoria*, 2d ed. (Horace Cox, 1904), p. 101. Judge Dillon has testified to the same truth in his *Laws and Jurisprudence of England and America* (Boston, 1894), pp. 17–18.
55. This utterance presents a supreme example of balance and proportion.
56. The fusion or merger of law and equity does not abolish the distinction between legal rights and legal remedies, on the one hand, and equitable rights and equitable remedies on the other. It only means the vesting of the powers of awarding legal and equitable remedies in the same court. The court has two sets of remedies at its disposal, and exercises a wide discretion as to which kind of relief to apply to a particular case in the light of its circumstances and with a view to doing substantial justice.
57. *A Concise History of the Common Law*, p. 609.
58. Maitland, *Equity* (*Cambridge*, 1936), p. 17.
59. William Roper, *The Life of Sir Thomas More*, ed. by E. V. Hitchcock, pp. 44–5.
60. See Chambers, *Thomas More*, p. 271.
61. Aside from European writers such as De Tocqueville, Boutmy, and James Bryce, I was told by Archbishop Thomas Boland that he had read a book of memoirs written by a Chinese diplomat in America in the nineteenth century, who traced the strength of America to Christianity.
62. Holland, *Jurisprudence*, 11th ed. (Oxford, 1910), p. 40.
63. Pound, *Law and Religion*, Rice Institute Pamphlet No. 28 (April, 1940), 109 at 144. See also *The Spirit of the Common Law*, p. 43.
64. *Ibid.*, p. 45.
65. *Ibid.*, p. 44.
66. *Ibid.*, p. 58.
67. These words apply to Morley, not to Pound.
68. "Law and Conscience" (November 13, 1949). See Pius XII, *Discorsi agli Intellettuali: 1939–1954*, pp. 211–12.

69. *Communism and Man*, p. 201.
70. Dr. Friedman, in his *Legal Theory* (2d ed., Stevens, 1949), makes the observation that "the Catholic theory of society makes the community supreme over the individual" (p. 430). In this I think he has been misled by Gierke, who had projected his own collectivistic and organismic interpretation of society upon medieval thought. Professor Ewart Lewis has presented a more objective picture. In his article on "Organic Theories in Medieval Thought," in *American Political Science Review*, October 1938, he wrote: "In short, on this question of the ends of groups and the ends of individuals I have been unable to find any evidence which clearly supports Gierke's interpretation, and on the contrary, considerable evidence to support De Wulf's contention that medieval thinkers recognized no destiny except the destiny of individuals, assigned no purpose to the State or other social groups except the service of individual ends, and understood the 'common good' as equivalent to the good of a totality of individuals." See also an excellent paper by Andrew Beck, A.A., on "The Common Good in Law and Legislation" in O'Sullivan's *The King's Good Servant*, pp. 71 ff.
71. To Savigny (1779–1861), the *Volksgeist* ("folk-soul") is the sole source of all laws and customs of a people. That a people has a soul of its own, over and above the souls of the individual persons, is a sheer myth on a par with Hegel's exaltation of the Prussian State as the embodiment of the Absolute.
72. *The Spirit of the Common Law*, p. 46.
73. *Youngstown Sheet & Tube Co. v. Sawyer* (1952), 72 S.Ct. 863, at 888–9.
74. Quoted in Garrigou-Lagrange, *Reality* (Herder, 1950), pp. 378–9.
75. *Ibid.*, p. 385.
76. Ps. 1.
77. See Matt. 21:23–7.
78. Acton, *Essay on Freedom and Power* (Beacon Press, Boston, 1949), pp. 56–7.
79. Holliday, *Life of Lord Mansfield*, 260–1.
80. See Luke 9:51–5.
81. Kent, *Commentaries on American Law*, 12th ed. by O. W. Holmes, Jr., vol. I, pp. 35–7.
82. *Ho Ah Kow v. Nunan* (1879), 5 Sawy. 552, 12 Fed. Cas. 253.
83. *The Analects of Confucius*.
84. *The Chung Yung*, I. 1. (*The Doctrine of the Golden Mean*).
85. *China in the Sixteenth Century: The Journals of Matthew Ricci: 1583–1610*, trans. by Louis J. Gallagher, S.J. (Random House, 1953), p. 155.
86. Mark 8:28.

87. P. 150.
88. *S. T.*, I–II, 99. 2. *ad* 2.
89. *Ibid.*, 109. 4. *in corp.*
90. Plucknett, *A Concise History of the Common Law*, pp. 8–9.
91. *De legibus*, fol. 2b.
92. *Institutes*, Vol. III, p. 107.
93. See F. B. Sayre, "Public Welfare Offences," *Columbia Law Review*, Vol. 33, p. 55. Jerome Hall, "Prolegomena to a Science of Criminal Law," *University of Pennsylvania Law Review*, Vol. 89, p. 549.
    These writers maintain that while civil liabilities may be based in some cases on considerations of public welfare, apart from personal fault, criminal responsibility, except for the most trifling cases, must always be based upon fault. See also Stallybrass, "The Eclipse of Mens Rea," *Law Quarterly Review*, Vol. 52 (1936), pp. 60–1.
94. 342 U.S. 246 (1951).
95. "The Puritan," a speech delivered February 12, 1886, on the 250th Anniversary of the First Church in Cambridge. See *Speeches by Oliver Wendell Holmes* (Boston, 1900), p. 20.
96. *The Works of Mencius.*
97. *De legibus*, fol. 107b.
98. Acts 5:29; 4:9–20.
99. *Ecclesiastical Polity*, Book I, Sec. 16.
100. *People v. Sustek* (1953), 724 N.Y.S. 2d 641.
101. Foss, *A Biographical Dictionary of the Judges of England: 1066–1870* (London, 1870), pp. 351–2.
102. *Ibid.*, pp. 353–4.
103. Holdsworth, *Some Makers of English Law*, p. 170.
104. *Merchant of Venice*, Act VI. The point is that a judge who loves justice as much as Portia loved Antonio will naturally be more ingenious than one who does not.
105. George W. Constable, "What Does Natural Law Jurisprudence Offer?", *The Catholic University of America Law Review*, Vol. 4 (1954), p. 17.
106. "Nobiltà della Scienza e della Professione guridica alla Luce dell' Inseguamento Cattolico" (November 6, 1949). See Pius XIII, *Discorsi Agli Intellettuali*, p. 202.
107. *Ibid.*, p. 203–4.
108. *Ibid.*, p. 205.

EPILOGUE

THE ART OF LAW

THE ART OF LAW

IT was Bracton who said that the term law (*ius*) "is sometimes used to signify *the art of law* instead of the law which may be found in the exercise of that art. For the law does not prescribe everything: on the contrary, it leaves certain things at discretion."[1] This is why, he said further, "law is called *the art of what is good and equitable*, by virtue of which people honor us with the title of priests, inasmuch as we worship justice and minister the law, which is a sacred thing."[2]

St. Thomas, too, spoke of law as an art, "the art of directing or ordering the life of man."[3] If this is the case, as I think it is, it is easy to see that the art of law is among the noblest of all human arts. To introduce order and harmony into human relations and affairs is an art which can only be exercised by "straining all the faculties by which man is likest to a god."[4]

The essence of law is justice, which all existing laws should endeavor to embody as perfectly as possible. Now, justice is, in the words of Aristotle, "the most excellent of virtues . . . more glorious than either the evening or morning star."[5] In the Christian ideology, it is true, love is even more noble than justice, as it is the crown of perfection. Among the moral virtues, at any rate, justice is the queen. Furthermore, what is love but a higher form of justice? For, as Christ tells us, unless our justice abound more than that of the scribes and Pharisees, we shall not enter the kingdom of heaven.

What Christ commands us to do is to cultivate, by the help of grace, a more abundant justice, which seems to me but another name for love.[6]

But it is in God alone that love and wisdom, justice and mercy, goodness and beauty, are one, for, as Frank Sheed says, "there is no distinction between God's attributes and God, and therefore no difference between one of God's attributes and another."[7] Take, for instance, justice and mercy. "Infinite justice and infinite mercy are not two opposing tendencies in God: they are one same God. . . . The mercy of God is an infinite reality. The justice of God is an infinite reality. In the being of God they are the same reality."[8]

On the human plane, however, all these attributes do not fuse into one. They are quite distinct, although they are interrelated and point to their common ontological origin. What is true may not be good, what is good may not be beautiful, and so forth. We are living in a world of limitations, where good qualities cannot be fully developed and are seldom found together.

But the excellence of justice, even as it is in the human world, consists precisely in the fact that it is compounded of the true, the good and the beautiful. It does not contain this triad of ultimate values in their wholeness; and yet there is something of each in its composition. Truth is the foundation of justice, goodness is its end, and beauty constitutes its essential quality. The justice of a law or a judgment depends upon whether it is based on truth, whether it is directed toward the good life, and whether its dispositions are fittingly adapted to the end.

Justice and Truth

Truth enters into the philosophy of law on two different planes. First, on the metaphysical plane, we must visualize the human law as a rivulet flowing from the natural law, which, in turn, flows from the eternal law. The fountainhead of all law is God. If we do not realize this, then we are not true realists, but blind gropers in the realm of passing shadows. Then the words of Jeremias would apply to us: *Be astonished, O ye heavens, and ye gates thereof, be very desolate, saith the Lord. For my people have done two evils. They have forsaken me, the fountain of living water, and have digged to themselves cisterns, broken cisterns, that can hold no water* (Jer. 2:13).

Secondly, on the empirical plane, we must see law in its relation to the other sciences and the actualities of life.

The first requisite of a just judgment is that it must be based upon the facts. In fact, the popular notion of justice is inseparably bound up with truth. Our imagination is excited and our hearts cheered up, whenever we observe that the truth is found out in a puzzling case. Solomon was called a wise man and a just judge mainly because of his ability to find the real facts. Nothing is so agonizing as to see an innocent person condemned; it is only a little less agonizing to see a murderer go free. For justice is owed not only to the accused, but also to the victim of another's crime.

Now, our capacity to find the relevant truth grows with our scientific knowledge. It is in this respect that the progress of physical and psychological sciences has contributed immensely to the administration of justice. As an Oklahoma court put it, "This court is of the opinion, that we should favor the adoption of scientific methods for crime detection, when the demonstrated accuracy and reliability has become established and recognized. Justice is truth in action, and any instrumentality which aids justice in ascertainment of truth, should be embraced without delay."[9] This was said in connection with applying the Drunkometer to a defendant charged with driving an automobile while intoxicated.

In bastardy proceedings, where the question is the paternity of the illegitimate child, the courts adopt the blood grouping tests, which are generally considered conclusive where the results are negative. In the courts of old China, the test was more clumsy. They put two drops of blood—one from the reputed father and one from the child—into a bowl of water. If the two drops stuck together and fused into one, the paternity was established, while if they repulsed each other, it was excluded. I do not know how accurately this worked, and I am afraid that many a man must have had another man's child foisted on him in this way.

But what delights me most is to see the American judges making
use of the psychological insights which modern analytical psychology has contributed toward the understanding of human nature.

In a case of sexual outrage, perpetrated upon a working girl by
two young ruffians, Judge Powell, dealing with the defenses put up
by the prisoners, had the following to say:

> They would have the girl "resist to the utmost," which
> would amount to resisting to the death when attacked by one
> or more lustful males bent on satisfying vicious appetites
> where the circumstances were all too indicative of prior plan-
> ning that had built them up to any extreme in accomplishing
> their purpose. It is further claimed that because the girl was
> not hysterical when she reached home, the defendants should
> be told in effect to go hence and sin no more.
>
> The nature of different individuals varies. Here was a girl
> forced at a tender age to make her own living and live in a
> hovel, when compared to average standards. She was appar-
> ently more or less stoical, but her mother said that, when she
> was awakened by Nadine, the girl was standing by her bed
> "and very much upset." Dr. Beddoe, who examined her a
> couple of hours or so later, said that she was "concerned" but
> not hysterical.
>
> What good would it have done for the victim to have
> screamed in the secluded spot where the acts occurred? She
> was in fear that to scream might cause her to forfeit her life.
> She had good reason by the fact of the almost daily account
> of the number of females who met their deaths while resisting
> to the utmost when resistance was useless. The fact that one
> may be an introvert rather than an extravert and when they
> lose their all and their hour seems blackest they stand in dumb
> and stunned silence, rather than screaming to the capacity of
> their lungs, makes their suffering no less acute, and can de-
> prive them under proper circumstances of no less credence
> than the female who becomes hysterical in recounting the
> facts of her ravishment. This is a common characteristic
> among persons where the vicissitudes of life have from in-
> fancy brought about everything but cheerfulness and a nor-
> mal existence and a sound foundation for hopefulness of a

brighter day. Their emotional reactions often may be quite different from those whose environment and circumstances have been more favorable.[10]

The above examples should be enough to show how close justice stands to truth. And yet justice cannot be identified with truth. This will be clear if we consider some other cases where for some reason truth is deliberately excluded from judicial cognizance. Take, for instance, the famous "Stomach-pumping" case, *Rochin v. People of California,* decided by the Supreme Court of the United States in 1952.[11] The facts are stated by the court as follows:

> Having "some information that the petitioner here was selling narcotics," three deputy sheriffs of the County of Los Angeles, on the morning of July 1, 1949, made for the two-story dwelling house in which Rochin lived with his mother, his common-law wife, brothers and sisters. Finding the outside door open, they entered and then forced open the door to Rochin's room on the second floor. Inside they found petitioner sitting partly dressed on the side of the bed, upon which his wife was lying. On a "night stand" beside the bed the deputies spied two capsules. When asked "Whose stuff is this?" Rochin seized the capsules and put them in his mouth. A struggle ensued, in the course of which the three officers "jumped upon him" and attempted to extract the capsules. The force they applied proved unavailing against Rochin's resistance. He was handcuffed and taken to a hospital. At the direction of one of the officers a doctor forced *invito* an emetic solution into Rochin's stomach by means of a tube. This "stomach pumping" produced vomiting. In the vomited matter were found two capsules which proved to contain morphine.

The question was whether the capsules were admissible as evidence. The Supreme Court said that "they are inadmissible under the Due Process Clause." Justice Frankfurter, speaking for the court, made this significant remark:

> We are compelled to conclude that the proceedings by which this conviction was obtained do more than offend some fastidious squeamishness or private sentimentalism about com-

batting crime too energetically. It is conduct that shocks the conscience. Illegally breaking into the privacy of the petitioner, the struggle to open his mouth and remove what was there, the forcible extraction of his stomach's contents—this course of proceeding by agents of government to obtain evidence is bound to offend even hardened sensibilities. They are methods too close to the rack and the screw to permit of constitutional differentiation.

Coerced confessions offend the community's sense of fair play and decency. So here, to sanction the brutal conduct which naturally enough was condemned by the court whose judgment is before us, would be to afford brutality the cloak of law. Nothing would be more calculated to discredit law and thereby to brutalize the temper of a society.

If truth were the sole consideration in the administration of justice, one could hardly imagine more substantial evidence than the two capsules freshly pumped from the stomach. But here human dignity and other values are involved which clamor for recognition and override even the interests of crime detection.

Without going into the law of evidence, I think the following quotation from James B. Thayer on judicial notice will serve to bring out both the intimate relation between justice and truth and the restricted nature of this relation:[12]

> The maxim that what is known need not be proved, *mani-festa* [or *notoria*] *non indigent probatione*,[13] may be traced far back in the civil and the canon law; indeed, it is probably coeval with legal procedure itself. We find it as a maxim in our own books, and it is applied in every part of our law. It is qualified by another principle, also very old, and often over-topping the former in its importance,—*non refert quid notum sit judici, si notum non sit in forma judicii*.[14] These two maxims seem to intimate the whole doctrine of judicial notice. It has two aspects, one regarding the liberty which the judicial functionary has in taking things for granted, and the other the restraints that limit him.

This leads us to the relation between justice and the good.

Justice and the Good

The good enters into the art of law also in a twofold way. Vertically, the ultimate end of law is identical with the ultimate end of man, which is union with God. Horizontally, whatever things can help toward the realization of this ultimate end are values to be recognized and protected by the law to the fullest possible extent of its limited capacity. St. Thomas Aquinas synthesizes both these views when he says: "Private good is subordinated to the end of the common good: for the being of a part is for the sake of the being of the whole; hence the good of the race is more godlike than the good of the individual man. But the sovereign good, which is God, is the common good, since the good of the whole community depends on Him: while the goodness which marks any given thing is its own private good, and also the good of other things which depend upon it. All things therefore are subordinate to the end of one good, which is God."[15] Thus, both the individual and society are *sub Deo et sub lege*.

All goods or values short of the supreme good—that is, God— are relative, because they are means or stepping stones to an end. But so far as they are necessary means or steps, they derive their significance from the end. "Exterior riches are necessary to the good of virtue, inasmuch as by them we support the body and succor other people . . . Riches therefore are so far forth good as they make for the exercise of virtue. But if that measure is exceeded, and the exercise of virtue impeded by them, they are no longer to be counted among good but among bad things."[16] All private rights are relative to the end, and limited in scope. But within the proper scope, they are to be valued on account of the end which they serve, and must be protected by the law.

Values are, however, not a hotch-potch existing independently of the human person. They are centered on the well-being of man. Some values are inherent in the human person, such as life, liberty and the moral, intellectual, and spiritual virtues. Other values are instrumental, such as private property and industrial and commercial enterprises.

In the child-custody cases, modern American courts have frequently said that the paramount consideration is the welfare of the child, which includes its physical, intellectual, moral, and spiritual well-being. While this principle has come to the fore on the occasion of the cases relating to children, it gives a clue to the heart and the mind of the law, to the philosophy which underlies its attitude *vis-à-vis* the human being as such. If it does not directly concern itself with the well-being of normal adults in all its manifoldness, as when dealing with the infants, it is only because the adults can take better care of themselves and do not need the protecting arms of the law so desperately and thoroughgoingly as does a child. It certainly does not mean that the law has no concern for the fourfold well-being of men and women within the limits of propriety and practicability and in proportion to actual needs.

According to the Christian philosophy of law, all legal institutions, including the State, have as their end the well-being of man, who is made in the image of God. As Frank Sheed says, "If there be no God, everything loses background."[17] Instead of the State ministering to the needs of men in accordance with law, men would become slaves of the State which perverts the law into an instrument of oppression.

It has been the fashion among modern intelligentsia to speak of humanism apart from Christianity. But it cannot be overemphasized that whatever dignity the human person as such has acquired in the West can be traced to the uplifting influence of Christianity. As Monsignor John K. Cartwright has truly observed, "At bottom our law has its chief nobility, not because of borrowings from the Roman Code and not because of some racial capacity for law in our ancestry, but because there has been a light that comes from the Holy Law of Sinai and from the sermon on the Mount of the Beatitudes."[18] And needless to say, "What was once necessary for the origin of our system of law remains necessary for its maintenance and survival."[19]

Christianity brought a new note of love into the world, by which man's dignity has increased by infinite proportions. To quote Sheed again, "It is not always realized how closely the personal value is bound up with the Christian revelation. Before the coming of Christ, men were valued as kings or generals or rich men or poets or gladiators, but not as men. The notion that man was valuable simply because he was a man may have occurred to an occasional philosopher, but had not penetrated into the mind of society at large. It was the Christian message that man, every man, was not only a being of value, but a being of eternal value, and this message revolutionized the world."[20]

But by and large, the peoples of the Christian countries have behaved very much like the children of a rich and aristocratic family who, not realizing the infinite value of the treasures stored in their own house, run desperately after strange things of no value. Like the prodigal son, they are hungry after the husks fit to feed the swine.

At the present juncture, I am happy to see far-sighted lawyers awake to the importance of spiritual values for the science and profession of law. Robert G. Story, President of the American Bar Association, in his Annual Address delivered at Boston in 1953, under the title *Under God and the Law*, concluded with these words:

> It is, after all, our responsibility to bring law into the supremacy which it must attain in a world of free men. We have not yet found the key to universal peace; nor have we built a temple of justice for all mankind. Let us give of our best efforts, individually and through the legal profession, to establish a society based upon morality, dedicated to justice tempered by mercy, and to adopt a sincere, true and basic philosophy of living and acting "Under God and the Law." Then may we truly say—"Liberty Under Law" shall be eternal.

Professor Shelden D. Elliott, President of the Association of American Law Schools, in his recent Message to the Association, quoted with warm approval some significant words from Dean James A. Pike of New York's Cathedral of St. John the Divine, which I take liberty to reproduce in part:

> What we need is a recognition that every man is under the call of His Creator to serve with his whole mind, soul, and

strength; in other words, to use his peculiar gifts—fully and all the time—the way which will most fully aid the achievement of the will of God in society. This is, in short, to make his daily work—whether it be teaching, social work, bricklaying, or the law—a ministry, and it can be as high a ministry as what we generally call by that name. Thus a lawyer accepting such a claim will view every decision, every service to—and influence upon—his client, the way he distributes his time among various claims upon him, what he is willing to take on and not willing to take on—as under judgment, recognizing that there is a higher claim upon him than legal requirements or the rules of a bar association.[21]

In the judicial decisions, too, there are signs of a growing sense of moral values. In a disbarment case, Justice Terrell of the Supreme Court of Florida had this to say: "The administration of justice is a composite rather than an individual concept. It is a derivative of Christian ethics and with us has attained a significance that it has nowhere else on earth. It contemplates the righteous settlement of every controversy that arises affecting the life, liberty or property of the individual. Lawyers and judges are stewards of the law provided for this purpose."[22]

It was Justice Cardozo who said,[23] "Some relations in life impose a duty to act in accordance with the customary morality and nothing more. In those the customary morality must be the standard for the judge. *Caveat emptor*[24] is a maxim that will often have to be followed when the morality which it expresses is not that of sensitive souls. Other relations in life, as, e.g., those of trustee and beneficiary, or principal and surety, impose a duty to act in accordance with the highest standards which a man of the most delicate conscience and the nicest sense of honor might impose upon himself. In such cases to enforce adherence to those standards becomes the duty of the judge. Whether novel situations are to be brought within one class of relations or within the other must be determined, as they arise, by considerations of analogy, of convenience, of fitness and of justice."

At present, even outside of fiduciary relations, moral standards applied by the courts have advanced. As Judge Goodrich observes in a case of unfair trade practice, "We are in a field where the tendency of the law 'has been in the direction of enforcing increasingly higher standards of fairness or commercial morality in trade. The tendency still persists.' "[25]

In the famous segregation cases,[26] Chief Justice Warren of the Supreme Court of the United States reduced the notions of due process and equal protection to the common denominator of "the American ideal of fairness."[27] In a rent case, Justice Drapeau said, "In this, as in every contract, there is the implied covenant of good faith and fair dealing, that neither party will do anything that would result in injuring or destroying the right of the other to enjoy the fruits of the agreement."[28]

Speaking of the underlying philosophy of the National Labor Relations Act, Chief Judge Hutcheson pointed out that "it was enacted not to engender an atmosphere or climate of hate or ill will, or to prevent exchange by employers and employees of courtesies and kindnesses essential to the maintenance of common human relations, but to discourage such an atmosphere or climate and to encourage such exchanges."[29] In a note, he underscores the distinction between the gospel of love and "the gospel of hate."[30]

This leads me to the profound insight of St. Thomas: "The end of the law is love, and there is no stinting about ends, but only with means."[31]

In this insight is contained a whole philosophy of the relations and differences between law and morals. Law and morals share the same end, but they differ in the means they employ for the attainment of the end. No one has, to my knowledge, treated with such lucidity as St. Thomas the thorny question about law and morals, which Ihering used to call "The Cape Horn of jurisprudence." To my knowledge, St. Thomas is the only writer who has really rounded the cape with complete success. Therefore I want to reproduce here a new translation[32] of two articles from *The Treatise on Law* in the *Summa Theologica* under the question of the extent and limitations of the power of human law.

Question 96—The Extent and Limitations of the Power of Human Law.

Article 2—Whether or not it is within the province of human law to prohibit all evil actions.

In the second article we proceed thus. It seems that it might be within the province of human law to prohibit all evil actions.

1. Because Isidore says (*Etymologies*, V, 20) that laws were made so that in apprehension of them the rash deeds of men might be checked. But rash deeds would not be checked effectively unless each and every evil act were prohibited. Therefore human law must prohibit all evil acts.

2. Furthermore it is the intent of the legislator to make good citizens. But no one can be good unless he refrains from all evil acts. Therefore it is within the province of human law to prohibit all evil acts.

3. Besides, human law is derived from natural law, as was said before (Q. 95, A. 2). Now all evil acts are opposed to natural law. Therefore human law must prohibit all evil acts.

But on the contrary, there is the argument given in *De Lib. Arb.* L, 5, viz., "It seems to me that the law which is written for the government of people, properly permits these things [i.e., certain evil acts] while it leaves to Providence to punish them." But Divine Providence punishes nothing but evil acts. Therefore human law properly permits some evil acts by not prohibiting the same.

I answer that, as was said above (Q. 90, A. 1, 2), the law is enacted as a kind of rule or measure of human acts. But a measure must be suitable in the nature of things to that which is measured, as stated in *Metaphysics*, X, for different things are measured by different measures. Hence it must be that laws too are imposed on men according to their condition; for, as Isidore says, the law must be possible both in regard to the nature of things and in regard to the customs of the country. Now the power or the faculty to act proceeds from the interior habit or disposition and an act is not equally possible for him who has not the habit or virtue as it is for him who has the habit; just as it is not equally possible for a boy as it is for a full grown man. And because of this, the same law is not imposed on children as on adults; since many things are allowed to children which the law punishes or severely censures in adults. Likewise, many things must be permitted in men not advanced in goodness which would not be tolerated in good men.

Moreover, human law is set up for the mass of men, the majority of whom are imperfect in virtue. And therefore human law does not forbid all evil acts from which the good abstain, but only the more serious ones from which the majority of men are able to abstain; and, in particular, those evil acts which are harmful to others, without the prohibition of which human society could not survive, for example, murder and theft, are forbidden by human law.

To the first objection, I say that rash deeds appear to be a wrong to others. Hence they are grouped most properly with those sins which do harm to our fellow men and which are forbidden by human law, as has been said before.

To the second objection, I say that the purpose of human law is to lead men to virtue, but not abruptly, only step by step. And so human law does not require at once from the majority of men, who are imperfect, that which is required of men already advanced in virtue, namely, that they refrain from all evil. Otherwise, imperfect men being unable to obey such precepts would fall into greater wrong, as is said in Proverbs (30:33): "He who violently presses the nose brings forth blood," and Matthew (9:17) says that *if new wine*, that is, the precepts of a perfect life, *be placed in old skins*, that is, men who are imperfect, *the skins shall burst and the wine be spilt*, that is, the precepts would be held in contempt, and out of contempt men would fall into greater wrong.

To the third objection, I say that the natural law is a certain participation in us of the eternal law; but human law falls short of the eternal law. Indeed, St. Augustine says (I *De Lib. Arb.*): "That which is enacted for the government of States yields to many considerations and leaves unpunished things which are punished by Divine Providence. And because the law does not accomplish everything, this is no reason for finding fault with what it does accomplish." Hence human law is not able to prohibit everything which the natural law prohibits.

Article 3—Whether the human law prescribes acts of all the virtues.

In the third article we proceed thus. It would seem that human law does not prescribe acts of all the virtues.

1. Because acts of vices are opposed to acts of virtue. But human law does not prohibit all vices, as was said before. Therefore human law does not command acts of all the virtues.

2. Furthermore acts of virtue proceed from virtue. But virtue is the purpose of law; and so what proceeds from virtue cannot fall under the precept of the law. Therefore human law does not command acts of all the virtues.

3. Besides, the law is directed to the common good, as has been said already (Q. 90, A. 2). But certain acts of virtue are not directed to the common good, but rather to private well-being. Therefore the law does not prescribe the acts of all the virtues.

On the contrary, there is the argument which the Philosopher gives (*Ethics*, V, 1), namely that the law prescribes the acts of bravery, those of temperance as well as those of meekness; and likewise as to the other virtues and vices, enjoining the former and forbidding the latter.

I answer by saying that the different kinds of virtues are distinguished according to their objects, as is obvious from what was said above. Now all the objects of the virtues can be related either to the private well-being of a person or to the common good of a community; for example, the object of fortitude can be carried out either for the protection of the community or for the protection of the rights of a friend; and the same for the other virtues. Now the law, as we have said above, is directed to the common good, and even though there is no virtue whose acts the law cannot prescribe, yet human law does not prescribe all the acts of all the virtues, but only those which are related to the common good, either immediately, as when certain things are done directly for the common good, or mediately as when some things pertaining to good order are prescribed by the law-maker through which the citizens are instructed to support the common good in the form of justice and of peace.

To the first objection, I reply that human law does not prohibit all acts of vice under the obligation of a commandment, just as it does not prescribe all acts of virtue. But it does prohibit some acts of the different vices, just as it prescribes some act of the different virtues.

To the second objection, I reply that acts are said to be virtuous in two senses. First in the sense that certain acts which a man does are virtuous, thus the act of justice is to do what is right and the act of fortitude is to do what is courageous. And in this sense the law prescribes some acts of the virtues. In the other sense, acts are called acts of virtue because man does them in the manner and spirit in which a virtuous man would do them. And such an act always proceeds from virtue; nor does this act fall under the commandment of the law, but it is the end toward which the law-maker would lead men.

To the third objection, I reply that there is no virtue whose acts cannot be directed to the common good as was said above, either immediately or mediately.

St. Thomas looks at the whole picture of the social life of men. Both ethics and law are founded on the natural law. Both have for their subject-matter human conduct. Both aim at the establishment of orderly concord and friendship amongst men. But they have different functions and work by different sanctions. In the case of law, the sanction is mainly exterior; in the case of ethics, it is mainly interior. In his *Summa Contra Gentiles* is to be found an illuminating passage on this point:

There is then orderly concord amongst men, when to each there is rendered his own, which is the act of justice; and therefore it is said: *The work of justice is peace* (Isa. xxxii, 17). To the observance of this justice man is inclined both by an interior and an exterior principle. By an interior principle, in so far as a man has a will to observe the precepts of the divine law, which is done by his bearing love to God and to his neighbour: for whoever loves another renders him his due spontaneously and with pleasure, and even adds more by liberality: hence the whole fulfilment of the law hinges upon love (Rom. xiii, 10: Matt. xxii, 40). But because some are not so inwardly disposed as to do of their own accord what the law commands, they have to be dragged by an exterior force to the fulfilment of the justice of the law; and so they fulfil the law under fear of penalties, not as freemen but as slaves. Hence it is said: *When thou shalt do thy judgments upon the earth* by punishing the wicked, *the inhabitants of the earth shall learn justice.* (Isa. xxvi, 9.) Others are so disposed as to do of their own accord what the law bids them. They are a law to themselves, having charity, which bends their wills in place of a law to generous conduct. There was no need of an exterior law enacted for them: hence it is said: *The law is not made for the just, but for the unjust:* which is not to be taken to mean that the just are not bound to fulfil the law, as some have misunderstood the text, but that the just are inclined of themselves to do justice even without a law.[33]

This reminds me of what Confucius had said: "If you guide the people by laws, and keep them in order by penalties, they will avoid the penalties, but they will lose all self-respect. But if you guide them by the practice of virtue and keep them in order by the rules of propriety, they will not only keep their self-respect but will become good of their own accord."[34]

There is, however, an important difference between Confucius and St. Thomas. Confucius speaks in terms of either-or, as though one had to choose between law and morality. St. Thomas, more realistic than Confucius, sees the necessity and the educative value of laws and penalties. In fact, he thinks that law can prepare men for virtue. For instance, it is written in Deuteronomy (23:24): *Going into thy neighbour's vineyard, thou mayest eat as many grapes as thou pleasest; but must carry none out with thee.* This is a precept of law. *Love thy neighbor as thyself*—this is a principle of ethics. St. Thomas weaves these two together without a seam. He writes:

As the Apostle says (Rom. 13:8), *he that loveth his neighbour hath fulfilled the law:* because, to wit, all the precepts of the law, chiefly those concerning our neighbour, seem to aim at the end that men should love one another. Now it is the effect of love that men give their own goods to others: because, as stated in 1 John 3:17: *He that . . . sees his brother go in want; if he steels his heart against his brother, how can we say that the love of God dwells in him?* Hence the purpose of the Law was to accustom men to give of their own to others readily: thus the Apostle (I Tim. 6:18) commands the rich *to give easily and to communicate to others*. Now a man will not give easily to others if he will not suffer another man to take some little thing from him without any great injury to himself. And so the Law laid down that it should be lawful for a man, on entering his neighbour's vineyard, to eat the fruit there: but not to carry any away, lest this should lead to the infliction of a grievous harm, and cause a disturbance of the peace: for among well-behaved people, the taking of a little does not disturb the peace; in fact, it rather strengthens friendship and accustoms men to give things to one another.[35]

Justice and the Beautiful

For a law or a judgment to be just, it must be *based upon* the true, it must *aim at* the good, and finally it must *be* beautiful. In a real sense, therefore, the idea of beauty has a closer and more internal relation with justice than the ideas of the good and the true.

I must not be understood as speaking of physical beauty, nor even of the literary qualities of judicial opinions and juristic writings. I am thinking only of the beauty of judgment itself. Here again St. Thomas comes to our aid. "Clearness and proportion," he said, "go to compose the beautiful or handsome. Dionysius says that God is beautiful, for he is the cause of the consonance and clearness of all things. Bodily beauty consists in well-shaped members with freshness of complexion; *spiritual beauty, which is the same as honorable good, in fair dealing according to the candor of reason*."[36]

In fact, the Spirit Himself called God "the beauty of justice."[37] The ultimate source of beauty lies in the supreme Harmony of the Holy Trinity. The beauty of God is reflected in all His works, external as well as internal. As the Scripture says, "He hath beautified the glorious works of his wisdom . . . Oh how lovely are all his works, and what we can know is but as a spark! . . . All things he has made in pairs, balanced against one another; never a fault of symmetry; to each one its own well-being assured. His glory contemplating, thou shalt never have thy fill" (Ecclus. 42:21, 23–26).

One of the greatest of the tragedies that have befallen the spirit of man is that he is so "civilized" as to have lost the fresh sensibilities of a child's heart. Has man experienced a second Fall? How is it that he is no longer thrilled by the joy of living in such a wonderful universe? How long must God display His supreme art to the blind of vision?

If we had the heart and the eye of a child or a poet, what a wonderland the world would be! "Like a jewel the vault of heaven is set above us; the sight of it is glory made visible. Plain to our view is the sun's passage as it shines out, a very masterpiece of His workmanship, who is the most High. . . . The moon, too, whose changes serve mankind for a calendar, to mark the passing of time, and give the signal when feast days come round! . . . Look up at the rainbow, and bless the maker of it; how fair are those bright colours that span heaven with a ring of splendour, traced by an almighty hand" (Ecclus. 43:1–2, 6, 12–13).

The reader may wonder what relevance these speculations have for jurisprudence. The truth is that without a keen awareness of the beauty of the landscape of reality, a jurist would be oblivious of the fountain of justice, and he would end by being a mediocre lawyer.

The spirit of childhood is absolutely indispensable to the attainment of true wisdom and true happiness. Christ Himself has proclaimed this truth in the clearest and most emphatic words: "Unless you be converted, and become as little children, you shall not enter into the kingdom of heaven" (Matt. 18:3). The spirit of childhood comprehends humility, but, as the beloved sister of St. Thérèse of Lisieux, Sister Geneviève, has pointed out, it is more than humility.[38] It means boundless confidence in God; it means the restoration, as far as possible, of the mind and the heart to the virginal freshness of vision and affection of Adam and Eve before their tragic Fall; it means the ineffable joy of feeling at home in the universe as a member of Our Father's house; finally, it means a simplicity nourished by the infinite variety of things which it sees as flowing from a single source.

Unless a lawyer be converted into a child, he will not be "a scribe steeped in the kingdom of heaven," he will not hunger and thirst after justice, and hence he is no lawyer worthy of the name. All his learning will be a lifeless mass of information, which brings no delight to himself and no happiness to others. Legal science without legal wisdom is bound to degenerate into a dustbin of precedents and a cobweb of technicalities. Lit up by the morning light of wisdom, even these can be transmuted into a divine spark.

It was St. Augustine who distinguished the knowledge of the angels into *morning* and *evening* knowledge.[39] St. Thomas gave a very interesting comment on this:

> As dawn is the opening and dusk the close of the ordinary day, so the knowledge of the original being of things in the Word is described as the morning light, while the knowledge of them as they stand in their own natures is described as the evening light. The Word is the source, as it were, from which realities stream, flowing into the very being things have within themselves.[40]

As applied to human beings, we may say that *wisdom belongs to the morning light, while science belongs to the evening light.* Jurisprudence, which is "the knowledge of things human and Divine,"[41] embraces both species of knowledge. It takes the *morning* light to realize the existence of the eternal law and to perceive the clear principles of the natural law, which are nothing else than the dictates of the natural reason of man. Our empirical knowledge of positive law, on the other hand, belongs to the *evening.* Needless to say, *evening* knowledge cannot be dispensed with in the study of jurisprudence. Positive law must be thoroughly mastered. But to allow such *evening* knowledge to dominate and occupy the whole field of jurisprudence without an awareness of its vital connection with the *morning* light is to fall into the bottomless pit of positivism.

It is true that the *morning* knowledge alone does not constitute jurisprudence. It takes both *morning* and *evening* to make a whole day. But it must be emphasized that the *morning* knowledge is the foundation and the only guide capable of keeping *evening* knowledge on the right track. The rootlessness of modern civilization in general and modern jurisprudence in particular is due to an exclusive attachment to and absorption in the *evening* knowledge. The modern age is just like an adolescent boy who despises the very idea of childhood. Only when one has become truly mature will one return to childhood. For, as Lao Tse says, "When one's virtue and wisdom reach ripeness, one becomes like a child again."[42] "A great man," says Mencius, "is one who preserves intact the heart of a newborn baby."[43]

Many modern jurists, even of the idealistic type, have cudgelled their brains searching after postulates and criteria of justice, but they have failed because they have resorted to complicated methods in their search for simple truths, and they search in the wrong direction. Why seek for the living among the dead? Can the natural law be found in the musty records? Is it not written on the fleshly tablets of your heart? Or do you want to put up an air of respectability and win credit with the world by a show of erudition and dialectical power? But can you ever establish the natural law by such unnatural means? What we need is simplicity and perfect candor.

His Holiness Pius XII has put the matter into a nutshell, when he says, "The profoundest or subtlest science of law could not point out a criterion for distinguishing just from unjust laws, mere *"legal law"* from the true law, other than that which is already perceptible in the light of natural reason from the nature of things, and perceptible by man himself from the law written in man's heart by the Creator (Rom. 2:14–15), and expressly confirmed by revelation."[44]

These words coming from a supreme scientist of law, who has for many years studied and pondered juridical problems from all angles, should warn us against vain endeavors to seek the natural law or an objective criterion of justice outside our own heart. But the mind of modern man is so blinded by the cobwebs of false reasoning and trivialized knowledge that unless he returns to simplicity and the spirit of childhood, he will not be able to see even the simplest and most obvious truths. The modern jurist is de-naturalized to such a point that the very name of "natural law" sounds very unnatural to his ears.

Lao Tse says, "To be great is to go on, to go on is to be far, to be far is to return."[45] Have we not gone far enough? Is it not time to return to the simple and natural? If human civilization is to be put on the right track again, we must retrace our steps to our origins, and begin with the beginning.

To begin with the beginning is nothing else than to start from the Word. Only thus can we recapture the spirit of the morning. In one of the noblest of the Messianic Psalms is to be found this verse of superb beauty: *With thee is sovereignty in the splendor of holiness on the day of thy birth: before the morning star, like the dew, I have begotten thee* (Ps. 109:3).

Begotten of the Father from "the womb of the morning,"[46] perennially fresh like the dew, the Son radiates the morning light and the spirit of childhood from eternity to eternity. This eternal generation of the Word is the source of all life, law and delight for the whole creation. The Word gives to all things the laws of their nature, each according to its place in the scale of being. In creatures lower than man, the laws of their nature are followed instinctively without any hitch. The stars praise God by their harmonious course; all the elements of nature praise God by performing their functions within the limits He has assigned to them; the trees praise God by bringing forth, in due season, blossoms and fruits after their kind; the birds praise God by their singing; all animals praise God by fulfilling the instincts He has placed in them.

All things below man evidently follow the laws of their proper nature. Only in the human world do we find disheartening discords and execrable crimes. What has man made of man? Is it possible that God, who gave laws to all creatures according to their nature, should have forgotten to give laws conformable to the nature of our being? Or have we become so rebellious that we do not even wish to think of these God-made laws, but prefer to make our own "laws" in oblivion and defiance of the natural law? I think the latter is the more likely.

Let us see where we are. Of all animals man alone is endowed

with reason and liberty. But modern man has turned liberty into
self-will and licence, which he has tried to justify with his marvelous powers of reasoning. He observes with admiration the order and harmony prevailing in the lower stages in the scale of
being, and he has come to fancy that by following *their* laws we
are likely to attain a like order and harmony in the human world.
He holds his mirror to the lower order of nature, rather than to
his own nature. The unprecedented successes of the natural sciences have re-enforced this tendency on the part of social and
moral scientists, who aspire to mould their sciences upon the pat-
tern of the natural sciences. For a time all talk about the ultimate
ends and the hierarchy of values was hushed down by fashionable
sociologists and jurists as being "unscientific." All that they would
accept into their legitimate domain were quantitative measure-
ments and statistics. Efficient causality became their only idol, and
any mention of teleology was suspect. Determinism was introduced
into human conduct and relations, and the idea of responsibility
was lost sight of.

Jurisprudence followed the general downward current, and
fell so low as to exclude from its field the consideration of justice.
Morris Cohen gave a testimony of this tendency which I can con-
firm by my own experience:

> To the great majority of people, law is a special technique.
> It is something exclusively for lawyers and their clients. I re-
> member a class in which a student complained that he didn't
> see the justice of a decision in a given case. The professor re-
> plied, "This is a class in law, not in justice." Now there is of
> course some measure of truth in this reply. It is unfortunately
> true that many laws are unjust and are none the less part of
> our law, to be observed and analysed. But from the historic
> and moral point of view this is surely not the final answer. The
> law arises to meet social needs and can maintain itself in the
> long run only if it serves those needs both justly and to the
> general satisfaction of the community.[47]

The slogan of those early days of this present century was "Facts,
facts, and more facts." Laws were also facts, to be proved by their
actual enforcement by the courts. The students of law did not

realize that the "criterion of simple fact" is valid only for the Supreme Being, whose Essence consists in His Existence, and that all existing things under Him must justify their existence by their progressive embodiment of their essence. They did not realize that the essence of law is justice and that any law which does not bear within itself this aspiration toward its essence is not a "true" law.

A law which is not ordained to the good cannot be called a "true" law. Sir William Scott put it very well in the case of *Santa Cruz:* "when I say the *true rule,* I mean only the rule to which civilized nations, attending to just principles, ought to adhere."[48] Here the word "true" does not refer to merely empirical facts, but to the higher realm of *being.*

Dom Marmion has made an illuminating observation on this matter:

> By nature, man is a reasonable being. He cannot, like an animal destitute of reason, act only by instinct: what distinguishes him from all other beings of the earthly creation, is that he is endowed with reason and liberty. Reason must therefore be sovereign in man; but, as a creature, reason must itself be subject to the Divine Will on which it depends, and that is manifested by the natural law, and by positive laws.
>
> To be "true," which is the first condition necessary in order to be pleasing to God, each human action must be in conformity with our condition as free and reasonable creatures, subject to the Divine Will; otherwise this action does not correspond to our nature, to the properties belonging to it and the laws that govern it: it is false.[49]

Now, it may be asked, where are we to find the first principles of the natural law? The answer has been given in the clearest terms by His Holiness Pius XII:

> It is impossible to observe with attention the universe, corporeal and spiritual, physical and moral, without being struck with admiration at the sight of the order and harmony that reign throughout all the various grades in the scale of being. In man, up to that line of boundary where his unconscious activity ends and the conscious and free action begins, that order and that harmony are strictly realized according to the

laws placed by the Creator in the existing being. Beyond that line the ordaining will of God is still in force; however, its actualization and its development are left to the free determination of man, which can be either conformed or opposed to the Divine Will.[50]

It is, then, in the borderline between the instinctive and the rational, in the nature of man, that the seeds or the first beginnings of the natural law are to be found.

It takes the *morning* light and the *morning* spirit to have a clear perception and a firm grasp of what the still, small voice of conscience teaches us just at the point where we pass from the unconscious to the conscious, from the inarticulate to the articulate, from the instinctive to the rational. Of course, rationality is distinctively human; but even the instincts of humanity are, as St. Thomas has observed, richer and nobler than those of lower animals.[51] To St. Thomas, as to Pius XII, the instincts or the inborn inclinations of man furnish the basic materials to be refined by reason. Thus, their conception of the natural law is at once existential and essential; psychology and logic, ontology and ethic, are woven into a seamless tunic. But what is distinctively new in Pius XII's philosophy is that he puts his finger on the exact point at which the seeds of the Logos are preparing to yield fresh shoots in the form of spontaneous dictates of natural reason and conscience. Written in the unconscious, they are "promulgated" and recognized in the conscious. This is the region where reason dawns, where the morning light is clear, where the dew is fresh, where the Eternal passes into the temporal with "the whisper of a gentle breeze" (3 Kings 19: 12).

This simple truth is revealed, as Our Lord has declared, not to the so-called wise and prudent, but only to little children (Matt. 11: 25). Sometimes, too, a genuine poet like Robert Browning has a momentary glimpse of the perennial beginnings:

> The year's at the spring
> And day's at the morn;
> Morning's at seven;
> The hillside's dew-pearled;
> The lark's on the wing;

> The snail's on the thorn:
> God's in his heaven—
> All's right with the world!

This is one of the profoundest poetic visions that I know of. Yet it has been scoffed at as a shallow optimism by creatures of the *evening*. Indeed, to the superficial, all things are superficial. The trouble with the modern world is that God can find no room in the heart of man, which, so far as this world is concerned, is supposed to be His garden of delight, His heaven.

Speaking of the theologian, Mr. Sheed has thrown out a deep insight. "In that *awareness* of reality which is so vital, the poet has something to give the theologian."[52] Then he goes on to say

> Wordsworth's
> > The moon doth with delight
> > Look round her when the heavens are bare
> and Virgil's "*Sunt lachrymae rerum*" witness over eighteen hundred years to the same truth: the poets cannot be happy with the idea that nature is dead. They feel the life in it, though they do not always know what the life is that they feel. The Christian is exactly the reverse: he knows what the mystery is, but for the most part does not feel it. . . . What the Christian knows as a truth, the poet responds to as a living fact.[53]

This is also true of the lawyer. The art of law has for its materials the whole gamut of human relations and activities. Out of a welter of conflicts and discords the legal artist is to create order and harmony in consonance with the music of the spheres. The matters with which the law deals may be very sordid, but the manner in which it deals with them can be very beautiful. Wrongs are base and mean, but the righting of them is noble and godlike. Just as the exposure of darkness is light, so the redressing of wrongs is justice.[54] How godlike this task is should be clear from the magnificent prophecy of Isaias:

> Thrills the barren desert with rejoicing; the wilderness takes heart, and blossoms, fair as the lily. Blossom on blossom, it will rejoice and sing for joy; all the majesty of Lebanon is

bestowed on it, all the grace of Carmel and of Saron. All alike shall see the glory of the Lord, the majesty of our God. Stiffen, then, the sinews of drooping hand and flagging knee; give word to the faint-hearted, *Take courage, and have no fear; see where your Lord is bringing redress for your wrongs, God himself, coming to deliver you!* (Isaias 35: 1–4).

Law is the meeting ground of the actual and the ideal, of the human and Divine. Like the lotus, it stretches its roots deep in the mud, but sends forth its graceful flowers heavenward.

St. Thomas says, "In the human scene prudence becomes wisdom when all conduct is oriented to the proper end of human living. Hence, he who considers the highest cause of the whole universe, namely God, deserves the title of wise man with least reservation."[55]

It is only by linking the juridical order to the cosmic order that a student of law can attain wisdom, and wisdom alone can make him a jurist worthy of the name. As Joseph Story has said:

> Many of our most illustrious statesmen have been lawyers, but they have been lawyers liberalized by philosophy, and a large intercourse with the wisdom of ancient and modern times. The perfect lawyer, like the perfect orator, must accomplish himself for his duties by familiarity with every study. It may truly be said, that to him nothing, that concerns human nature or human art, is indifferent and useless. He should search the human heart, explore to their sources the passions, and appetites, and feelings of mankind. . . . He should for this purpose make the master-spirits of all ages pay contribution to his labors. He should walk abroad through nature, and elevate his thoughts, and warm his virtues, by a contemplation of her beauty, and magnificence, and harmony. He should examine well the precepts of religion, as the only solid basis of civil society; and gather from them, not only his duty, but his hopes; not merely his consolations, but his discipline and his glory.[56]

The need of a broad culture for a lawyer has also been brought out by Chief Justice Vanderbilt, who says, "The study of law and its practice consist in problem-solving, and the mind requires the balance that is afforded by the cultivation of the emotions and the sense of beauty through the best in the field of art in the broadest sense of the term."[57]

It was Cardozo who said that in a judge there should be a touch of the qualities which make the poet. It was precisely this touch that made Cardozo such a great judge. For him, justice is an idea far more subtle and comprehensive than mere obedience to a rule of positive law. It is "a synonym of an aspiration, a mood of exaltation, a yearning for what is fine or high."[58] At times, "when talking of justice, the quality we have in mind is charity, and this though the one quality is often contrasted with the other."[59]

Cardozo further compares the art of judgment to the art of cooking. "The ingredient which sours if left alone, is preserved by an infusion, sweetening the product without changing its identity. You may give what recipes you will. A trained sense of taste, approving or rejecting, will pass judgment on the whole."[60]

Dealing with the demands of logical symmetry and the demands of change, he said, "There is emancipation in our very bonds. The restraints of rhyme and metre, the exigencies of period and balance, liberate at times the thought which they confine, and in imprisoning release."[61] Let me give a concrete illustration of this from one of his own decisions. In *De Cicco v. Schweizer*,[62] a father promised in writing to pay an annuity to his daughter in consideration of her forthcoming marriage to an Italian Count, to whom she was already engaged at the time of the promise. The question in the case was whether there was a valid consideration to support the promise. Now, according to the general principles of common law governing contracts, a consideration must either be a benefit to the promisor or detriment to the promisee. In this case, so the defendant argued, not only was there no benefit to the father, but there was no detriment to the daughter, because at the time of promise, she was already legally engaged to marry. This is true as a general rule, for nothing which one is already legally bound to do can constitute a consideration. Judge Cardozo held that there was a consideration. He stretched the concept of consideration to an unprecedented extent, but not to the breaking point. "The defendant," he said, "knew that a man and a woman were assuming the responsibilities of wedlock in the belief that adequate provision had been made for the woman and for future offspring. He offered this inducement to both while they were free to retract or to delay. That they neither retracted nor delayed is certain. It is not to be expected that they should lay bare all the motives and promptings, some avowed and conscious, others perhaps half-conscious and inarticulate, which swayed their conduct. It is enough that the natural consequence of the defendant's promise was to induce them to put the thought of rescission or delay aside. From that moment there was no longer a real alternative. There was no longer what philosophers call a 'living' option. This in itself permits inference of detriment." At the end of the opinion, Judge Cardozo made a refreshingly candid confession of the real judicial motive in stretching the concept of consideration in such cases. "The law favors marriage settlements, and seeks to uphold them. . . . It strains, if need be, to the uttermost the interpretation of equivocal words and conduct in the effort to hold men to the honorable fulfilment of engagements designed to influence in their deepest relations the lives of others."

Now, this is what I would call a *beautiful* decision, where natural reason and juristic reason work in harmony. If the judge is subtle, he does not indulge in subtlety for subtlety's sake. If his reasoning is sinuous and serpentine, his heart is simple and straight. It shows that justice is not really blind, but open-eyed. Justice is impartial but not neutral; it has its smiles and its frowns. It smiles on what is honorable and fair, and frowns on what is unreasonable and mean.

The function of logic and precedent is to preserve the symmetry and order of the law. But, to quote Cardozo again, "As new problems arise, equity and justice will direct the mind to solutions which will be found, when they are scrutinized, to be consistent with symmetry and order, or even to be starting points of a symmetry and order theretofore unknown."[63] In the art of law, as in all other arts, "we can never rid ourselves of our dependence upon intuitions or flashes of insight transcending the contributions of mere experience."[64]

Nothing can be more interesting than to see how the courts

weigh the conflicting interests involved in the cases before them, and how they adjust their judgments to the circumstances and exigencies of each case.

Most of the legal rights and wrongs are relative to time and place. "A nuisance," said Justice Sutherland, "may be merely a right thing in the wrong place, like a pig in the parlor instead of the barnyard."[65] This would make it seem as though the law were extremely fickle, like a weathercock. But it should be noted that often it is the very immutability of basic principles which compels their specific determinations to be variable. Take, for instance, *Omychund v. Barker*,[66] a case decided by the English Chancery in 1744. The question was whether an Indian witness should be allowed to take an oath according to the Hindu rites. The Court held that he could, even in the absence of a statute. What interests me is a remark made by one Mr. Murray, a young man of thirty-nine, who appeared as Solicitor General. "All occasions," he said, "do not arise at once: now a particular species of *Indians* appears; hereafter another species of *Indians* may arise; a statute seldom can take in all cases, therefore the common law, *that works itself pure* by rules drawn from the fountain of justice, is for this reason superior to an act of Parliament."[67] This remark, thrown out in a most casual way in the course of argument, embodies one of the profoundest insights into the nature of the common law. The fountain of justice is permanent, while the rules drawn from it are variable. Immutability and change are found in union here. No wonder that Mr. Murray should grow to be Lord Mansfield.

Of all English judges, Lord Mansfield is still the most frequently quoted in contemporary American decisions. I have the impression that American jurisprudence is saturated with the spirit of Lord Mansfield. In many cases one finds a very salutary combination of a dynamic tendency with a lofty moral idealism. Instances are innumerable. Let me give one sample: "There is no virtue, per se, in rigid and inflexible adherence to the doctrine of stare decisis. Times change, customs alter, and despite our human sins of omission and commission, the history of mankind continues to testify to the nearer approach to some constant and unchanging ideals, one of which is the concept of justice, predicated upon humanitarian considerations."[68]

What is of jurisprudential significance is that it is precisely because the best judges of the common law fix their eyes upon the constant and unchanging principles of justice and equity that they have become so flexible and reasonable in handling instrumental doctrines and concepts. It was Confucius who said, "Where art overrides nature, you get the pedantry of a scribe. Where nature overrides art, you get the boorishness of a rustic. Only when art and nature blend in harmony do you become a man of true culture."[69] Measured by this yardstick, there have been a goodly number of men of true culture in the history of common law.

Taken at its best, the common law has its sublime aspects as well as its beautiful spots. It can be flexible where flexibility is called for; it can be tough where toughness is in order. Teaching the art of law through carefully selected cases from the common law can keep the feet of the star-gazers solidly on the ground, and lift the eyes of the earth-bound to the things above. It will help to quicken and subtilize the rigid mind, and warn dynamic and flexible natures against being lost in the journey. It will serve to plant in the student a passionate love for fairness and justice, a sense of balance, a habit of striving after the happy mean, a ready response to the rhythms of life, a discernment of what is important and what is not, a singlehearted fidelity to the immutable principles of law together with a versatile resourcefulness in devising the means of their implementation. It will awaken him to the indescribable nobility of his profession by showing him in concrete examples how the great men in the law have moved between the finite and the Infinite, between time and Eternity; how patiently they have untied little knots as for the love of God. They will teach him how a warm heart and a cool head can work together in promoting the happiness of mankind so far as law can do it. Finally, they will call his attention to the persistent antinomies and paradoxes of legal science, such as the immanent and the transcendent, the one and the many, permanency and change, the ideal and the actual, nature and art, reason and will, order and liberty, the individual and the group, and many other problems. But these problems will not be solved by trying to stop the swinging of the pendulum, nor by attempting a compromise, still less by taking sides, but by rising to a higher plane of thought where partial truths are woven into a whole and discordant notes are resolved into a cosmic harmony. For what is impossible with man alone is possible with the help of God. Only upon the realization of this will the student begin to taste for himself the joy that comes from "the gladsome light of Jurisprudence," from "the beauty of justice."

NOTES

1. *De legibus,* fol. 3.
2. *Ibid.,* fols. 2 and 3.
3. *S. T.,* I–II, 104. 4. *in corp.*
4. Holmes, *Collected Legal Papers,* p. 26.
5. *Ethics,* Book V.
6. Matt. 5:20.
7. *Theology and Sanity,* p. 52.
8. *Ibid.,* p. 52.
9. *Toms v. State,* 239 P. 2d at p. 821. See also *People v. Kovacik,* 128 N.Y.S. 2d 492.
10. *Kidd v. State* (1953), 261 P. 2d 224.
11. 72 S.Ct. 205.
12. Thayer, *A Preliminary Treatise on Evidence at the Common Law* (Little, Brown & Co., 1898), pp. 277–8.
13. "What is obvious stands in no need of proof."
14. "What is known personally to the judges, but not known through the form of judicial proceeding, cannot be the basis of judgment."
15. *Summa Contra Gentiles,* III. 17. 5. I am using the translation of Joseph Rickaby, S.J., *Of God and His Creatures* (Newman, 1950), p. 197.
16. *Ibid.,* p. 305.
17. *Communism and Man,* p. 136. See also the penetrating remarks of President Eisenhower: "Without God, there could be no American form of government, nor an American way of life. Recognition of the Supreme Being is the first—the basic—expression of Americanism. The Founding Fathers [recognized] God as the author of individual rights. . . . But in many lands the state claims to be the author of human rights. . . . If the state gives rights, it can—and inevitably will—take away those rights." (As reported in the *New York Herald Tribune,* February 21, 1955.)

18. In a sermon. It was published in the Congressional Record, February 4, 1954, as extension of remarks of Hon. Edith Nourse Rogers of Massachusetts.
19. *Ibid.*
20. *Communism and Man,* p. 135.
21. *Journal of Legal Education,* Vol. 7 (1954) p. 275.
22. *Lambdin v. State* (1942), 150 Fla. 814, 9 So. 2d 192.
23. *The Nature of the Judicial Process,* pp. 109–10.
24. "Let the buyer beware."
25. *Q-Tips, Inc. v Johnson & Johnson* (1953), 206 F.2d 144 at 145.
26. *Brown v. Board of Education of Topeka* (1954), 74 S.Ct. 686. *Bolling v. Sharpe* (1954), 74 S.Ct. 693.
27. 74 S.Ct. 694.
28. *Brawley v. Crosby, etc. Foundation* (1954), 267 P. 2d 28.
29. *National Labor Relations Board v. Valentine Sugars* (1954), 211 F. 2d 317, at 320.
30. The judge's point is that the underlying philosophy of labor relations is the background against which the Act in question is to be interpreted.
31. *S. T.,* II–II, 184. 3. *in corp.* I am using here Gilby's translation in his *St. Thomas Aquinas: Philosophical Texts,* p. 330.
32. I owe the translation of these articles to Rev. Anthony Lo Gatto.
33. Rickaby, *Of God and His Creatures,* p. 291.
34. *The Analects of Confucius.*
35. *S. T.,* I–II, 105. 2. *ad* 1.
36. *Ibid.,* II–II, 145. 2. *in corp.* Gilby, *St. Thomas Aquinas: Philosophical Texts,* p. 78.
37. Jer. 31:23; 50:7.
38. Ste. Thérèse de l'Enfant-Jesus: *Conseils et Souvenirs,* recueillis par Soeur Geneviève de la Sainte Face (Carmel de Lisieux, 1952), pp. 30–40.
39. St. Augustine, *De Genesi ad litteram,* 2:8.
40. *S. T.,* I, 58. 6. *in corp.*
41. Justinian, *Institutes,* 1. 1. 1. *Digest,* 1. 1. 10.
42. *Tao Teh Ching,* chap. 55.
43. *Works of Mencius,* 4. 2. 12.
44. Allocution on "Law and Conscience"; see *Discorsi agli Intellettuali: 1939–1954,* p. 213.
45. *Tao Teh Ching,* chapter 25.
46. See Callan and McHugh, *The Psalms Explained* (Wagner, 1929), p. 399, note 3. According to the authors, the Hebrew of this verse may be rendered: *Thy people shall offer themselves willingly in the day of Thy power, in adornment of holiness; from the womb of the morning shall come to Thee the dew of Thy youth.*

47. Cohen, *The Faith of a Liberal* (Henry Holt, 1946), p. 42.
48. *The Santa Cruz* (1798), 1 C. Robinson 49. Sir William Scott, later Lord Stowell, was the greatest builder of the Prize Law.
49. Dom Marmion, *Christ, The Life of the Soul* (Herder, 1922), p. 215.
50. "Law and Conscience"; see *Discorsi agli Intellettuali: 1939–1954,* p. 211.
51. *S. T.*, I–II, 94. 2. *in corp.*
52. *Theology and Sanity,* pp. 316–7.
53. *Ibid.,* p. 317.
54. See Ephes. 5:13.
55. *S. T.*, I, 1. 6. *in corp.*
56. *Miscellaneous Writings* (1852), pp. 527–8.
57. Vanderbilt, "A Report on Prelegal Education," *New York University Law Review,* Vol. 25 (1950), p. 215.
58. Cardozo, *The Growth of the Law,* p. 87.
59. *Ibid.,* p. 87.
60. *Ibid.,* p. 88.
61. *Ibid.,* p. 89.
62. (1917), 221 N.Y. 431, 117 N.E. 807.
63. *The Growth of the Law,* p. 88–9.
64. *Ibid.,* p. 89.
65. *Euclid v. Ambler Realty Co.* (1926), 272 U.S. 365, 47 S.Ct. 114 at 118.
66. (1744), 26 English Rep. 15.
67. *Ibid.,* pp. 22–23.
68. Judge Hardy in *Long v. Northern Soil Conservation Dist. of La.,* (1954), 72 So. 2d 543.
69. *The Analects of Confucius.*

EXPLANATIONS AND
ACKNOWLEDGMENTS

I.

THE word "lawyers" as used in this book designates not only practicing attorneys, but also judges and other law officers, law teachers and law students, legislators and legal scholars. It includes the Bench and the Bar, the Chair and the Stool. In this sense it comes near to "lawyers," "doctors of laws," and "scribes" in the Gospel. These terms are used interchangeably there to signify that class of men in the Jewish community who devoted their lives to the study of the Mosaic Law. Originally the scribes were priests. For instance, Esdras, a scion of Aaron, was "a ready scribe in the law of Moses, which the Lord God had given to Israel" (1 Esdras 7:6). "For Esdras had prepared his heart to seek the law of the Lord, and to do and to teach in Israel the commandment and judgment" (*Ibid.* 7:10).

The scribes, then, were those priests whose special function was to interpret the Law, or, what amounts to the same thing, Holy Scripture. But, unlike the sacrificial and ritualistic functions, which only a priest could perform, the study and exposition of the Law could be engaged in by pious and learned laymen. As time went on, the scribal profession was gradually differentiated from the priesthood. At the time of Christ, the scribes had become leaders of the new party of Pharisees, who were extreme nationalists, in opposition to an increasing number of priests, who favored the Hellenistic tendencies which had made themselves felt among them. The scribes, as Dr. James F. Driscoll has told us, "never wielded any political power, but they were admitted to the Sanhedrin on a par with the chief priests and elders and thus enjoyed official recogni-

tion. With the increasing formalism, which their influence doubtless helped to develop, the character of the scribes and their activities underwent a marked change. They neglected the deeper and
more spiritual aspects of the Law, and from men of sacred letters
they became mainly jurists who devoted most of their attention to
mere quibbles and subtle casuistry" (*Catholic Encyclopedia*).

Due partly to the ill effects of specialization—which, whether
among Jews or gentiles, ancients or moderns, tends to make its vo-
taries unable to see the wood for the trees—and partly to the lack of
a sound philosophy of law, which could help them to distinguish
the spirit from the letter and interpret the Divine *positive* laws in
the light of the Divine *natural* law, the scribes found themselves in
a situation in which they were compelled to resort to highly technical and artificial ingenuities in order to adapt old laws to new
conditions and circumstances of life. To some extent this embarras-
sing situation is the common lot of the jurists of all countries, particularly at certain periods of their legal history. The law is permanent, and yet it has to cope with the changing conditions and manners of the people. This problem was not unknown to the Roman
jurists. But with the scribes, the problem was particularly knotty
because they were dealing with *Divine* laws. They got around it
by inventing, unconsciously rather than deliberately, the fiction
that God revealed to Moses more laws than he could actually re-
duce to writing. The oral part of the revelation was said to be
transmitted to them through Esdras. This fiction served as the
foundation of a whole legal tradition of which the scribes were the
guardians. The ever-accumulating mass of legal traditions and legal
decisions was known as *Halaka*, "the way."

In other words, the scribes introduced new legal measures under
the pretext of merely applying the old law. This was how Hillel,
who was an elder contemporary of Jesus, instituted the Prosbol. As
is well known, there is a prescription in Deuteronomy (15:1 et
seq.) about the remission of debts in the seventh year: "He to
whom anything is owing from his friend or neighbor or brother,
cannot demand it again, because it is the year of remission of the
Lord" (Deut. 15:2). This is followed up with a thoughtful reminder: "Beware lest perhaps a wicked thought steal in upon thee,

and thou say in thy heart: 'The seventh year draweth near,' and thou turn away thy eyes from thy poor brother, denying to lend him that which he asketh . . ." (*Ibid.* 15:9). But given human nature, and as manners decayed through the generations, more and more people yielded to this thought and saw the imprudence, from their worldly point of view, of lending anything to their poor neighbors, when the year of remission was drawing near. And perhaps the borrowers were not all in good faith either. Some were probably too eager in taking advantage of the sabbatical year. Be that as it may, Hillel thought that a modification was called for, and he instituted the Prosbol, according to which it sufficed for the creditor to submit to the judges a document reserving his right to recover his debt *at any time*, in order to be immune from the operation of the remission rule. (See Lagrange, *Le Judaism avant Jésus-Christ*, 3d ed., p. 299.) This, to my mind, is not in the same class as the institution of "Corban." In the Corban case, a natural law is circumvented, whereas here a positive law is amended.

From the standpoint of juristic methodology, the scribes have made contributions comparable to the jurisprudence of any other country. They had a highly developed system of judicial reasoning. They knew how to proceed inductively from the minor to the major, how to draw conclusions from analogies; how to marshall all the texts of the law, in order to elucidate a provision of the same nature; how to formulate a general principle on the basis of two or more provisions; how to explain the meaning of a law by resorting to a similar passage; and how to find the solution of a case in the light of the context. (See Strack, *Einleitung in den Talmud*, 5th ed. pp. 97 ff.)

The scholarship and juridical accomplishments of the scribes are not to be slighted. If only they were instructed in the kingdom of God, in a right philosophy of law and justice, they could have been magnificent householders, drawing from their storeroom things new and old.

2.

Although this book is not a volume of collected legal papers but possesses a unity of its own, yet it should be pointed out that in composing it I have drawn liberally upon a number of papers I have published or delivered on various occasions during the past four years. The Prologue is based upon an article on *Law* that Rev. Vincent C. Hopkins, S. J., requested me to write for the *Catholic Encyclopedia Supplement*, which he has been editing. I have embodied many parts of the article in the Prologue, and I wish to express my gratitude to the Gilmary Society for its permission to do so.

The genesis of Part One of the present work has been given in a special introductory note. It is based upon an article published in the *Fordham Law Review*, March, 1954. But as the reader will see, it has been expanded considerably, and the second section dealing with the common law in its new home has practically been rewritten. I am, however, deeply indebted to the *Fordham Law Review* for its permission to reproduce the article which forms, as it were, the scaffolding for this part of the book.

Part Two of the book, dealing with the juridical wisdom of Christ and the Christian influences on the Common Law, constitutes a further development of Part One. The two have an organic connection, although they were conceived at different times. The idea of studying Christ's wisdom in the law and art of judgment was sown in my mind about forty years ago when I began to study law and became a Christian (a Methodist) almost at the same time. But it was on September 8, 1951, when I was attending a Holy Mass in celebration of the Nativity of Our Lady in the lovely chapel of Seton Hall University, that the idea took definite shape. I do not claim inspiration, but I certainly felt the kind of thrill a hen must feel in watching her chick break its shell. After coming back home, I quickly jotted down in a note-book all the thoughts that had shot through my mind during Mass. Shortly afterwards, Rt. Rev. Monsignor Robert E. McCormick invited me to give an address to the New York Guild of Catholic Lawyers in one of its regular meetings. I went and talked on "Christ the Judge." The talk lasted more than an hour, but the judges and attorneys were not bored. On the contrary, they were so delighted with my talk that, at the instance of Mr. Robert G. Burke, the retiring President, I was elected unanimously to be an honorary life member of the Guild. I certainly am appreciative of the honor, but even more do I value the friendship. Honors pass; but friendship lasts.

Some time later, Rev. Anthony Lo Gatto invited me to give a talk at an annual meeting of the Italian Board of Guardians in Brooklyn, N. Y. Many prominent lawyers were present. I talked about "Law and Equity in Christ's Art of Judgment." That too was received with a warmth extraordinary even for those of Italian blood; for, believe me, I was adopted as a fellow-Italian!

I sought only Christ and His justice, and these other things have been added to me.

I have not incorporated in the present work those two addresses, because on both occasions I talked *ex tempore*. But I feel grateful to both organizations, because their approval gave me courage to write "In the School of Christ," which constitutes Part II of the book.

As to the Epilogue, dealing with the art of law and expounding a theory of justice, I must acknowledge that it grew from a paper I had read before the National Association of Women Lawyers at their Annual Banquet held in New York on September 15, 1951. A summary of the address was later published under the title "Toward a Christian Philosophy of Law" in *Women Lawyers Journal* (Vol. 37, No. 4). It happened to be the first address I was invited to deliver since I came to this part of the country. Not having been advised beforehand against speaking too long, especially on a Saturday evening, I talked on and on until midnight! But the women lawyers, who were gathered from all parts of this country, were so kind and patient that they stayed through that ordeal up to the very end. It was no ordeal to me. On the contrary, it was one of the most pleasant experiences I have ever had. But it must have taxed their patience. What, therefore, was my surprise when I came to read in their report, "Dr. Wu's address was scholarly and was directed to the source of law and justice. His presentation was a compliment to the members of our Association." Oh the sportsmanship of these lady lawyers! I am especially grateful to the then retiring President, J. Helen Slough, and the newly elected President, Mary H. Zimmerman.

But throughout the book, I have also used materials contained in several other papers. None of them has been published, but since I have incorporated parts of them here and there, it is only fair that I should mention this fact and express my gratitude to those whose kind invitations have compelled me to prepare the papers and whose warm appreciation has encouraged me to elaborate certain ideas contained in them.

1. "The Cape Horn of Jurisprudence," delivered on December 12, 1952, before the St. Thomas More Society, organized by a group of students of the Harvard Law School. On that occasion I had the pleasure of meeting many brilliant students of law, notably the then President of the Society, Mr. Robert Kennedy. Mr. Kennedy was so thoughtful as to invite Professor Warren A. Seavey to preside at the meeting; it was the first time that I had the privilege of seeing the man who was a great teacher of law in my own country before he began to teach in this country.

2. "Justice Holmes and the Natural Law," delivered in the Winter of 1951 before the Brandeis Society in Philadelphia, at the invitation of Mr. Arthur Cowan.

3. "Justice Holmes: A New Estimate," delivered in the Spring of 1952 to the Root-Tilden Scholars of the New York University School of Law, at the instance of Chief Justice Vanderbilt.

4. "American Jurisprudence through Chinese Eyes," delivered on May 5, 1954, before a meeting of Indianapolis Bar Association, at the invitation of Mr. John K. Ruckelshaus, whom I discovered to have been my classmate at Harvard in 1923.

5. "Morals and Public Policy in the Light of Comparative Jurisprudence," delivered on May 6, 1954, at the Indiana University School of Law, at the invitation of Dean Leon Wallace and Professor Jerome Hall. From Bloomington and Indianapolis I have brought home many pleasant memories.

6. "Contemporary Trends in American Jurisprudence," delivered in October, 1954, at a meeting of the legislative council of The Contemporary Club of Newark, at the invitation of Mrs. Masucci.

7. "Jurisprudence as a Cultural Study," delivered at the Round Table Meeting on Jurisprudence held on December 29, 1954, at the Annual Meeting of the Association of American Law Schools. I am

grateful to Professor Reginald Parker, Chairman of the Round Table, for his invitation, which gave me an opportunity to formulate some fundamental ideas of law and jurisprudence which were floating about in my mind, and to meet many jurists whom I had wished to meet, such as Dr. Brendan Francis Brown, Prof. Paul Sayre, Prof. Thomas Cowan, Rev. Thomas Davitt, S. J., Rev. William F. Cahill, Rev. James F. Orford, S. J., and Judge Jerome Frank. On top of all I had a very interesting and fruitful exchange of views with my dear friends Rev. William James Kenealy, S. J., and Dr. Yuen-Li Liang.

3.

In the writing of this book, the greatest help I have received is from the Rt. Rev. Monsignor John L. McNulty, who has been my theological and spiritual adviser ever since I came to Seton Hall University in 1951. What the friendship of this great priest of Christ has meant to me is not easy to put in words. He is one of those men whose holiness makes them able to read one's soul like an open book. There is a current saying among the students of Seton Hall about their beloved President: "His words echo our thoughts." As for me, I cannot thank God enough for bringing me into intimate relation with Msgr. McNulty. Were it not for his wise guidance, constant encouragement, and timely corrections, neither *The Interior Carmel* nor *Fountain of Justice* could ever have been written. All the papers I have mentioned above have passed under his eyes, at once critical and sympathetic.

On the juristic side, I am deeply indebted to Dr. Miriam T. Rooney, Dean of the Seton Hall University School of Law, in many ways. But here I need only to mention one thing in particular. It was through reading her remarkable book, *Law, Lawlessness and Sanction*, that I began to take a serious interest in the works of Bracton. This interest has grown with the years, and my eyes have gradually been opened to the background and spirit of the Common Law. It was also through Dr. Rooney that I have come to know many wonderful friends, the latest being Rev. David C. Bayne, S. J.

For use in this book, I have made a new version of the introductory part of Bracton's *De legibus et consuetudinibus angliae* with the generous and invaluable help of Rev. Edward Synan. I made the first draft, and he meticulously checked it against the best available Latin edition and made a number of corrections. In producing the first draft, however, I profited also by the co-operation of my son Peter, and my daughter Teresa, fresh with her Latin grammar learned at Marylawn of the Oranges.

In retranslating the passages from St. Thomas Aquinas, it was Rev. Anthony Lo Gatto of Brooklyn who prepared the first draft. He has most generously spent many hours with me in order to make the translation as accurate, simple and readable as possible.

Next I must acknowledge my deep indebtedness to Rev. Peter Philip Reilly, O. P. I have known Father Reilly for years. Whenever he comes to Newark, he favors me with a visit. He has read over my manuscripts and made many suggestions which I have eagerly adopted.

It was Rev. John M. Oesterreicher who made the thoughtful suggestion that I should bring out the distinction between "lawyers" in the Biblical sense and "lawyers" in the popular sense. As we have seen, the lawyers or scribes in the Gospel have more in common with professors of law and supreme court judges than with advocates.

I am grateful, too, to Rev. Thomas Reardon and Dr. Alfred D. Donovan for taking the trouble to read over the whole manuscript, and for saying that it was no trouble but a pleasure! I am grateful to Thomas Cardinal Tien, Archbishop Paul Yupin, Archbishop Thomas A. Boland, Bishop James A. McNulty, and Bishop Raymond A. Lane, M. M., for their encouragement of my work in the field of legal philosophy. In one way or another, I feel deeply indebted to Rev. Nicholas Maestrini, to my godson and friend Dr. Paul Sih, Rev. John T. S. Mao, Rev. Paul Chan, Monsignor Lokuang, Monsignor William F. Furlong, Rev. Raymond de Jaegher, Rev. John Davis, Rev. William Noe Field, Monsignor John A. Abbo, Rev. Albert B. Hakim, Rev. Charles Murphy, Monsignor Joseph H. Brady, Rev. Harold C. Gardiner, S. J., Rev. John H. McDonald, S. M., Dr. Jean Charlot, Mrs. Denis M. O'Brian, Dr. Leon Smith, Rev. Matthew Hoehn, O. S. B., Aelred Wall,

O. S. B., Rev. Joseph S. McGrath, C. S. C., Rev. John Stanley Murphy, Rev. Joseph L. N. Maxwell, S. J., Rev. Philip Marquart, O. F. M., Dr. Stanley Ho, and Mr. John F. McLaughlin.

Among my learned colleagues at the Law School, who have called my attention to significant cases and books, are Judge Arthur O'Dea, Mr. Arthur Murphy, Mr. Daniel Degnan, Professors John T. Fitzgerald, John Kean, John Loftus, John L. Grant, Francis Coughlin, Joseph Slowinski, and Rodman C. Herman.

I have also derived much inspiration and consolation from my students in the Law School, who have shown a keen intelligent interest in all the problems discussed in this book.

I wish to express my hearty thanks to Sister M. Zita who read the book in manuscript.

John C. H. Wu

June 14, 1955
3 Reynolds Place,
Newark 6, N. J.

INDEX